The Vietnam War Era

Southeast Asia

The Vietnam War Era

A PERSONAL JOURNEY

Bruce O. Solheim

Westport, Connecticut
London

Library of Congress Cataloging-in-Publication Data

Solheim, Bruce Olav.
    The Vietnam War era : a personal journey / Bruce O. Solheim.
      p. cm.
    Includes bibliographical references and index.
    ISBN 0-275-98308-0 (alk. paper)
    1. Vietnam War, 1961–1975—United States.   2. Vietnam War, 1961–1975.
    3. United States—History—1945–   I. Title.
    DS558.S64 2006
    959.704'3—dc22   2006025641

British Library Cataloguing in Publication Data is available.

Library of Congress Catalog Card Number: 2006025641
ISBN: 0-275-98308-0

First published in 2006

Praeger Publishers, 88 Post Road West, Westport, CT 06881
An imprint of Greenwood Publishing Group, Inc.
www.praeger.com

Printed in the United States of America

The paper used in this book complies with the
Permanent Paper Standard issued by the National
Information Standards Organization (Z39.48-1984).

10 9 8 7 6 5 4 3 2 1

Contents

III. FIGHTING FOR PEACE, 1968–1972

IV. BACK IN THE WORLD, 1973–1975

List of People Profiled

Creighton Abrams
Muhammad Ali
Peter Arnett
George Ball
Malcolm Browne
McGeorge Bundy
William Calley
Stokely Carmichael
Eldridge Cleaver
Clark Clifford
William E. Colby
Walter Cronkite
Bao Dai
Peter Dewey
Ngo Dinh Diem
Pham Van Dong
Bob Dylan
Dwight D. Eisenhower
Gloria Emerson
Bernard Fall
Jane Fonda
Gerald R. Ford
William Fulbright
Vo Nguyen Giap
Wallace M. Greene, Jr.
David Halberstam
Tom Hayden

Richard Helms
Seymour Hersh
Abbie Hoffman
Daniel "Chappy" James, Jr.
Lyndon B. Johnson
George F. Kennan
John F. Kennedy
Robert F. Kennedy
John Kerry
Martin Luther King, Jr.
Henry Kissinger
Nguyen Cao Ky
Edward Lansdale
Robert McNamara
Duong Van Minh
Ho Chi Minh
Bill Moyers
Huey Newton
Ngo Dinh Nhu
Richard M. Nixon
Archimedes Patti
Dean Rusk
Harrison Salisbury
Jonathan Schell
Neil Sheehan
Benjamin Spock
James Stockdale

Acknowledgments

I dedicate this book to my friend and colleague David Willson. David is a Vietnam veteran and author of many well-received and critically acclaimed books on the war (*REMF Diary*, *the REMF Returns*, and *In the Army Now*, among others). I would not know anything about the Vietnam War without having met this kind and funny man, who also happens to be a fine scholar.

I would like to thank the more than 2000 students of my Vietnam War history course. I have learned more from you than you will ever know.

I would also like to thank all of my Vietnam War veteran friends, including my brother, who is among those brave warriors; Dr. Gary Hess, my mentor from Bowling Green State University; Dr. Bruce Haulman, the man who allowed me to teach the Vietnam War the first time; and my editor Hilary Claggett, who has been very professional, creative, supportive, and more than patient.

And, last, but not least, I want to thank my wife, Heather, who helped me edit this manuscript and has built a wonderful home for our family.

Preface

This book came about as a result of twelve years of teaching the Vietnam War and because I realized how much that war had affected me and my family. This book, essentially, documents a personal journey. Moreover, this personal journey is one that each of us has taken who remember the Vietnam War. Being a historian, I have integrated my personal journey with that of my nation and of many others around the world, in a narrative history of the Vietnam era. In a 1963 publication put out by an American organization known as the Friends of Vietnam, they said more than they knew when they wrote that Americans do not realize how much of that faraway place is in all of us.

The Vietnam War Era: A Personal History provides readers with an integrated, lengthy, and detailed timeline of events in American and Vietnamese history, biographical sketches of more than fifty key figures (Vietnamese and American), a narrative history of America's war in Vietnam, and my personal history as it relates to the Vietnam War. No other book provides readers with this combination. The basic premise is that history both begins and ends with the individual. This book will help readers better comprehend the American war in Vietnam through its integration of the national and personal histories and its insights into the impact of the Vietnam era on Americans today.

Chronology

2,000 BC to 200 AD	The Viet people, a fusion of peoples from China and indigenous people from Vietnam, form in Red River Valley. Vietnamese historians claim the Dong Son culture as the start of the Vietnamese nation.
208 BC	Trieu Da, a Chinese general, conquers Au Lac in the northern mountains of Vietnam. He builds a capital and makes himself emperor of what he calls Nam Viet.
111 BC	Chinese armies reconquer Vietnam and incorporate it into the expanding Han empire. Vietnamese resistance continues sporadically.
39 AD	The most famous of several early Vietnamese revolts was led by the Trung sisters, both widows of local aristocrats. Their revolt was successful, and the older sister, Trung Trac, ruled an independent state for three years.
43 to 203	China reconquers Vietnam. It is again ruled by the Han dynasty, but Vietnamese rebellions continue sporadically during Chinese rule.
939	The Chinese are finally driven out of Vietnam (now known as Dai Viet), and Ngo Quyen sets up an independent Vietnamese state.
982	Expansion to the south begins.
1260s–1270s	The Mongol armies of Kublai Khan attack Vietnam to reintegrate it into the Chinese empire, but are

	defeated in several battles and driven back across the border.
1400	Vietnam battles the Kingdom of Champa south along the central coast near Da Nang. After decades of conflict, Vietnamese forces defeat the Chams and destroy their kingdom.
1500	Dai Viet conquers Anghor.
1535	Portuguese conduct the first-known Western visit of the region.
1500s–1600s	Further expansion south to the Mekong and then westward begins to pit the Vietnamese against the waning Khmer state.
1613	Civil war between northern and southern Dai Viet.
1627	Alexandre de Rhodes, a French missionary, adapts Vietnamese language to Roman alphabet.
1802	Nguyen dynasty established, capital moved to Hue, country now known as Vietnam.
1820	Captain John White of Massachusetts is the first American to set foot in Vietnam.
1842	The Opium Wars give Europeans control over China through a series of unfair treaties.
1845	USS *Constitution* lands in Da Nang. A company of U.S. Marines moves overland to Hue and rescues a French bishop who had been captured by the Vietnamese. America's first combat involvement in Vietnam. Exactly 120 years later, two battalions of U.S. Marines will return to Vietnam via Da Nang.
1847	French vessels bombard Da Nang.
February 1859	French forces capture Saigon.
February 1861	The French defeat the Vietnamese army and gain control of Gia Dinh and surrounding provinces.
1867	France had conquered all of southern Vietnam, which became the French colony of Cochinchina.
1880	France divides up Vietnam into three regions: Tonkin, Annam, and Cochinchina.
1887	Cambodia joins the French holdings in Vietnam to form French Indochina (the Indochina Union).

1890	Ho Chi Minh born (Nguyen Tat Thanh).
1893	Laos is added to French Indochina.
1900	Resistance against the French by Modernization Society led by Phan Boi Chau.
1911	Ho Chi Minh leaves Vietnam for a thirty-year exile.
1919	Nguyen Ai Quoc (Ho Chi Minh) emerges in Paris at the end of World War I and tries to petition President Woodrow Wilson for self-determination of Vietnam.
1920	VNQDD (non-Communist nationalists) attempts armed uprising against the French.
1920	Ho Chi Minh is one of the founding members of French Communist Party.
1924	Ho Chi Minh leaves Paris and moves to Moscow, where he becomes a full-time Communist agent.
1930	Indochinese Communist Party founded by Ho Chi Minh.
1932	Bao Dai returns to Vietnam from France and ascends the throne.
1940	Japan invades Vietnam, restricting local French administrators to figurehead authority.
1941	Communist activist Ho Chi Minh secretly returns to Vietnam after thirty years in exile and forms a nationalist organization known as the League for the Independence of Vietnam (Viet Minh).
1941	Japanese troops occupy Vietnam. The Vichy French colonial government is allowed by the Japanese to continue to administer Vietnam, and French repression continues.
1941–1945	The Viet Minh resists Japanese occupation with the help of the United States and China. Ho teams up with Vo Nguyen Giap. The Viet Minh army is developed.
1942	The U.S. Office of Strategic Services (OSS, the forerunner of the CIA) allies with Ho Chi Minh and his Viet Minh guerrillas to harass Japanese troops and to help rescue downed American pilots.
30 April 1945	Major Archimedes Patti of the U.S. Office of Strategic Services (OSS) meets with Ho Chi Minh, who shows his support for America.

May–July 1945	Severe famine leads to 2 million deaths from starvation, out of a population of 10 million in Vietnam.
8 May 1945	Following the Nazi defeat, Chinese nationalists will move in and disarm the Japanese, north of the 17th parallel, while the British will move in and do the same in the south.
August 1945	Ho Chi Minh's guerrillas occupy Hanoi and proclaim a provisional government in the north of Vietnam.
September 1945	The head of the OSS mission in Saigon, Colonel Peter Dewey, is shot by the Viet Minh, becoming the first American to die in Vietnam.
23 September 1945	French troops return to Vietnam and clash with Communist and nationalist forces and seize power in the south, with British help.
23 November 1946	French bombard Haiphong and occupy it, killing 6,000 Vietnamese civilians. Ho appeals for U.S. support for the last time. French-Viet Minh War begins.
4 February 1947	French opinion poll shows 36 percent favored use of force, 42 percent favored negotiations, 8 percent thought France should leave Indochina altogether.
April 1948	France recognizes an "independent" state of Vietnam in the south.
July 1949	The French establish the (South) Vietnamese National Army.
October 1949	Mao Zedong's Communist forces victorious in China. U.S. leaders fear spread of Communism worldwide.
January 1950	The People's Republic of China and the Soviet Union recognize Ho Chi Minh's Democratic Republic of Vietnam.
February 1950	The United States and Britain recognize Bao Dai's French-controlled South Vietnam government. France requests U.S. military aid.
7 February 1950	Era of "McCarthyism" begins as Senator Joseph R. McCarthy of Wisconsin capitalizes on the hysterical fear of Communism in America.
8 May 1950	United States military involvement in Vietnam begins as President Harry Truman authorizes

	$15 million in military aid to the French. American military advisors will accompany the flow of U.S. tanks, planes, artillery, and other supplies to Vietnam. Over the next four years, the United States will spend $3 billion on the French war, and by 1954 will provide 80 percent of all war supplies used by the French.
30 June 1950	Communist North Korean army crosses the 38th Parallel. President Harry S Truman orders U.S. ground troops into Korea. In his message to the American people, Truman describes the invasion as a Moscow-backed attack by "monolithic world Communism."
27 September 1950	The United States establishes a Military Assistance Advisory Group (MAAG) in Saigon to aid the French army.
22 December 1950	Napalm is used for the first time in Vietnam against Viet Minh forces at Tien Yen.
November 1951	U.S. Senator John F. Kennedy visits Vietnam and declares, "In Indo-China we have allied ourselves to the desperate effort of the French regime to hang on to the remnants of an empire."
20 January 1953	Dwight D. Eisenhower increases U.S. military aid to the French in Vietnam to prevent a Communist victory. The Domino Theory will be used by a succession of presidents and their advisors to justify ever-deepening U.S. involvement in Vietnam.
3 March 1953	Soviet leader Josef Stalin dies and is succeeded by Nikita Khrushchev.
27 July 1953	The Korean War ends and an armistice is signed, dividing the country at the 38th parallel into Communist North and Democratic South.
20 November 1953	The French begin construction of a series of entrenched outposts protecting a small air base in the isolated jungle valley at Dienbienphu in northwest Vietnam.
13 March 1954	50,000 Viet Minh under General Giap begin their assault against the fortified hills protecting the Dienbienphu air base.
7 May 1954	Dienbienphu falls. More than 10,000 French soldiers surrender at Dienbienphu, depriving

	France of any bargaining power at Geneva. By now, an estimated 8,000 Viet Minh and 1,500 French have died.
8 May 1954	The United States, Britain, China, Soviet Union, France, Vietnam (Viet Minh and representatives of Bao Dai), Cambodia, and Laos meet at the Geneva Conference on Indochina to negotiate a solution for Southeast Asia. The Geneva Accords divide Vietnam in half at the 17th parallel.
7 July 1954	Ngo Dinh Diem chosen premier of South Vietnam.
August 1954–May 1955	The first of the waves of North Vietnamese move to South Vietnam under the Geneva Accord. By May 1955, about 1 million refugees had fled south as opposed to some 90,000 Communists in the south going north. At the same time, nearly 10,000 Viet Minh fighters are instructed by Hanoi to quietly remain behind.
8 September 1954	South East Asia Treaty Organization (SEATO) is formed.
11 October 1954	Following the French departure from Hanoi, Ho Chi Minh returns after spending eight years hiding in the jungle. The Viet Minh formally assume control over North Vietnam.
1 January 1955	Direct U.S. aid to South Vietnam begins. Americans begin training the South Vietnamese army.
12 February 1955	U.S. advisors begin training South Vietnamese troops.
July 1955	Ho Chi Minh visits Moscow and agrees to accept Soviet aid.
20 July 1955	South Vietnam refuses to take part in the unifying elections called for by the Geneva agreements, charging that free elections are impossible in the Communist North.
26 October 1955	The Republic of Vietnam (South Vietnam) is declared. Bao Dai installs Ngo Dinh Diem as president. The Republic of Vietnam is recognized by more than 100 countries.
December 1955–December 1956	Rise of Martin Luther King, Jr., at the Montgomery Bus Boycott.

December 1955

In North Vietnam, radical land reforms by Communists result in landowners being hauled before "people's tribunals." Thousands are executed or sent to forced labor camps by Ho Chi Minh.

28 April 1956

An American Military Assistance Advisory Group (MAAG) takes over the training of South Vietnamese forces. The French Military High Command disbands, and French troops leave South Vietnam.

January 1957

The Soviet Union proposes permanent division of Vietnam into North and South, with the two nations admitted separately to the United Nations.

8–18 May 1957

Diem pays a state visit to Washington, where President Eisenhower labels him the "miracle man" of Asia and reaffirms U.S. commitment.

October 1957

Viet Minh guerrillas begin a widespread campaign of terror in South Vietnam, including bombings and assassinations. By year's end, over 400 South Vietnamese officials are killed.

March 1959

The armed revolution begins as Ho Chi Minh declares a "people's war" to unite all of Vietnam under his leadership. Thus begins the Second Indochina War.

May 1959

Construction of the Ho Chi Minh trail begins. The trail will eventually comprise a 1500-mile-long network of jungle and mountain passes extending from North Vietnam's coast along Vietnam's western border through Laos, parts of Cambodia, funneling a constant stream of soldiers and supplies into the highlands of South Vietnam.

April 1960

North Vietnam imposes universal military conscription with an indefinite tour of duty.

11–12 November 1960

A failed coup against President Diem by disgruntled South Vietnamese army officers brings a harsh crackdown against all enemies of the state. Kennedy wins close election versus Richard Nixon.

20 December 1960

The National Liberation Front (NLF) is established by Hanoi as its Communist political organization for Viet Cong (VC) guerrillas in South Vietnam.

January 1961	Soviet premier Nikita Khrushchev pledges support for "wars of national liberation" throughout the world, encouraging North Vietnamese Communists to escalate their armed struggle to unify Vietnam.
January 1961	President Eisenhower warns us of a Military Industrial Complex in his farewell speech.
20 January 1961	John Fitzgerald Kennedy is inaugurated as the 35th U.S. president. He is advised in private by outgoing President Eisenhower that troops may be needed in Southeast Asia.
9 April 1961	President Diem is reelected as president of South Vietnam. U.S. ambassador Frederick Nolting reveals that Diem "did not want combat troops in Vietnam."
May 1961	President Kennedy sends 400 Green Berets as Special Advisors to South Vietnam to train South Vietnamese soldiers in methods of counterinsurgency in the fight against VC guerrillas.
August 1961	VC launches several successful attacks on South Vietnamese troops. Diem then requests more military aid from the Kennedy administration.
11 October 1961	Kennedy announces that his aides Maxwell Taylor and Walt Rostow will visit Vietnam to examine the deteriorating situation. The president decides against sending any combat troops.
24 October 1961	The number of military advisors sent by Kennedy will eventually surpass 16,000.
16 November 1961	As a result of Taylor's mission, President Kennedy decides to increase military aid to South Vietnam, without committing U.S. combat troops.
December 1961	VC guerrillas control much of the countryside in South Vietnam and frequently ambush South Vietnamese troops. The cost to America of maintaining the 200,000-man ARVN army and managing the overall conflict in Vietnam rises to a million dollars per day.
31 December 1961	U.S. military personnel in Vietnam total 3,200.
6 February 1962	MACV, the U.S. Military Assistance Command for Vietnam, is formed. It replaces MAAG-Vietnam,

	the Military Assistance Advisory Group, established in 1950.
27 February 1962	Two renegade South Vietnamese pilots flying American-made World War II–era fighter planes bomb the presidential palace in Saigon, killing three and wounding twenty. President Diem and his brother Nhu escape unharmed.
March 1962	Strategic Hamlet resettlement program begins.
May 1962	Defense Secretary McNamara visits South Vietnam and reports, "[W]e are winning the war."
June 1962	Formation of SDS and the writing of the Port Huron statement.
23 July 1962	The Declaration on the Neutrality of Laos, signed in Geneva by the United States and thirteen other nations, prohibits U.S. invasion of portions of the Ho Chi Minh trail inside eastern Laos.
August 1962	A U.S. Special Forces camp is set up at Khe Sanh to monitor NVA infiltration down the Ho Chi Minh trail.
October 1962	Cuban Missile Crisis brings the United States and the Soviet Union to the brink of nuclear war. The point of conflict was the stationing of intermediate range nuclear missiles in Cuba.
May 1963	Buddhists riot in South Vietnam after they are denied the right to display religious flags during their celebration of Buddha's birthday.
June–August 1963	Buddhist demonstrations spread. Several Buddhist monks publicly burn themselves to death as an act of protest. Diem imposes martial law.
24 August 1963	President Kennedy and top aides begin three days of heated discussions over whether the United States should in fact support the military coup against Diem.
28 August 1963	March on Washington and the "I have a dream" speech by Martin Luther King.
2 September 1963	President Kennedy describes Diem in an interview with Walter Cronkite as "out of touch with the people" and adds that South Vietnam's government might regain popular support "with changes in policy and perhaps in personnel."

1 November 1963	The coup begins.
2 November 1963	Realizing the situation is hopeless, Diem and Nhu offer to surrender from inside a Catholic church. They are then taken into custody by rebel officers and placed in the back of an armored personnel carrier. While traveling to Saigon, the vehicle stops and Diem and Nhu are assassinated.
22 November 1963	President John F. Kennedy is assassinated in Dallas.
31 December 1963	South Vietnam has 16,300 American military advisors and received $500 million in U.S. aid during 1963.
30 January 1964	General Minh is ousted from power in a bloodless coup led by General Nguyen Khanh, who becomes the new leader.
March 1964	U.S.-backed mercenaries flying World War II American fighter planes start bombing the Ho Chi Minh trail inside Laos.
6 March 1964	Defense Secretary McNamara visits Vietnam and states that General Khanh has U.S. support, adding, "We'll stay for as long as it takes."
March 1964	McNamara advises President Johnson to increase military aid to the ARVN. Cost of the war in Vietnam rises to 2 million dollars per day.
May 1964	Work begins on a congressional resolution supporting the president's Vietnam policy. The work is postponed because of lack of support in the Senate, but later surfaces as the Gulf of Tonkin resolution.
Summer 1964	Over 56,000 VC spread guerrilla war throughout South Vietnam, reinforced by NVA regulars pouring in via the Ho Chi Minh trail. Responding to this escalation, President Johnson orders U.S. Navy warships in the Gulf of Tonkin, including the destroyer USS *Maddox*, to conduct electronic surveillance.
1 July 1964	President Johnson appoints General William C. Westmoreland as the new U.S. military commander in Vietnam (MACV).
2 August 1964	Three North Vietnamese patrol boats attack the American destroyer USS *Maddox* in the Gulf of

| | Tonkin, ten miles off the coast of North Vietnam. They fire three torpedoes and machine-guns. A single machine-gun round hits the *Maddox*. There were no casualties. |

2 August 1964 · U.S. Navy fighters from the carrier *Ticonderoga*, led by Commander James Stockdale, attack the patrol boats, sinking one and damaging the other two.

2 August 1964 · President Johnson reacts cautiously, sending a diplomatic message to Hanoi, warning of "grave consequences" from further "unprovoked" attacks and ordering the *Maddox* to resume operations in the Gulf of Tonkin. U.S. forces worldwide go on alert.

3 August 1964 · USS *Turner Joy* and USS *Maddox* open fire on apparent targets without any actual enemy sightings.

4 August 1964 · Despite lack of information and possible doubts about the second attack, the Joint Chiefs of Staff recommend a retaliatory bombing raid against North Vietnam. American press reports embellish the second attack with spectacular eyewitness accounts, although no journalists had been present. President Johnson orders retaliatory bombing of North Vietnamese oil facilities and naval targets.

4 August 1964 · Lieutenant Everett Alvarez pilots one of two navy jets shot down during the bombing raids, and becomes the first American prisoner of war (POW) and the first inhabitant of the infamous POW camp called "Hanoi Hilton."

4 August 1964 · In a midnight television appearance, President Johnson tells Americans, "We still seek no wider war."

5 August 1964 · With opinion polls showing 85 percent public support, Johnson's aides lobby Congress to pass a White House resolution giving the president a free hand in Vietnam.

7 August 1964 · U.S. Congress overwhelmingly passes the Gulf of Tonkin resolution that allows the president "to take all necessary steps, including the use of armed force," to prevent further attacks against U.S. forces.

26 August 1964	President Johnson is nominated at the Democratic National Convention, and states, "We are not about to send American boys nine or ten thousand miles away from home to do what Asian boys ought to be doing for themselves."
September 1964	Free Speech movement begins in Berkeley.
October 1964	Martin Luther King wins Nobel Peace Prize.
16 October 1964	China tests its first atomic bomb. China masses troops along its border with Vietnam as a message to the United States.
1 November 1964	A predawn mortar assault kills five Americans, two South Vietnamese, and wounds nearly a hundred others at Bien Hoa Air Base twelve miles north of Saigon.
3 November 1964	Democrat Lyndon B. Johnson is reelected as president of the United States.
December 1964	More than 10,000 NVA soldiers arrive in the Central Highlands, carrying modern Chinese and Soviet weapons.
1 December 1964	President Johnson's top aides, including Secretary of State Dean Rusk, National Security Advisor McGeorge Bundy, and Defense Secretary McNamara, recommend a policy of gradual escalation of U.S. military involvement in Vietnam.
20 December 1964	General Khanh, and young officers led by Nguyen Cao Ky and Nguyen Van Thieu, oust older generals including General Minh from the government and seize control.
24 December 1964	A VC car bomb set off during happy hour at the Brinks Hotel, an American officers' residence in downtown Saigon, kills two Americans and wounds fifty-eight.
31 December 1964	American military advisor troop strength in South Vietnam is 23,000. An estimated 170,000 VC/NVA fighters have begun coordinated battalion-sized attacks against ARVN troops around Saigon.
27 January 1965	National Security Advisor McGeorge Bundy and Defense Secretary Robert McNamara send a memo to the president, stating that America's limited military involvement in Vietnam is not succeeding,

and that the United Sates has reached a "fork in the road" in Vietnam and must either soon escalate or withdraw.

6 February 1965

VC guerrillas attack the U.S. military compound at Pleiku in the Central Highlands, killing eight Americans, wounding 126, and destroying ten aircraft.

7–8 February 1965

President Johnson approves Operation Flaming Dart. Polls indicate a 70 percent approval rating for the President and an 80 percent approval of U.S. military involvement in Vietnam. Johnson now agrees to a long-standing recommendation from his advisors for sustained bombing against North Vietnam.

7–8 February 1965

In Hanoi, Soviet prime minister Kosygin is pressured by the North Vietnamese to provide unlimited military aid to counter the American "aggression." The Soviets give North Vietnam surface-to-air missiles (SAMs).

21 February 1965

Malcolm X assassinated.

22 February 1965

President Johnson sends two battalions of U.S. Marines to protect the American air base at Da Nang from 6,000 VC massed in the vicinity.

2 March 1965

Operation Rolling Thunder begins with over 100 American fighter-bombers attacking the Ho Chi Minh Trail and targets in North Vietnam. Scheduled to last eight weeks, Rolling Thunder will go on for three years.

9 March 1965

President Johnson authorizes the use of napalm.

11 March 1965

Operation Market Time, a joint effort between the U.S. Navy and South Vietnamese navy, disrupts North Vietnamese supplies into the South. The operation is successful in cutting off coastal supply lines. North Vietnamese are forced to use the more difficult land route along the Ho Chi Minh trail.

29 March 1965

VC terrorists bomb the U.S. embassy in Saigon.

1 April 1965

President Johnson authorizes two more marine battalions and up to 20,000 logistical personnel. The president authorizes American combat troops to conduct patrols in the countryside. His decision

	to allow offensive operations is kept secret from the American press and public for two months.
7 April 1965	President Johnson delivers his "Peace without Conquest" speech at Johns Hopkins University, offering Hanoi "unconditional discussions" to stop the war in return for massive economic assistance in modernizing Vietnam.
17 April 1965	In Washington, 15,000 students gather to protest U.S. bombing.
20 April 1965	Johnson's top military and civilian aides meet in Honolulu and recommend sending 40,000 more troops to Vietnam.
24 April 1965	President Johnson announces that Americans in Vietnam are eligible for combat pay.
3 May 1965	First army combat troops (173rd Airborne) arrive in Vietnam.
13 May 1965	First unilateral bombing pause initiated to spur negotiations.
19 May 1965	U.S. bombing of North Vietnam resumes.
18 June 1965	Nguyen Cao Ky takes power in South Vietnam as the new prime minister, with Nguyen Van Thieu functioning as official chief of state. They lead the tenth government in twenty months.
28 July 1965	President Johnson announces to the press that he will send forty-four combat battalions to Vietnam, increasing the U.S. military presence to 125,000 men. Monthly draft calls are doubled to 35,000.
3 August 1965	After seven marines were killed nearby, film crews record a marine company destroying suspected VC villages near Da Nang. CBS TV shows the film and generates controversy in America.
4 August 1965	President Johnson asks Congress for an additional $1.7 billion for the war.
18–24 August 1965	Marines conduct Operation Starlight as a preemptive strike against the VC at Chu Lai.
31 August 1965	A law is signed making draft-card burning a criminal act subject to a five-year prison sentence and $1,000 fine.

16 October 1965	Antiwar rallies occur in forty American cities and in international cities including London and Rome.
19 October 1965	NVA troops attack the U.S. Special Forces camp at Plei Me in a prelude to the Battle of Ia Drang Valley.
14–16 November 1965	The Battle of Ia Drang Valley marks the first major battle between U.S. troops and NVA inside South Vietnam.
27 November 1965	More than 35,000 antiwar protesters circle the White House, then march on to the Washington Monument for a rally.
9 December 1965	The *New York Times* reports the United States is unable to stop the flow of North Vietnamese soldiers and supplies into the South, despite extensive bombing.
25 December 1965	The second unilateral pause in the bombing of North Vietnam is announced with hopes of encouraging a negotiated peace.
31 December 1965	U.S. troop levels in Vietnam reach 184,300. An estimated 90,000 South Vietnamese soldiers deserted in 1965, while an estimated 35,000 soldiers from North Vietnam infiltrated the South via the Ho Chi Minh trail. Up to 50 percent of the countryside in South Vietnam is now under some degree of VC control.
31 December 1965	General William Westmoreland is chosen as *Time* magazine's 1965 "Man of the Year."
31 January 1966	President Johnson announces bombing will resume.
31 January 1966	Senator Robert F. Kennedy criticizes President Johnson's decision to resume the bombing. His comments infuriate the president.
February 1966	The largely antiwar Senate Foreign Relations Committee, chaired by Senator J. William Fulbright, holds televised hearings examining America's policy in Vietnam.
3 February 1966	Newspaper columnist Walter Lippmann attacks President Johnson's strategy in Vietnam.

26 March 1966	Antiwar protests are held in New York, Washington, Chicago, Philadelphia, Boston, and San Francisco.
12 April 1966	B-52 bombers are used for the first time against North Vietnam.
13 April 1966	VC attack Tan Son Nhut airport in Saigon.
2 May 1966	Secretary of Defense McNamara privately reports that the North Vietnamese are infiltrating 4500 men per month into the South.
4 June 1966	More than 6,400 teachers and professors sign a three-page antiwar advertisement in the *New York Times*.
6 July 1966	Hanoi Radio reports that captured American pilots have been paraded though the streets of Hanoi through jeering crowds.
11 July 1966	Bombing raids intensify against the Ho Chi Minh trail in Laos.
15 July 1966	Operation Hastings is launched by U.S. Marines and ARVN troops in Quang Tri Province. Largest combined action to date.
30 July 1966	Americans bomb NVA troops in the DMZ for the first time.
30 August 1966	Hanoi announces China will provide economic and technical assistance.
1 September 1966	While visiting Cambodia, French president Charles de Gaulle calls for U.S. withdrawal from Vietnam.
12 September 1966	NVA supply lines and coastal targets attacked by more than 500 aircraft in the heaviest air raid of the war to date.
14 September–24 November 1966	During Operation Attleboro, 20,000 U.S. and ARVN soldiers conduct a successful search-and-destroy mission fifty miles north of Saigon, near the Cambodian border.
3 October 1966	The Soviet Union announces it will provide military and economic assistance to North Vietnam.
25 October 1966	President Johnson conducts a conference in Manila with America's Vietnam Allies: Australia, Philippines, Thailand, New Zealand, South

Korea, and South Vietnam. The Allies pledge to withdraw from Vietnam within six months if North Vietnam will withdraw completely from the South.

26 October 1966   President Johnson visits Cam Ranh Bay.

12 November 1966   The *New York Times* reports that 40 percent of U.S. economic aid sent to Saigon is stolen, or winds up on the black market.

8–9 December 1966   North Vietnam rejects a proposal by President Johnson for discussions concerning treatment of POWs and a possible exchange.

31 December 1966   U.S. troop levels reach 389,000 with 5,008 combat deaths and 30,093 wounded. American Allies fighting in Vietnam include 45,000 soldiers from South Korea and 7,000 Australians. An estimated 89,000 soldiers from North Vietnam infiltrated the South via the Ho Chi Minh trail in 1966.

8–26 January 1967   Operation Cedar Falls involves 16,000 American and 14,000 South Vietnamese soldiers clearing out VC from the Iron Triangle area, twenty-five miles northwest of Saigon.

10 January 1967   UN Secretary-General U Thant expresses doubts that Vietnam is essential to the security of the West.

10 January 1967   In his State of the Union address before Congress, President Johnson declares, "We will stand firm in Vietnam."

23 January 1967   Senator Fulbright advocates direct peace talks between the South Vietnamese government and the VC.

2 February 1967   President Johnson states there are no "serious indications that the other side is ready to stop the war."

13 February 1967   President Johnson resumes full-scale bombing of North Vietnam.

22 February 1967   The war's largest operation, Junction City, targets the NVA's Central Office headquarters in South Vietnam.

19–21 March 1967	President Johnson meets in Guam with South Vietnam's prime minister Ky and pressures him to hold national elections.
April 1967	Antiwar protests in New York and San Francisco.
14 April 1967	Nixon visits Saigon and says that antiwar protests back in the United States are "prolonging the war."
15 April 1967	Antiwar demonstrations occur in New York and San Francisco, involving nearly 200,000. Martin Luther King declares that the war is undermining President Johnson's Great Society social reform programs.
20 April 1967	U.S. bombers target Haiphong harbor in North Vietnam for the first time.
24 April 1967	General Westmoreland condemns antiwar demonstrators.
2 May 1967	British antiwar activist and philosopher Bertrand Russell organizes a mock war crimes tribunal in Stockholm to condemn the United States.
13 May 1967	A New York City fire captain leads a 70,000-person march in support of the war.
18–26 May 1967	U.S. and ARVN troops enter the DMZ for the first time and engage in a series of firefights with NVA.
June 1967	U.S. Mobile Riverine Force using U.S. Navy "Swift" boats and army troops attempt to halt VC usage of inland waterways in the Mekong Delta.
June 1967	"Summer of Love" begins in Haight-Ashbury.
July 1967	Race riots in many U.S. cities.
July 1967	Westmoreland requests an additional 200,000 reinforcements on top of the 475,000 soldiers already scheduled to be sent to Vietnam. Johnson agrees to only 45,000.
7 July 1967	North Vietnam decides to launch a widespread offensive against South Vietnam (Tet Offensive).
29 July 1967	The USS *Forestall* catches fire in the Tonkin Gulf from a punctured fuel tank that kills 134 U.S. crewmen, the worst naval accident since World War II.
18 August 1967	California governor Ronald Reagan says the United States should get out of Vietnam, citing the

	difficulties of winning a war when "too many qualified targets have been put off limits to bombing."
21 August 1967	The Chinese shoot down two U.S. fighter-bombers that accidentally crossed their border during air raids in North Vietnam along the Chinese border.
1 September 1967	North Vietnamese prime minister Pham Van Dong publicly states Hanoi will "continue to fight."
October 1967	Antiwar demonstrators march on the Pentagon.
21–23 October 1967	"March on the Pentagon" draws 55,000 protesters. In London, protesters try to storm the U.S. embassy.
31 October 1967	President Johnson reaffirms his commitment to maintain U.S. involvement in South Vietnam.
17 November 1967	President Johnson tells the American public on TV that progress is being made.
29 November 1967	Robert McNamara resigns as Defense Secretary during a press briefing.
30 November 1967	Antiwar democrat Eugene McCarthy announces he will be a candidate for president, opposing Lyndon Johnson.
4 December 1967	Four days of antiwar protests begin in New York. Among the 585 protesters arrested is "baby doctor" Benjamin Spock.
6 December 1967	VC murder 252 civilians in the hamlet of Dak Son.
23 December 1967	Johnson makes his second and final presidential visit to Vietnam.
31 December 1967	U.S. troop levels reach 463,000, with 16,000 combat deaths to date. Over a million American soldiers have served in Vietnam, most in support units. An estimated 90,000 soldiers from North Vietnam infiltrated into the South via the Ho Chi Minh trail in 1967, bringing overall estimated VC/NVA troop strength throughout South Vietnam to 300,000.
31 January 1968	Tet Offensive is launched as Communists attack over a hundred cities and towns throughout South Vietnam.
February 1968	Walter Cronkite admits that it does not look like we are winning in Vietnam.

1 February 1968	In Saigon, a suspected VC guerrilla is shot in the head by South Vietnam's police chief General Nguyen Ngoc Loan.
2 February 1968	President Johnson calls the Tet Offensive "a complete failure."
24 February 1968	U.S. Marines defeat the NVA in the Battle of Hue.
27 February 1968	Walter Cronkite reports war is stalemated.
28 February 1968	General Westmoreland asks President Johnson for an additional 206,000 soldiers and mobilization of reserve units.
2 March 1968	Hue is retaken after a month of fighting by the ARVN and U.S. Marines in the heaviest fighting of the Tet Offensive.
10 March 1968	The *New York Times* breaks the news of Westmoreland's troop request. Secretary of State Dean Rusk is grilled by the Senate Foreign Relations Committee about the troop request and the overall effectiveness of Johnson's war strategy.
12 March 1968	Public opinion polls taken after the Tet Offensive revealed Johnson's overall approval rating has slipped to 36 percent, while approval of his Vietnam War policy slipped to 26 percent.
14 March 1968	Senator Robert F. Kennedy offers to stay out of the presidential race if Johnson will renounce his Vietnam strategy and appoint a committee, including Kennedy, to chart a new course in Vietnam. Johnson turns down the offer.
16 March 1968	Robert F. Kennedy announces his candidacy for the presidency. Polls indicate Kennedy is now more popular than President Johnson.
16 March 1968	Over 300 Vietnamese civilians are slaughtered in My Lai.
26 March 1968	The "Wise Men" gather at the White House and most advocate U.S. withdrawal from Vietnam.
31 March 1968	Feeling betrayed, Johnson announces he will not seek reelection.
4 April 1968	Dr. Martin Luther King, Jr., is assassinated in Memphis. Racial unrest then erupts in over 100 American cities.

11 April 1968	Defense Secretary Clifford announces that General Westmoreland's request for 206,000 additional soldiers will not be granted.
23 April 1968	Antiwar activists at Columbia University seize five buildings.
27 April 1968	200,000 New York students refuse to attend classes as a protest.
10 May 1968	Peace talks begin in Paris.
5 June 1968	Robert F. Kennedy is assassinated in Los Angeles after winning the California Democratic primary.
1 July 1968	General Creighton W. Abrams replaces General Westmoreland as commander of MACV and U.S. ARV.
1 July 1968	The Phoenix program is established to destroy VC infrastructure in South Vietnam.
19 July 1968	President Johnson and South Vietnam's president Thieu meet in Hawaii.
8 August 1968	The Republican Party chooses Richard M. Nixon as the Republican presidential candidate. He promises "an honorable end to the war in Vietnam."
28 August 1968	During the Democratic National Convention in Chicago, more than 26,000 police and national guardsmen confront 10,000 antiwar protesters.
October 1968	Operation Sealord begins the largest combined naval operation of the entire war as over 1,200 U.S. Navy and South Vietnamese navy gunboats and warships target NVA supply lines extending from Cambodia into the Mekong Delta.
October 1968	Black Power demonstrations at Mexico City Olympics.
31 October 1968	Operation Rolling Thunder ends as President Johnson announces a complete halt of U.S. bombing of North Vietnam in the hope of restarting the peace talks.
5 November 1968	Republican Richard M. Nixon narrowly defeats Democrat Hubert Humphrey in the U.S. presidential elections.
27 November 1968	President-elect Nixon asks Harvard professor Henry Kissinger to be his national security advisor.

31 December 1968	U.S. troop levels reach 495,000 with 30,000 American deaths to date.
20 January 1969	Richard M. Nixon is inaugurated as the thirty-seventh U.S. president.
25 January 1969	Peace talks open in Paris, attended by the United States, South Vietnam, North Vietnam, and the VC.
4 March 1969	VC offensives in the South prompt President Nixon to threaten to resume bombing North Vietnam in retaliation.
March 1969	Letters from Vietnam veteran Ronald Ridenhour result in a U.S. Army investigation into the My Lai massacre.
17 March 1969	President Nixon authorizes the secret bombing of Cambodia by B-52s in Operation Menu, targeting North Vietnamese supply sanctuaries.
9 April 1969	At Harvard University, 300 antiwar students seize the administration building.
30 April 1969	U.S. troop levels peak at 543,400, with a total of 33,641 Americans killed.
May 1969	The New York Times breaks the news of the secret bombing of Cambodia. As a result, Nixon orders FBI wiretaps of four journalists and thirteen government officials to determine the source of news leak.
10–20 May 1969	In the A Shau Valley near Hue, the 101st Airborne fight a ten-day battle at "Hamburger Hill." Prompts change in strategy.
8 June 1969	Nixon meets Thieu at Midway Island and informs him U.S. troop levels are going to be sharply reduced. During a press briefing with Thieu, Nixon announces Vietnamization of the war and a U.S. troop withdrawal of 25,000 men.
27 June 1969	Life magazine displays portrait photos of all 242 Americans killed in Vietnam during the previous week.
17 July 1969	Secretary of State William Rogers accuses Hanoi of mistreating American POWs.
25 July 1969	The "Nixon Doctrine" is made public. It advocates U.S. military and economic assistance to

	nations around the world struggling against Communism.
30 July 1969	President Nixon visits U.S. troops and President Thieu in Vietnam. This is Nixon's only trip to Vietnam during his presidency.
August 1969	Woodstock music festival takes place in New York State.
4 August 1969	Henry Kissinger conducts his first secret meeting in Paris with representatives from Hanoi.
3 September 1969	Ho Chi Minh dies of a heart attack at age seventy-nine.
5 September 1969	The U.S. Army brings murder charges against Lt. William Calley concerning the massacre of Vietnamese civilians at My Lai in March of 1968.
5 September 1969	Nixon starts Draft Lottery.
16 September 1969	President Nixon orders the withdrawal of 35,000 soldiers from Vietnam and a reduction in draft calls.
October 1969	An opinion poll indicates 71 percent of Americans approve of President Nixon's Vietnam policy.
15 October 1969	Moratorium peace demonstration is held in Washington and several U.S. cities.
15 November 1969	Mobilization peace demonstration draws an estimated 250,000 in Washington for the largest antiwar protest in U.S. history.
15 December 1969	President Nixon orders an additional 50,000 soldiers out of Vietnam.
31 December 1969	More than 115,000 troops have been sent home. American lives lost stands at 40,024.
2 February 1970	B-52 bombers strike the Ho Chi Minh trail in retaliation for the increasing number of VC raids throughout the South.
18 March 1970	Prince Sihanouk of Cambodia is removed by General Lon Nol. Pol Pot will later oust Lon Nol and begin radical "reforms" that result in the death of 2,000,000 people (the Killing Fields).
10 April 1970	Paul McCartney publicly announces that he has left the Beatles.

20 April 1970	President Nixon announces the withdrawal of another 150,000 troops.
30 April 1970	President Nixon shocks Americans by announcing a U.S. incursion into Cambodia.
1 May 1970	President Nixon calls antiwar students "bums blowing up campuses."
2 May 1970	American college campuses erupt in protest over the invasion of Cambodia.
4 May 1970	Four students killed at Kent State University in Ohio.
9 May 1970	Protests shut down 400 colleges.
3 June 1970	NVA begins a new offensive toward Phnom Penh in Cambodia. The U.S. provides air strikes to prevent the defeat of Lon Nol's inexperienced young troops.
22 June 1970	American usage of jungle defoliants in Vietnam is halted.
24 June 1970	The U.S. Senate repeals the 1964 Gulf of Tonkin resolution.
30 June 1970	U.S. troops withdraw from Cambodia.
11 August 1970	South Vietnamese troops take over the defense of border positions from U.S. troops.
24 August 1970	Heavy B-52 bombing raids occur along the DMZ.
5 September 1970	Operation Jefferson Glenn, the last U.S. offensive in Vietnam, begins in Thua Thien Province.
24 October 1970	South Vietnamese troops begin a new offensive into Cambodia.
12 November 1970	My Lai massacre trial begins.
20 November 1970	American troop levels drop to 334,600.
25 November 1970	Unsuccessful raid on POW camp near Hanoi.
10 December 1970	President Nixon warns Hanoi that more bombing raids may occur if North Vietnamese attacks continue against the South.
31 December 1970	American troop levels drop to 280,000 by year's end.
4 January 1971	President Nixon announces, "The end is in sight."
30 January 1971	Operation Lam Son 719, an all–South Vietnamese ground offensive, occurs as 17,000 South

	Vietnamese soldiers attack 22,000 NVA inside Laos in an attempt to sever the Ho Chi Minh trail. Aided by heavy U.S. artillery and air strikes, ARVN troops advance but are unsuccessful.
March 1971	Opinion polls indicate Nixon's approval rating among Americans has dropped to 50 percent, while approval of his Vietnam strategy has slipped to just 34 percent.
1 March 1971	The Capitol building in Washington is damaged by a bomb apparently planted in protest of the invasion of Laos.
10 March 1971	China pledges complete support for North Vietnam's struggle against the United States.
29 March 1971	Calley is found guilty.
April 1971	500,000 people protest in Washington, D.C.
1 April 1971	President Nixon orders Calley released pending his appeal.
19 April 1971	Vietnam Veterans Against the War begin a week of nationwide protests.
24 April 1971	Another mass demonstration is held in Washington, attracting nearly 200,000.
29 April 1971	Total American deaths in Vietnam surpass 45,000.
30 April 1971	The last U.S. Marine combat units depart Vietnam.
3–5 May 1971	A mass arrest of 12,000 protesters occurs in Washington.
13 June 1971	The *New York Times* begins publication of the Pentagon Papers.
18 June 1971	The *Washington Post* begins its publication of the Pentagon Papers. Nixon attempts to stop the publication, and the case ends up before the U.S. Supreme Court.
28 June 1971	The source of the Pentagon Papers leak, Daniel Ellsberg, surrenders to police.
30 June 1971	The U.S. Supreme Court rules in favor of the *New York Times* and *Washington Post* publication of the Pentagon Papers.
15 July 1971	President Nixon makes a major diplomatic breakthrough and announces he will visit Communist China in 1972.

17 July 1971	Nixon aides John Ehrlichman and Charles Colson establish the Plumbers in the White House to investigate Daniel Ellsberg and plug various news leaks.
18 August 1971	Australia and New Zealand announce the pending withdrawal of their troops from Vietnam.
9 October 1971	The U.S. 1st Air Cavalry Division soldiers refuse to go on a mission.
17 December 1971	U.S. troop levels drop to 156,800.
26–30 December 1971	Heavy bombing of military installations in North Vietnam.
25 January 1972	President Nixon announces a proposed eight-point peace plan for Vietnam and also reveals that Kissinger has been secretly negotiating with the North Vietnamese. However, Hanoi rejects Nixon's peace overture.
21–28 February 1972	President Nixon visits China and meets with Mao Zedong and Prime Minister Zhou Enlai.
10 March 1972	The U.S. 101st Airborne Division leaves Vietnam.
23 March 1972	The United States stages a boycott of the Paris peace talks.
4 April 1972	Nixon authorizes a massive bombing campaign in North and South Vietnam.
15 April 1972	Hanoi and Haiphong harbors are bombed by the United States.
15–20 April 1972	Protests against the bombings erupt in America.
27 April 1972	Paris peace talks resume.
30 April 1972	U.S. troop levels drop to 69,000.
1 May 1972	South Vietnamese abandon Quang Tri City to the NVA.
8 May 1972	Nixon orders mining of North Vietnam's harbors and initiates Operation Linebacker I. The announcement brings international condemnation and ignites more antiwar protests in America.
8 May 1972	South Vietnamese pilots accidentally drop napalm on South Vietnamese civilians, including children.
22–30 May 1972	Nixon visits Soviet Union to establish better diplomatic relations with the Communist nation.
June 1972	Break-in at Democratic National Headquarters at the Watergate Hotel.

9 June 1972	Senior U.S. military advisor John Paul Vann is killed.
17 June 1972	Five burglars are arrested inside the Watergate building in the Democratic National Committee offices in Washington.
28 June 1972	South Vietnamese troops begin a counteroffensive to retake Quang Tri Province.
14 July 1972	Democrats choose antiwar senator George McGovern of South Dakota as their presidential nominee.
18 July 1972	During a visit to Hanoi, actress Jane Fonda broadcasts antiwar messages via Hanoi Radio.
1 August 1972	Henry Kissinger meets again with Le Duc Tho in Paris.
29 September 1972	Heavy U.S. air raids against airfields in North Vietnam destroy 10 percent of their air force.
8 October 1972	The stalemate between Henry Kissinger and Le Duc Tho finally ends as both sides agree to major concessions.
22 October 1972	Operation Linebacker I ends.
24 October 1972	President Thieu publicly denounces Kissinger's peace proposal.
26 October 1972	Radio Hanoi reveals terms of the peace proposal and accuses the United States of attempting to sabotage the settlement.
7 November 1972	Richard M. Nixon wins the presidential election in the biggest landslide to date in U.S. history.
30 November 1972	American troop withdrawal from Vietnam is completed, although there are still 16,000 army advisors and administrators remaining to assist South Vietnam's military forces.
18 December 1972	Operation Linebacker II (the "Christmas bombings") begins. The bombing is denounced by many American politicians, the media, and various world leaders including the Pope.
26 December 1972	North Vietnam agrees to resume peace negotiations within five days of the end of bombing.
29 December 1972	Operation Linebacker II ends.
23 January 1973	President Nixon announces that an agreement has been reached that will "end the war and bring peace with honor."

27 January 1973	Secretary of Defense Melvin Laird announces the end of the draft.
27 January 1973	Lieutenant Colonel William B. Nolde becomes the last American soldier to die in combat in Vietnam.
12 February 1973	Operation Homecoming begins with the release of 591 American POWs.
29 March 1973	The withdrawal of all American troops from South Vietnam is complete.
29 March 1973	The release of 590 American POWs.
1 April 1973	Captain Robert White, the last-known American POW, is released.
30 April 1973	The Watergate scandal results in the resignation of top Nixon aides, H. R. Haldeman and John Ehrlichman.
22 May 1973	Henry Kissinger and Le Duc Tho end their talks on implementation of the Vietnam truce agreement.
19 June 1973	U.S. Congress passes the Case-Church Amendment, which forbids any further U.S. military involvement in Southeast Asia.
1 July 1973	U.S. Congress votes to end all bombing in Cambodia after August 15.
16 July 1973	The U.S. Senate Armed Forces Committee begins hearings into the secret bombing of Cambodia during 1969–1970.
17 July 1973	Secretary of Defense James Schlesinger testifies about bombing raids in Cambodia. This results in first call for Nixon's impeachment.
14 August 1973	U.S. bombing of Cambodia halted.
22 August 1973	Henry Kissinger is appointed by President Nixon as the new secretary of state, replacing William Rogers.
22 September 1973	Henry Kissinger replaces William Rogers as secretary of state and retains national security advisor post.
10 October 1973	Political scandal results in the resignation of Vice President Spiro T. Agnew. He is replaced by Congressman Gerald R. Ford.

7 November 1973	Congress passes the War Powers Resolution requiring the president to obtain the support of Congress within ninety days of sending American troops abroad.
7 November 1973	U.S. Congress overrides presidential veto of War Powers Act.
9 May 1974	Congress begins impeachment proceedings against President Nixon stemming from the Watergate scandal.
9 August 1974	Richard M. Nixon resigns the presidency as a result of Watergate. Gerald R. Ford is sworn in as the thirty-eighth U.S. president.
September 1974	The U.S. Congress appropriates only $700 million for South Vietnam. This leaves the South Vietnamese army underfunded and results in a decline of military readiness and morale.
16 September 1974	President Gerald R. Ford announces a clemency program for draft evaders and military deserters. The program runs through March 31, 1975, and requires fugitives to take an oath of allegiance and also perform up to two years of community service. Out of an estimated 124,000 men eligible, about 22,500 take advantage of the offer.
16 September 1974	President Ford signs a proclamation offering clemency to Vietnam War–era draft evaders and military deserters.
October 1974	North Vietnam decides to launch an invasion of South Vietnam in 1975.
19 November 1974	William Calley is freed after serving a little more than three years under house arrest following his conviction in the My Lai massacre.
13 December 1974– 6 January 1975	In violation of the Paris treaty, North Vietnamese attack South Vietnamese positions.
18 December 1974	Based on President Ford's ineffective response and his hamstringing by Congress, North Vietnam's leaders meet in Hanoi to form a plan for final victory.
8 January 1975	North Vietnamese politburo orders major offensive to "liberate" South Vietnam by NVA cross-border invasion.

14 January 1975	Secretary of Defense James Schlesinger testifies to Congress that the United States is not living up to its earlier promise to South Vietnam's president Thieu of "severe retaliatory action" in the event North Vietnam violated the Paris peace treaty.
21 January 1975	President Ford tells a press conference that the United States is unwilling to reenter the war.
5 February 1975	NVA General Van Tien Dung crosses into South Vietnam to take command of the final offensive.
9 March 1975	The Battle of An Loc begins.
10 March 1975	25,000 NVA attack Ban Me Thuot, II Corps, which falls to NVA attack. The next day, half of the 4,000 South Vietnamese soldiers defending it surrender or desert.
14 March 1975	President Nguyen Van Thieu decides to abandon the Highlands region and two northern provinces and orders withdrawal of ARVN forces.
18 March 1975	NVA leaders meet and decide to accelerate their offensive to achieve total victory before May 1.
19 March 1975	Quang Tri Province, I Corps, falls to NVA attack.
26 March 1975	City of Hue falls to NVA attack after a three-day siege.
30 March 1975	More than 100,000 South Vietnamese soldiers surrender after being abandoned by their commanding officers. Da Nang falls.
1 April 1975	Cities of Qui Nhon, Tuy Hoa, and Nha Trang are abandoned by the South Vietnamese, yielding the entire northern half of South Vietnam to the North Vietnamese.
1 April 1975	Cambodian president Lon Nol abdicates. U.S. Navy operation Eagle Pull commences to evacuate U.S. embassy staff from Phnom Penh.
14 April 1975	American airlift of homeless children to the United States from South Vietnam ends. A total of about 14,000 arrived.
17 April 1975	Cambodia falls as Khmer Rouge troops capture Phnom Penh and government forces surrender.
20 April 1975	U.S. ambassador Graham Martin meets with President Thieu and pressures him to resign,

	given the gravity of the situation and the unlike-lihood that Thieu could ever negotiate with the Communists.
21 April 1975	President Thieu resigns.
23 April 1975	More than 100,000 NVA soldiers advance on Saigon, which is now overflowing with refugees.
27 April 1975	NVA troops encircle Saigon, which is defended by some 30,000 ARVN troops, many of whose leaders have fled. NVA starts rocketing the city.
28 April 1975	"Big" Minh becomes the new president of South Vietnam and appeals for a cease-fire. The NVA ignores this request.
29 April 1975	NVA begins attack on Saigon, shelling Tan Son Nhut Air Base, killing two marines. President Ford activates Operation Frequent Wind to evacuate 7,000 Americans and South Vietnamese from Saigon.
29–30 April 1975	U.S. Navy conducts Operation Frequent Wind to evacuate all U.S. personnel and selected South Vietnamese from Vietnam. Three U.S. aircraft carriers off the coast of Vietnam process the incoming refugees.
30 April 1975	The final ten marines from U.S. embassy depart by chopper at 8:35 a.m.
30 April 1975	NVA captures the presidential palace by 11 a.m.
30 April 1975	President Minh broadcasts a message of unconditional surrender.
April–August 1975	Research shows an extremely strong probability that at least 65,000 Vietnamese perished as victims of political executions in the eight years after Saigon fell.
28 May 1975	35,000 NVA prepare to attack Da Nang, and artillery fire falls on the city.
2 June 1975	Official Communist Party newspaper *Saigon Gai Phong* declares that the Southerners must pay their "blood debt" to the revolution.
1975–1978	Border tension with the Communist government in Cambodia escalated rapidly after the fall of Saigon, and tension remained high throughout

	the Pol Pot regime's forced relocation and mass murders of their population.
1975–1985	A massive exodus from Vietnam began with the change in government—2 million people tried to escape.
1976	The first Vietnamese "boat people" come ashore on the northern beaches of Australia, after traveling 4,800 km in leaky fishing boats. Over the next decade, tens of thousands of Vietnamese will flee Vietnam as boat people.
1976	South Vietnam and North Vietnam are united in a new Socialist Republic of Vietnam.
9 September 1976	Chinese leader Mao Zedong dies.
20 September 1977	Vietnam admitted to United Nations.
1978	Vietnamese prime minister Pham Van Dong declared that a million people who had "collaborated with the enemy" (about 7 percent of the South Vietnamese population) had been returned to civilian life from reeducation camps and jail.
21 December 1978	The Vietnamese PAVN forces invade Cambodia and install a pro-Vietnamese government. They will remain for twelve years, with the last Vietnamese troops leaving Cambodia in 1990.
17 February 1979	China launches invasion of Vietnam, with Chinese suffering approximately 50,000 casualties.
5 March 1979	Chinese forces withdraw from Vietnam under a UN-brokered agreement. With this, General Vo Nguyen Giap has defeated the Japanese, the French, the Americans, the Cambodians, and the Chinese.
December 1986	Doi Moi, "New Openness," declared. Free market economy reforms begin.
1991	Cold War ends with the collapse of the Soviet Union.
1994	United States removes a trade embargo against Vietnam.
1995	Vietnam and the United States agreed to exchange low-level diplomats, although full diplomatic relations (which involves opening embassies and

appointing ambassadors) had not yet been established.

November 2000   Outgoing president Bill Clinton became the first U.S. president to visit Vietnam since the Vietnam War.

Introduction: A People's History

Who controls the past controls the future, and who controls the present controls the past.

—George Orwell, 1984

"W hat was it like over there . . . in Vietnam?" a young student asked his father. The fifty-year-old man stood up, faced his son, and then suddenly swung his fist violently at his son's face, stopping just an inch or two from the boy's nose.

"Like that," his father said, "only all the fucking time." Of all of the stories I have heard from students and veterans, this one continues to impact me the most.

I am not sure anything could have prepared me for teaching the Vietnam War history course at Green River Community College in the spring of 1994. The Vietnam War took over my life. It consumed me and I even began to have nightmares. The emotions evoked in the class carried over into my dreams and came out in strange ways. The theme of tragedy runs through all of those dreams. Each day in class, a mini-drama played itself out. The veteran who tortured himself by taking the class, tears flowing in silent agony, or the son or daughter of a veteran watching a film of their dad torching a village, those scenes occurred regularly. The sound of the helicopter was always in the background. Even the classroom where I taught had ghosts.

I had never developed my own course. I felt an awesome responsibility. My brother was a Vietnam veteran. In preparing to teach the course, I began to examine my own life in the 1960s and 1970s and how the war affected me—I had never truly realized how much it had. I was nervous and excited about my first day teaching the course. The college administration had not allowed the course to be taught for nearly four years because they had trouble with the professor who last taught it. Although the course was wildly popular with the students, the administration felt that the professor was out of control.

I thought I would start the class off with some video comedy. I chose clips from Eddie Murphy's movie *Trading Places* and Rodney Dangerfield's *Back to School*. I noticed that one man who sat in the back of the class was not laughing at the humorous scenes, unlike the other students. In fact, he looked very agitated. I finished my first-day routine, discussed my teaching philosophy, and released the class, when he came up to see me. Some other students lingered as he began to speak.

"That film clip showed something that I just cannot tolerate," he said.

"What was that?" I asked hesitantly.

"I cannot stand imposters . . . people who say that they were soldiers when they were not. That makes me god-damned mad!" I could see that he was in his late forties and that he was in a great deal of pain, perhaps both mentally and physically. He implied that I was lying when I had said I was a veteran. I told him I had indeed been in the army and would not lie about that. As luck would have it, I had my DD Form 214 (army discharge certificate) with me that day. It was a coincidence because I was making a copy of it to send in with a job application.

"I've put lots of imposters in the hospital," he said, "and I'm not afraid of the law." He was getting more angry and agitated and began inching closer to my face. His eyes were bulging and his fists began to squeeze harder. Without any further hesitation, I produced the document and gave it to him. He examined it closely, very closely. My adrenaline was pumping as I thought about how I would protect my students and myself. Then his shoulders heaved downward as if his anger had been released through a relief valve. He looked at me with sorrowful eyes and said:

"I'm sorry, you have to understand, my twin brother died in Vietnam, this is serious shit to me." He never came back to the classroom.

Another professor, who was very popular, had taught the Vietnam War course before I had. He was so obsessed by the course that he lived in the 1960s all the time. With a headband around his long gray hair, his outrageous "do your own thing" attitude, and his pot smoking, he acted out the 1960s for his students. He died in 1989. No one taught the course after that until I resurrected it for our department. The room had a historic feel. The walls had witnessed many years of the war. There was a familiar sound in the room that I noticed the first day I was there—it sounded like a Huey helicopter. After a few weeks, I tracked the sound to its source. The sound came from the back of the room by the clock. The clock hands did not move with a ticking sound; rather, they moved with a whop, whop, whop sound, like a Huey helicopter.

War does not end when the shooting stops. War lingers on, from generation to generation. Unfortunately, we never heal from one war, before another one begins. This book presents biographies of government officials, members of the military and media, entertainment figures, and protesters—some of whom are Vietnamese. Although not presented in this book, I have read over a thousand oral histories of common people whose lives were touched by the American war in Vietnam. All of these stories have helped me get a better sense of the war and its toll on individual lives. I have included my own personal history along with that of my brother, who served in Vietnam. This personal history was possible because my mother had saved more than a hundred letters that my brother had written home while he was in the military. It is important to keep in mind, when reading oral histories and recalling historical events, that memories

are typically constructed rather than emerging as the simple, unfiltered recollections of past events. Individuals and societies choose what they will remember about the past—and what they will forget. Second, memories are constructed to meet present needs. The process of collective memory formation within societies is tied with utilitarian ends. There are conscious purposes and goals behind these efforts; they never occur in a social or political vacuum. Third, the project of forging a collective memory of important episodes in the histories of nations or groups is invariably led by elites, with the state itself often playing a dominant role. Finally, collective memory formation is intimately related to larger questions of group, or national, purpose and identity.[1]

It has been said that we have the most to learn from those whom we hate. I have found this to be rather odd, but true nonetheless. Those who are our enemies do not flatter us—they take a kernel of truth and develop it in such a way as to make us out in the worst light. We react by hating them and doing likewise to them. But when you really think about it, their attack would only have stung if it contained some element of truth. We should be careful when we hate because hatred tends to cause blindness. American diplomat George Kennan told us in 1947 to do all we could to contain Soviet-Communist expansion, but he also warned us not to become overly hysterical about our anti-Communism, lest it become a blind crusade.

Conventional wisdom says that history is written by the winners. We may have won the Cold War, but we did not win in Vietnam. In the case of the American war in Vietnam, much has been written by the side that lost the war. This book looks at the Vietnam War through the lives of several key figures from the Vietnam War era and through my own personal perspective. The idea is that such a historical narrative, coupled with biographies, and a personal history, will reveal themes (some bold and some more subtle) that will help to answer the big question: Why America lost its war in Vietnam?

This book starts with the premise, Why study history unless we can draw lessons from it that can help us today? It is with this approach that I will attempt to tell the story of America's involvement in Vietnam. This book begins with the assumption that war is failure—failure to keep the peace. But it seems impossible to avoid war, because humans have been waging war since we stood up on two legs. War reveals that we are all part warrior, part peacemaker. War exposes the duality of man. As confusing as this may be, confusion is the nature of war. A recent film documentary called the *Fog of War* makes this point, as the film title implies, very clearly. It is not unusual for combat veterans to admire the very same people whom they kill in combat. There is a sense of mutual respect among warriors. This is very difficult for nonveterans to comprehend. In spite of the fact that war seems inevitable, the pursuit of peace is not futile. In the United States, we can begin by putting more effort and resources into studying peace.

The Vietnam War is the second most traumatic, contentious, and problematic event in U.S. history—the first being the Civil War. The Vietnam War remains a "zone of contested meaning."[2] In 2001, former U.S. Senator and Medal of Honor winner Bob Kerrey (D-Nebraska) was in the news for his role in the killing of Vietnamese women and children over thirty years ago. We are still in the grip of that war. The children of the Vietnam War generation live with the damaged psyches of their parents, who pretend to believe that the war is over but are constantly being reminded and unintentionally revisiting the anguish on the next generation. As conservative policy analyst Ernest W. Lefever lamented, "Vietnam won't go away.... Its ghosts still haunt the American psyche like fragments of a twisted nightmare."[3]

Wars are always fought with the last war in mind. Four recent events in American history have revealed lessons from Vietnam: (1) George H. W. Bush asked Congress for authorization in the Gulf War, (2) the idea that we should let the military fight its own war, (3) tight control of the media, and (4) George W. Bush asked Congress for authorization in the War on Terror. These congressional approvals gave the Bushes the support they needed and more people to blame if things went wrong. Lyndon B. Johnson's Tonkin Gulf resolution was a blank check to wage war in Vietnam. Careful scrutiny went into the drafting of the Gulf War and War on Terror resolutions with the Tonkin Gulf resolution in mind. After the Gulf War, George Bush remarked: "It's a proud day for Americans and by God, we've licked the Vietnam Syndrome once and for all."

In the run-up to the Gulf War in 1991, President George H. W. Bush relied on the Powell Doctrine. General Colin Powell postulated his doctrine based on the experience in Vietnam: The United States should not use force unless there was a public consensus that the national interest was directly threatened and that the use of overwhelming force could achieve the desired goal quickly and with little loss of life. According to Powell, "[W]ar should be the politics of last resort. And when we go to war, we should have a purpose that our people understand and support; we should mobilize the country's resources to fulfill that mission and then go in to win."[4]

The Vietnam War lives on in our lives. We witnessed the most extensive bombing in the history of human conflict. Even more appalling was that this destruction was delivered by a hegemonic power against a third world nation. Our idealism turned to disillusionment. We had little or no understanding of Vietnamese history. Had we understood a bit more about the Vietnamese peoples' struggle against outsiders, those clues would have guided us into more appropriate strategies.[5] I am reminded of Robert McNamara's words in the documentary the *Fog of War*: "If we can't persuade nations of comparable values of the merit of our cause, we better reexamine our reasoning."

This book hopes to answer a few vital questions about the American war in Vietnam: (1) What is the meaning and significance of the Vietnam War for Americans today? (2) What lessons have Americans learned from our defeat, and how should we apply that knowledge in implementing current foreign policy? (3) Who or what is to be blamed for the loss in Vietnam? (4) How can we heal our nation from the Vietnam War syndrome? and (5) How do we fit the Vietnam War era into our greater historical narrative?

I hope this book will tell the people's history of the Vietnam War. Now that my classes are filling with recently returned Iraq and Afghanistan War veterans, I feel even more inspired to pursue answers to these critical questions about the Vietnam War and perhaps gain practical and prudent wisdom that we can use to make good judgments in our current Iraq War and in the future. We must keep in mind that nations do not go to war, people do. This is a people's history. For it is with the individual that history both begins and ends.

I
ANCIENT ADVERSARIES, ADVENTURERS, AND ADVISORS, 1000 BC TO 1963

In the final analysis ... we all inhabit this small planet, we all breathe the same air, we all cherish our children's futures, and we are all mortal.

—John F. Kennedy

1

Origins of Vietnamese Nationalism

According to the ancient military treatise by Sun Tzu, the first rule of war is to know your enemy.[1] So what did Americans know of the Vietnamese when they started financing the French colonialists in their war against the Viet Minh in the early 1950s? Most Americans did not know that the Vietnamese had been struggling for their own identity since before the Common Era.[2] North Vietnamese premier Pham Van Dong said that Vietnamese history,

> from the time of the Hung kings and the Trung sisters, to the era of President Ho Chi Minh has been a history of great struggle. Throughout history, the Vietnamese people have always done their best to defend the country and to build the nation.[3]

The Vietnamese fought for almost a thousand years to evict the Chinese. Then they expanded south to their present borders, conquering the Champa culture and the Khmer empire, among others, along the way. The country expanded and then it fragmented in a series of civil wars. In spite of internal troubles, the Vietnamese regarded themselves as one people, but they were too divided and technologically inferior to stop the conquering French colonial forces in the nineteenth century.[4]

The Vietnamese emerged from a fusion of people who came from southern China, below the Yangtze River, and the indigenous population of Vietnam. So it was during the first millennium BC that the Viet people, who were to become the Vietnamese, came into being.[5] Chinese expansion reached Vietnam in 100 BC, and China dominated the Vietnamese until 900 AD. Consequently, China is considered the traditional enemy of Vietnam.[6]

The indigenous Vietnamese may have been very much like the Muong people who lived in the highland area on the southwestern fringe of the Red River Valley. The Vietnamese clung to their traditional values even during the 1000 years of Chinese rule. Patriotism is one of the most important Vietnamese attributes. The Vietnamese still celebrate the revolt led by the Trung sisters in 39 AD.[7] The Red River Valley and the Mekong River Delta are two very important rice-growing regions. It was in the Red River Valley that the Vietnamese emerged as a people (then called the Viet). The Vietnamese were finally able to expel the Chinese in 939. But they still faced the threat of another Chinese invasion as well as threats from the Champa kingdom to the south and the Cambodian (Khmer) empire to the west.

Ngo Quyen, the general who led the Vietnamese over the Chinese, founded the first dynasty, but died before he established firm control. The early Vietnamese also had to fight off the Mongols in 1284. Although they successfully defended themselves, the country was weakened. The Chinese invaded again in 1418 and were driven out in 1428. It was then that the Vietnamese began their conquests to the south and eliminated the Champa kingdom and the Khmer empire. This march down the coast took 250 years, ending when the Vietnamese finally reached the Mekong River Delta.[8]

The second phase of foreign domination began in the 1850s with the arrival of the French colonialists. On 31 August 1858, a French naval squadron attacked Da Nang, beginning a colonial conquest that was completed by 1884.[9] The French divided Vietnam into three regions (from north to south): Tonkin, Annam, and Cochinchina. The French instituted a rice-exporting economy, wherein large landowners took over from small traditional farmers who grew only enough to feed their own families. The rice export linked Vietnam to Western world markets.

The French introduced rubber to Vietnam in 1897. Rubber grew best in the south, which had been a sparsely populated region prior to the introduction of rubber. The French imposed high taxes on the peasantry, including taxes on salt, which was a staple of the Vietnamese diet. The French colonial system disrupted the traditional Vietnamese village structure, which in effect weakened the peasants' hold on the land. Yet the Vietnamese resisted the French.[10] An 1862 anti-French manifesto read:

> We fear your valor, but we fear Heaven more than your power. We vow that we shall fight everlastingly and without respite. When we have nothing left, we will arm our soldiers with branches. How then can you live among us?[11]

Although Vietnamese labor was cheap, only a few French companies profited. Indochina was not a financial success for the French. While the

French government spent millions of francs to protect and support the colony, companies like Michelin Rubber made millions on the backs of Vietnamese laborers, who worked under brutal conditions. The Vietnamese did not stage any major uprisings during the early period of French colonization. The Vietnamese were trying to adapt to French culture, Western fashions, ideas, and technology. Wealthy Vietnamese sought a Western education for their children. Consequently, the Vietnamese who headed the resistance to the French were French-educated.[12]

From 1900 to 1920, Phan Boi Chau led the Modernization Society. This society was dedicated to using Western ideas, technology, and science to create a modern Vietnamese state. The Modernization Society looked to Japan, an Asian country like Vietnam, as an example of what can happen when a society embraces modern technology. The idea was that if the Vietnamese could modernize themselves, the French would feel no need to maintain colonial control. The French, however, brutally suppressed the movement by killing its members or sending them to prison. The Modernization Society ultimately failed because of its narrow base of support (who were educated urbanites) and a poorly planned execution of strategy.[13]

By the 1920s, grassroots nationalist organizations sprung up in Vietnam. The most important of these was the Nationalist Party of Vietnam or VNQDD (*Viet Nam Quoc Dan Dang*) led by urban intellectuals. A 23-year–old teacher named Nguyen Thai Hoc established the VNQDD in 1927 around the Red River Delta region. Because they believed that only armed revolution could bring freedom from French rule, the VNQDD stockpiled weapons and infiltrated the army. The VNQDD attempted an uprising in 1930 but were quickly put down by the French. They failed for the same reasons that the Modernization Society had failed: narrow support base and a flawed execution of strategy.[14]

The question remains, how did Vietnamese nationalism come to be associated with Communism? This is unique in Asia, since other nationalist movements in Asia (e.g., in India and the Philippines) were dominated by Western concepts. One reason is that the French did not allow a Vietnamese middle class to emerge that would have embraced more Western ideas of nationalism. The French executed many Communists and were successful in keeping the movement down. But in 1930, the Indochinese Communist Party (*Dang Cong San Dong Duong*) was founded, and the roots of Communism began to grow strong in Vietnam.[15] Ho Chi Minh figured prominently in these early years. Born Nguyen Tat Thanh in 1890 in central Vietnam, Ho Chi Minh used several aliases. He was known for many years as Nguyen Ai Quoc (Nguyen the Patriot) and during World War II adopted his final name, which means "he who enlightens."

Ho Chi Minh's early life is not easy to decipher, partly because he did not allow many interviews. Ho was the son of a government official who resisted French rule. As a young man, Ho left Vietnam and worked as a merchant sailor and traveled around the world, including America, Britain, and France. Ho was a ruthless revolutionary and a dedicated nationalist. He was born into a high social status (his father being a civil administrator), was well educated, and prided himself as being a wandering scholar.[16]

Ho Chi Minh did not care much for Phan Boi Chau's Modernization Society because he did not want to work closely with, or model Vietnam after, Japan. In 1917, Ho moved to Paris, took the name Nguyen Ai Quoc, and began to plan for Vietnam's independence. He listened intently to Woodrow Wilson's 14 Points address,[17] especially the point that called for self-determination of peoples. He presented a petition of recognition to Western leaders, asking for his country's independence, while the Paris peace talks were ongoing following World War I. Although his petition was ignored by Western leaders in Paris, the attempt to gain recognition for Vietnam made him famous among the Vietnamese in France.

Ho Chi Minh became a devout Marxist-Leninist after his negative experience with Western nations in Paris and seized upon Lenin's ideas of building an anti-imperialist movement rooted in his country's strong nationalist tradition. He was one of the founding members of the French Communist Party in 1920 and formalized a plan for a successful revolution in Vietnam based on peasant involvement, capitalizing on anti-French nationalism, and emphasizing social and economic justice.[18] While in France, Ho edited an anticolonial paper called *Le Paria* (the Outcast). Ho received Communist training in Russia in 1923 and subsequently organized expatriate Vietnamese in Germany, China, Thailand, and France.[19]

Ho Chi Minh had to remain in exile because the French were purging Communists and nationalists in Vietnam. He spent a lot of time in China and studied the ways of the West. Ho saw Communism as a way to help solve economic problems and to drive the French imperialists out of Vietnam. He was a nationalist first and foremost and a Communist by design in order to facilitate Vietnam's independence. By the 1930s, Ho Chi Minh was the most well–known spokesman for Vietnamese nationalism.

2

French-Viet Minh War

In June 1940, three days after France fell to Nazi Germany, Japan landed forces in Indochina. Nguyen Ai Quoc returned home to Vietnam with a new name, after thirty years in exile: Ho Chi Minh. Seeing an opportunity to establish Vietnamese independence after the French acquiescence to the Japanese, Ho established the Viet Minh (*Viet Nam Doc Lap Dong Minh Hoi*), which means League for the Independence of Vietnam, in 1941.[1] The Viet Minh organized guerrilla bases, trained cadres, harassed the French and Japanese, and spread propaganda, urging the peasants to resist. The Vietnamese people suffered greatly under Japanese occupation. Famine, made worse by rice hoarding by the Japanese military, killed an estimated 2 million Vietnamese by 1945.[2]

Ho Chi Minh

Ho Chi Minh was born in Vietnam in 1890. His father, Nguyen Sinh Huy, was a teacher who worked for the French. He refused to learn French and lost his job. To survive, Nguyen Sinh Huy was forced to travel throughout Vietnam, offering his services to the peasants. This usually involved writing letters and providing medical care. As a nationalist, Nguyen taught his children to resist the French. Not surprisingly, they all grew up to be committed nationalists willing to fight for Vietnamese independence.

Although his father had refused to learn French himself, Ho Chi Minh went to a French school. After his studies, Ho became a schoolteacher. He then decided to become a sailor so he could travel to many different countries. Ho settled in Paris in 1917, where he read books by Karl Marx and other Communist writers and eventually became a Communist. Ho became one of the founding members of the French Communist Party. Ho, like other French Communists, had been inspired by the Bolshevik Revolution. In 1924, he visited the Soviet Union, and dedicated himself to fight for the freedom and independence of Vietnam.

However, Ho was aware that if he returned to Vietnam he was in danger of being arrested by the French authorities. He therefore decided to go and live in China on the Vietnam border. Here he helped organize other exiled nationalists into the Vietnam Revolutionary League.

In September 1940, the Japanese army invaded Indochina. With Paris already occupied by Germany, the French troops decided it was not worth putting up a fight and they surrendered to the Japanese. Ho Chi Minh and his fellow nationalists saw this as an opportunity to free their country from foreign domination and formed an organization called the Viet Minh. Under the military leadership of General Vo Nguyen Giap, the Viet Minh began a guerrilla campaign against the Japanese.

When the Japanese surrendered to the Allies, the Viet Minh were in a good position to take over control of the country. In September 1945, Ho Chi Minh announced the formation of the Democratic Republic of Vietnam. Unknown to the Viet Minh, Franklin D. Roosevelt, Winston Churchill, and Joseph Stalin had already decided what would happen to postwar Vietnam at a summit meeting at Potsdam. It had been agreed that the country would be divided into two, the northern half under the control of the Chinese and the southern half under the British.

After the Second World War, France attempted to reestablish control over Vietnam. In January 1946, Britain agreed to remove her troops, and later that year, China left Vietnam in exchange for a promise from France that she would give up her rights to territory in China. Negotiations broke down in 1946 and open hostilities began between French and Viet Minh forces.

In 1959, Ho Chi Minh sent Le Duan, a trusted advisor, to visit South Vietnam. Le Duan returned to inform his leader that Diem's policy of imprisoning the leaders of the opposition was so successful that unless North Vietnam encouraged armed resistance, a united country would never be achieved.

Ho Chi Minh agreed to supply the guerrilla units with aid. He also encouraged the different armed groups to join together and form a more powerful and effective resistance organization. This they agreed to do, and in December 1960, the National Front for the Liberation of South Vietnam (NLF) was formed.

Ho Chi Minh led his Communist forces successfully against the United States, bringing them to a standstill by February 1968 after the Tet Offensive. Ho did not live to see the Communist victory in April 1975. He died on 3 September 1969.

Ho associated his Viet Minh movement with the worldwide movement against Fascism. Since the French colonial administration collaborated with the Japanese when they invaded, the Viet Minh saw both the French and Japanese as enemies and saw themselves aligned with the United States (Ho had connections and worked with the OSS—Office of Strategic Services). Ho went by the nickname Uncle Ho, ostensibly due to his humbleness, and as a show of respect and familiarity among the common people. The Viet Minh were active in helping the peasantry as they suffered under two levels of oppression during World War II. The Viet Minh had a three-headed leadership. Ho Chi Minh was the revolutionary nationalist leader and founder, Vo Nguyen Giap (a former history teacher) was the military genius in the Viet Minh organizational apparatus, and Pham Van Dong was the Communist organizational leader.[3]

The Viet Minh organized the peasants during the war. They seized rice stockpiled for the Japanese and gave it to the peasants. When the war in Europe ended, Allied attention turned to Asia and the war against Japan. The Viet Minh, believing Allied statements supporting the rights of oppressed peoples and thinking that the Allies might eventually support Vietnamese independence, supplied them with intelligence information during the war. Oddly, the Americans and Ho Chi Minh's Viet Minh were working on the same side at this time. U.S. State Department official Abbot Low Moffat and OSS officer Archimedes Patti both agreed that Ho Chi Minh was a nationalist first, a Communist second. Based on this assessment, they believed that Ho could be allied with the United States after the war.

The sudden Japanese collapse in 1945 took many in French Indochina by surprise, but the Viet Minh were ready for what they called the "August Revolution." Ho Chi Minh declared an independent Vietnam and formed a government in Hanoi. The OSS was still working with the Viet Minh, which served to reinforce the idea of American support.

While Japan surrendered on 2 September 1945, the Vietnamese celebrated the formation of the Democratic Republic of Vietnam. Ho Chi Minh delivered

---

Archimedes Patti

Archimedes Patti was born in 1914 in New York. He began his military career in 1941. He was an infantry officer in Europe during World War II and was later assigned to the OSS in Hanoi, where he was awarded the Bronze Star. After his retirement in 1957, he worked for thirteen years as a crisis management specialist in the Office of Emergency Planning in Washington, helping to formulate contingency plans for the civil governance of the nation in the event of a nuclear attack.

In retirement, he wrote a book and several articles on Vietnam. In 1982, he wrote "Why Vietnam: Prelude to America's Albatross," which describes his relationship with Communist guerrilla leader Ho Chi Minh during the mid-1940s.

> Colonel Patti's thirty-three-year career was in both military intelligence and civil service. He headed the OSS team that flew into Hanoi in August 1945 to make preparations for the surrender of Japanese troops in North Vietnam and for the release of the allied POWs. He noted that Ho Chi Minh was more of a nationalist than a Communist and felt that the United States missed an opportunity to keep Ho Chi Minh on the U.S. side after World War II.
>
> Archimedes Patti died on 23 April 1998 and was buried at Arlington National Cemetery. His research and archival materials have been deposited with the University of Central Florida in Orlando.

a speech that began, "All men are created equal. They are endowed by their creator with certain inalienable rights..." Some in attendance, to add to the sense of irony, claimed that a U.S. plane circled over a cheering crowd as Ho read those words.

Ho Chi Minh appealed to President Harry Truman to aid his fledgling country, but Truman did not respond. Since Truman had been in office only four months in August 1945, it could be that he had not had time to formulate his foreign policy, especially one dealing with the complexities faced in Southeast Asia.

Ho Chi Minh's declared independence for Vietnam, the August Revolution, was legitimized by Emperor Bao Dai's abdication. Following Japanese surrender, China occupied the northern part of Vietnam, and Great Britain occupied the southern part. The Viet Minh had their base of power in the north. The situation became rather complicated when the British began to hand control back to the French. Ho Chi Minh made the decision to allow the French to come back to northern Vietnam in exchange for the Chinese leaving. China was busy ransacking the north and taking everything they could. Ho responded to fellow Vietnamese nationalists who criticized his decision, by saying, "I would rather smell French shit for five years than eat Chinese shit for one thousand years." Negotiations began between the French and the Viet Minh, but soon broke down, and Ho was quoted as saying, "If we have to fight, we shall fight. You will kill ten of our men, and we will kill one of yours, and in the end it will be you who will tire of it."[4]

Shortly thereafter, France and the Communist forces of Ho Chi Minh, the Viet Minh, were locked into a bloody war that lasted eight years (1946–1954). The Viet Minh fought a guerrilla war versus the French who were equipped to fight a conventional war. The French controlled the day, the Viet Minh the night. The French controlled the cities, the Viet Minh the countryside. It was called a "quicksand war." The war fought by France holds many ironic parallels to the war the United States would fight in Vietnam less than twenty years later.

In November 1946, the French shelled Haiphong. The French believed only force would stop the Viet Minh. By late 1946, Ho Chi Minh left Hanoi, and the Viet Minh were forced out of the cities. The French-Viet Minh War had started.

Peter Dewey

Born in 1917, Peter Dewey became the first American casualty in Vietnam on 26 September 1945. Dewey was an OSS (Office of Special Operations) lieutenant colonel. He was killed in action by the Communist Viet Minh near Hanoi.

During World War II, the OSS, predecessor of the CIA, trained and armed Viet Minh guerrillas in the jungles of northern Vietnam to fight the Japanese.

Ho Chi Minh had organized patriots of all ages and all types—peasants, workers, merchants, and soldiers—to drive both the Japanese and French out of Vietnam. His new organization, led by Communists, appealed to many Vietnamese nationalists. After the Japanese surrendered, Ho used the Viet Minh as a power base for a Vietnamese nationalist movement against the French.

Dewey irritated the French and the British authorities because of his contact with the Viet Minh. General Douglas D. Gracey, commander of a British force in Vietnam assigned to disarm the Japanese, suspected Dewey of intriguing with the Viet Minh and ordered him out of the country.

Before leaving, Dewey summed up the situation in Vietnam: "Cochinchina is burning, the French and British are finished here, and we [the United States] ought to clear out of Southeast Asia." On 26 September 1945, Dewey and a colleague, Captain Herbert J. Bluechel, headed for the Saigon airport in a jeep with Dewey driving.

Dewey took a shortcut past the Saigon golf course, where he noticed three Vietnamese in the roadside ditch. He shouted at them in French. The Viet Minh opened fire perhaps thinking he was French. Bluechel, unarmed, ran from the scene with a bullet knocking off his cap as he fled. Dewey's body was never recovered. French and Viet Minh spokesmen blamed each other for his death.

The French were confident that they could wipe out the Viet Minh army quickly. The French had a modern army with superior weapons bought with U.S. aid. The Viet Minh had widespread support among the peasants, whom the French were never really able to impress or pacify. The French picked Bao Dai, the former emperor of Vietnam, to head what they called the State of Vietnam to rival the Communist state. But this puppet regime did not convince many Vietnamese of its legitimacy. In 1950, China and the Soviet Union officially recognized Ho's government. The United States, signaling a Cold War competition in Southeast Asia, recognized Bao Dai's government as the legitimate Vietnamese state.

Though, initially, the Viet Minh under General Vo Nguyen Giap had great difficulty in coping with the better–trained and equipped French forces, the situation improved in 1949 after Mao Zedong and his Communist army defeated Chaing Kai-Shek in China. The Viet Minh now had a safe base where they could take their wounded and train new soldiers. By 1953, the Viet Minh controlled large areas of North Vietnam. The French, however, had a firm hold on the south. When it became clear that France was becoming involved in

---

Bao Dai

Bao Dai, the last emperor of Vietnam, was born in Hue on 22 October 1913. Educated in France, Bao Dai succeeded his father, Khai Dinh, as emperor on 6 November 1925. After officially ascending to the throne, he went back to resume school in France, leaving the administration of the country to the French. On 6 September 1932, Bao Dai returned to Vietnam to assume his imperial duty. In September 1940, the Japanese army invaded Indochina. With Paris already occupied by Germany, the French troops decided it was not worth putting up a fight and they surrendered to the Japanese. Bao Dai went into exile in Hong Kong in March 1946 and was allowed to return in June 1948. The following year the French installed Bao Dai as head of the state. This "Bao Dai" solution was meant to give South Vietnamese nationalism more credibility. In October 1955, the South Vietnamese people were asked to choose between Bao Dai and Ngo Dinh Diem to lead the country. Bao Dai did not win the election. After his defeat Bao Dai went into exile and lived for the next forty years in France. Bao Dai died in Paris on 31 July 1997.

---

a long-drawn–out war, the French government tried to negotiate a deal with the Viet Minh. They offered to help set up a national government and promised they would eventually grant Vietnam its independence. Ho Chi Minh and the other leaders of the Viet Minh did not trust the word of the French and continued the war.

French public opinion continued to move against the war. There were four main reasons for this:

1. Between 1946 and 1952, 90,000 French troops had been killed, wounded, or captured.
2. France was attempting to build up her economy after the devastation of the Second World War. The cost of the war had so far been twice what they had received from the United States under the Marshall Plan.
3. The war had lasted seven years and there was still no sign of an outright French victory.
4. A growing number of people in France had reached the conclusion that their country did not have any moral justification for being in Vietnam.

By May 1950, President Truman authorized direct U.S. aid for the French war in Indochina. The U.S. commitment deepened in Vietnam after North Korean troops invaded South Korea at the end of June 1950. U.S. policymakers took a harder line as they saw what they thought was monolithic Communism spreading in Asia. China's support of Ho's government gave the Viet Minh the means to sustain the war. By the end of 1953, America was paying 80 percent of the French war effort in Vietnam, over a billion dollars a year. Toward the end of their war in Vietnam, France initiated *Le jaunissement*, an attempt to hand the fighting over to their allied Vietnamese troops. This was but one of the many failed strategies employed by the French and later adopted by the United States in their war in Vietnam.

General Navarre, the French commander, tried one last strategy. French units were set up in a remote area in Dienbienphu, a valley surrounded by mountains, 170 miles from Hanoi. In November 1953, 12,000 French para-troopers dropped into the valley, confident that the Viet Minh would never be able to get enough troops to Dienbienphu, set up artillery, and keep supply lines open.

While these preparations were going on, Giap brought up members of the Viet Minh from all over Vietnam. By the time the battle was ready to start, Giap had 70,000 soldiers surrounding Dienbienphu, five times the number of French troops enclosed within.

Using antiaircraft guns and howitzers obtained from China, Giap was able to virtually stop French supply efforts to their forces in Dienbienphu. When Navarre realized that he was trapped, he appealed for help. The United States was approached, and some advisors suggested the use of tactical nuclear weapons against the Viet Minh. Another suggestion was that conventional air raids would be enough to scatter Giap's troops.

Vo Nguyen Giap

Vo Nguyen Giap was born in Quang-binh Province, Vietnam, in 1912. He was educated at the University of Hanoi, where he earned a doctorate in economics. After leaving the university he taught history in Hanoi. He later joined the Communist Party and took part in several demonstrations against French rule in Vietnam. Giap was arrested in 1939 but escaped to China, where he joined up with Ho Chi Minh, the leader of the Viet Minh. While in exile his sister was captured and executed. His wife was also sent to prison, where she died. From 1942 to 1945, Vo Nguyen Giap helped organize resistance to the occupying Japanese army. When the Japanese surrendered to the Allies after the atomic bombing of Hiroshima and Nagasaki in August 1945, the Viet Minh were in a good position to take control of the country, and Giap served under Ho Chi Minh in the provisional government.

Giap was a brilliant military strategist and one of the Big Three that ruled North Vietnam (along with Ho Chi Minh and Pham Van Dong). He was primarily responsible for the victory over the French at Dienbienphu in 1954 and also the victory over the Americans and the South Vietnamese government. Ultimately, Giap led his forces in victories over the French, the Americans, and the Chinese (after China's unsuccessful incursion into Vietnam in 1979).

The NLF arrived in Saigon on 30 April 1975. Soon afterwards, the Socialist Republic of Vietnam was established. In the new government, Vo Nguyen Giap was minister of defense and deputy premier.

The French faced 51,000 Viet Minh soldiers at Dienbienphu. On 13 March 1954, Giap began his attack with human wave assaults. Viet Minh artillery, hidden on the mountaintops, quickly destroyed the main airstrip. Four days into the battle, the Viet Minh controlled the perimeter of the French base. General Giap then dug in and encircled the French. The French tried to resupply by air, but most of the supplies fell into enemy hands. Dienbienphu was a disaster for the French. The French lost 1,500 dead, with 4,000 wounded and 10,000 taken prisoners. Many of the prisoners died in Viet Minh camps. The French were done.

Eisenhower refused to intervene unless he could persuade Britain and his other Western allies to participate. Winston Churchill, the British prime minister, declined, claiming that he wanted to wait for the outcome of the peace negotiations taking place in Geneva before becoming involved in escalating the war.

The French surrendered on 7 May 1954. French casualties totaled over 7,000, and a further 11,000 soldiers were taken prisoners. The following day, the French government announced that it intended to withdraw from Vietnam.

The negotiations began in Geneva in 1954. The Viet Minh were forced into negotiations by their fellow Communists. The unifying elections would take place in two years. The Soviets and Chinese feared that if the Viet Minh were not accommodating in the settlement, France would keep fighting and America would intervene. In the fall of 1954, the Viet Minh marched back into Hanoi after eight years of fighting the French.

The major agreements at Geneva were to divide Vietnam at the 17th parallel, thereby producing two separate Vietnamese states, and to hold unifying elections in two years (1956). The United States did not sign any agreements in Geneva and neither did the South Vietnamese delegation.[5]

The U.S. government, unfortunately, was unable to distinguish Vietnamese nationalism from Communism. The Communist-nationalist combination seemed to work in Vietnam because the Communists were better organized, had support from all classes including the peasantry, and had the superb leadership of Ho Chi Minh, Vo Nguyen Giap, and Pham Van Dong.

George F. Kennan

George Kennan was born in Milwaukee, Wisconsin, on 16 February 1904. After graduating from Princeton in 1925, Kennan joined the foreign services. He spent several years in Geneva and Berlin before being assigned in Moscow in 1933. After two years in the Soviet Union he was assigned to Vienna. This was followed by spells in Prague and Berlin.

On the outbreak of the Second World War Kennan was arrested by the Nazis but was eventually released and subsequently given diplomatic posts in Lisbon and Moscow. After the war Kennan returned to the United States, where George Marshall appointed him as director of the State Department's policy planning staff. Over the next couple of years Kennan developed the foreign policy of containment.

Kennan criticized U.S. foreign policy for its excessive moralism and legalism. He is known as the Father of Containment. His 1947 "X" article argued that the United States should hold a policy of long-term, vigilant containment of Russian expansionist tendencies. He said that all we needed to do, basically, was hold on until a new generation of Soviet leaders emerged that were more reasonable to deal with. Earlier, in his 1946 "Long Telegram," Kennan had warned that "the greatest danger that can befall us in coping with ... Soviet communism, is that we shall allow ourselves to become like those with whom we are coping." Most importantly, containment policy should stress economic, political, and psychological means over military force. He also advised the Americans to contain themselves as well. Almost as if he was predicting McCarthyism a few years later, Kennan said that we must guard against becoming hysterically anti-Communist. Kennan's restrained containment views were no longer acceptable by 1950 and he was driven out of government.

In 1956 Kennan was appointed as professor of historical studies at the Princeton Institute and while there revised his views on containment. Kennan now advocated a program of disengagement from areas of conflict with the Soviet Union. He was an unlikely antiwar critic during the American War in Vietnam. Books by Kennan include *Realities of American Foreign Policy* (1954), *Russia Leaves the War* (1956), *Memoirs: 1925–1950* (1967), and *The Nuclear Delusion* (1982). George Kennan died on 17 March 2005.

The groundwork for the American war in Vietnam was already being laid in the early 1950s. U.S. policymakers made three momentous decisions in Southeast Asia during the French-Viet Minh War:

1. The 1950 decision to support the Bao Dai government, and the financial support of the French war effort, which reached 80 percent by 1953
2. The decision in 1954 not to intervene in Dienbienphu
3. The decision not to engage in the diplomatic efforts in Geneva after the war, which would give the American government an excuse to not honor the agreements later.[6]

Because the United States did not take part in the Geneva agreement or sign them, they did not feel they were violating the agreements when they were subsequently broken.

Enter America

NATION BUILDING WITH EISENHOWER

Since U.S. president Dwight D. Eisenhower had begun to focus on the Third World during the 1950s, Vietnam seemed like a good place to hold the line against the spread of Communism. Eisenhower's foreign policy came to be known as the New Look. This policy relied heavily on the nuclear threat and brinkmanship. Brinkmanship might have worked with the Soviets, but did little good in nationalist wars in Third World countries. When Eisenhower left office, he warned us against a Military Industrial Complex.[1] Taken literally, he seemed to warn us about our system of government and cooperation between public and private industries. Our war industry could possibly destroy the very liberty it sought to protect. What is very clear is that in the 1950s, Eisenhower made a clear commitment to South Vietnam and President Ngo Dinh Diem.

Dwight D. Eisenhower

Dwight David Eisenhower was born in Denison, Texas, on 14 October 1890. He attended West Point and graduated in 1915. He was appointed commander of a heavy tank brigade in Pennsylvania but was not sent to Europe during the conflict.

After the war Eisenhower served under George Patton at Fort Meade, Maryland, where they became close friends. Promoted to the rank of major, Eisenhower was appointed chief of staff to Brigadier General Fox Connor when he was sent to Panama in 1922. Connor was a great influence on Eisenhower and introduced him to books written by philosophers and military strategists such as Plato, Tactitus, Clausewitz, and Nietzsche.

Eisenhower impressed General George Marshall, U.S. chief of staff, and, a week after Pearl Harbor, was recruited to help prepare the plans for war with Japan and Germany. In March 1942, Eisenhower was sent to England as head of European Theater of Operations (ETO). Recognized as an excellent coalition commander, Eisenhower was appointed head of the Supreme Headquarters Allied Expeditionary Force (SHAEF) and was given responsibility for Operation Overlord, the invasion of Europe.

The invasion was preceded by a massive aerial bombardment of German communications. This resulted in the destruction of virtually every bridge over the Seine. On 6 June 1944, 2,727 ships sailed to the Normandy Coast and on the first day landed 156,000 men on a front of thirty miles. It was the largest and most powerful armada that has ever sailed.

Eisenhower retired in 1948 and became president of Columbia University. In 1951 he returned to Europe as supreme commander of NATO. Although Eisenhower did not belong to a political party, in 1952 he was approached about being the Republican Party candidate for president. He accepted and in November easily defeated the Democratic Party candidate, Adlai Stevenson.

On 20 January 1953 Eisenhower became the first soldier-president of the United States since Ulysses S. Grant (1869–1877). Eisenhower's government was severely concerned about the success of Communism in Southeast Asia. Eisenhower was aware that he would have difficulty in persuading the American public to support another war so quickly after Korea. He therefore decided to rely on a small group of military advisors to prevent South Vietnam becoming a Communist state.

Eisenhower's Indochina policy was based on Containment. He had supported the French in the French-Viet Minh War with weapons, money, and technical assistance. But he did not intervene when the French were pinned down in Dienbienphu in 1954. He also did not like the fact that the French did not want to fight a broader war against Communism instead of a colonial war. Eisenhower took the lead in building SEATO (Southeast Asia Treaty Organization) in an attempt to join non-Communist countries together, much like NATO in Europe. Eisenhower supported the Diem regime in South Vietnam and their decision not to hold unifying elections in 1956. He supported Kennedy and Johnson's war policies except he did not think that Johnson did enough to win the war.

Eisenhower left office as one of the most popular presidents in American history. He was admired for his integrity, modesty, strength, and a flair for conciliation. He retired to his farm in Gettysburg and devoted much of his time to writing his memoirs, *Mandate For Change* (1963), *Waging Peace* (1965), and *At Ease* (1967). Dwight David Eisenhower died on 28 March 1969.

Throughout history, Laos and Cambodia have been influenced by events in Vietnam. Vietnam is much more populous than either of them. Laos was more of a political convenience than a nation. There was no strong sense of Laotian nationalism. Laos was created to serve French colonial interests. The Viet Minh penetrated the Laotian Communist movement, the Pathet Lao, demonstrating Vietnam's influence in the rest of Southeast Asia.

Cambodia, on the other hand, had a strong sense of national identity, based on the ancient Khmer empire. The royal family headed by Norodom Sihanouk galvanized Cambodian nationalism. Pol Pot was the Cambodian Communist leader. It is important to note that the struggle against Communism waged by the West in Southeast Asia was a struggle that involved the whole region, not just Vietnam.

By 1953, the U.S. National Security Council had warned, "[T]he loss of Indochina would be critical to the security of the United States." Ironically, when President Eisenhower was contemplating sending U.S. support to the French at Dienbienphu, Senator Lyndon B. Johnson of Texas railed against "sending American GIs into the mud and muck of Indochina on a bloodletting spree."[2] America had given France more than $2 billion to stop the Communist-led Viet Minh in Indochina.

In September of 1954, the U.S. advisory mission started training the South Vietnamese army, later called the ARVN (Army of the Republic of Vietnam). Ngo Dinh Diem was brought back from exile in a New York seminary to lead South Vietnam.

Ngo Dinh Diem

Ngo Dinh Diem was born in Vietnam in 1901. Diem was a Catholic whose ancestors had converted to Christianity in the seventeenth century. Diem, like previous generations of his family, was educated in French Catholic schools. After he graduated he was trained as an administrator for the French authorities in Vietnam. At the age of twenty-five he became a provincial governor. During the French-Indochina War, Diem left Vietnam for the United States. While in America he met influential Catholics like John F. Kennedy. He told them that he opposed both Communism and French colonialism and argued that he would make a good leader of Vietnam if the French decided to withdraw.

The United States delegation proposed Diem's name as the new ruler of South Vietnam during the Geneva Conference in 1954. Once Diem was in power, the Americans discovered that he was unwilling to be a puppet ruler. He constantly rejected their advice and made decisions that upset the South Vietnamese people. Several attempts were made to overthrow Diem; and, although the Americans were unhappy with his performance as president, they felt they had no choice but to support him. In October 1955, the South Vietnamese people were asked to choose between Bao Dai, the former emperor of Vietnam, and Diem for the leadership of the country. Diem won in a rigged election.

The main religion in Vietnam was Buddhism. The French, aware of the potential threat of Buddhism to their authority, passed laws to discourage its growth. After the French left Vietnam, the Catholics managed to hold onto their power in the country. Diem tended to appoint people to positions of authority who shared his religious beliefs. This angered Buddhists, especially when the new government refused to repeal the anti-Buddhist laws passed by the French. The Buddhists began a series of demonstrations against the Diem government to let the world know about his persecution of Buddhists.

After Thich Quang Duc's self-emulation in June 1963, Kennedy lost confidence in Diem. With the help of the CIA, South Vietnamese generals conducted a coup and removed President Diem from power. The generals killed Diem and his brother Nhu on 2 November 1963. With Diem's assassination ended the restriction on U.S. troops being deployed in great numbers in South Vietnam.

According to the Geneva cease-fire agreement, which imposed a temporary division of Vietnam, the French could retain their influence in the South. Ho Chi Minh took over the North. But the French decided to leave. To many Vietnamese, the Viet Minh were nationalist heroes. To America's leaders, Ho Chi Minh represented international Communism directed by Moscow, and was yet another example of the monolithic wall of Communism. In the South, America hoped to help build an anti-Communist state led by Ngo Dinh Diem, a less-than-well-known nationalist appointed prime minister during the Geneva Conference. Diem was a nationalist and had disliked French rule; now he took over a weak government bureaucracy, a downtrodden army, and a chaotic political situation in Saigon. Diem only had two years to win enough popular support to remain in power. The Geneva agreements called for unifying elections in 1956. If Ho Chi Minh won, the Communists would control all of Vietnam. The Eisenhower administration was less than certain about Diem. Diem, an austere Catholic, had been appointed by Bao Dai. He had no allies in South Vietnam.[3]

During the two-year period prior to the elections, the U.S.-backed South Vietnamese government did everything they could to consolidate power, including harassment of the North (i.e., use of astrologers to predict ruin and bad times in the north). By 1956, it was clear that Ho Chi Minh would easily win any Vietnamese election. Ngo Dinh Diem decided not to hold elections, and Eisenhower supported the decision since the United States and Diem had not signed the Geneva Accords. After the French were defeated at Dienbienphu, they did not take long to divest themselves from Vietnam. The United States was already involved in Vietnam through its military support of the French; consequently, the fledgling anti-Communist government in South Vietnam led by Ngo Dinh Diem was supported by the American government.

The concept of nation is not something that can be built overnight. The United States expected South Vietnam to be able to develop a strong enough sense of nationalism to resist Communist infiltration from North Vietnam. Nationalism takes many, many years to build. Our own experience with nationalism is a good example. Even after 100 years, the United States had to fight a civil war to settle differences related to competing concepts of what constituted an American nationality and proper government (Federalism versus anti-Federalism).[4]

From a Communist perspective, it looked like the United States was building a colony in South Vietnam not unlike what the French had done. This colonial stronghold could then be used strategically to dominate all of Southeast Asia. The United States began pouring millions of dollars into the anti-Communist regime in the South. The ARVN was built up dramatically during 1956–1960. Colonel Edward Lansdale arrived in Saigon to help Diem. He had been an OSS officer in World War II and had helped root out the Filipino Communists. The United States held Diem up as a model of anti-Communism and as the "Miracle Man of Asia." But Diem had trouble reaching the masses.

Diem had significant liabilities as president of South Vietnam. Not the least of these was his Catholicism. In a country that was 95 percent Buddhist, Diem was a Roman Catholic. He also was not a man of the people. He relied on a few members of his family and did not seek to win popular consensus. He actually spent time as a monk in upstate New York and seemed to possess personality traits that the clergy would have made that a better occupation for him. U.S. intelligence estimates were that South Vietnam was unlikely to develop its own independent sense of nationalism. This was due to poor leadership, the weakened state of the army, and the fact that 100,000 Communist operatives were actively working against the South Vietnamese government in South Vietnam. South Vietnam lacked the essentials of nation building. The United States kept Diem afloat financially, but Diem insisted that U.S. troops not be sent in. There were additional difficulties:

1. 25 million Vietnamese lived north of the 17th parallel
2. North Vietnam had a tightly organized government and a highly trained army
3. Ho Chi Minh was the most popular Vietnamese leader
4. The Viet Minh had defeated the French
5. Ho Chi Minh swore that he would reunite Vietnam
6. The South Vietnamese economy was totally dependent on the West and was in chaos
7. The South Vietnamese army was in ruins
8. Diem was tied to French despotism and was unpopular and inflexible.

Many challengers emerged from the political chaos in Saigon. Although Diem prevailed, he set a pattern where he would never compromise. Ho Chi

Minh's followers believed the elections in 1956 would bring him to power in a reunified Vietnam. Although the Viet Minh had pulled out of South Vietnam according to the Geneva agreements, they left behind political organizers to rally support for Ho. Diem, who had condemned the Geneva accords, decided to forego the election.

Since there were no nationwide elections in 1956, Vietnam remained divided, as Eisenhower promoted Diem as a hero. Without American support, Diem would never have survived. Diem welcomed U.S. aid, but he resisted American advice. During the late 1950s, Diem's problems grew. He tightened his inner circle under the pressure to stay in power and manage the chaos of South Vietnam. He was especially close to his brother Ngo Dinh Nhu and Nhu's wife. Their secret police, run by Nhu, set out to eliminate Communists and other dissidents.

Diem had his troubles in Vietnam. There were many competing sects and organizations fighting against Diem and his U.S.-backed government. Although Diem was successful in taking on his opponents, he curtailed democratic principles in order to preserve his power and authority. Early in 1960, Liberals and Conservatives alike in the United States supported the experiment with Diem in South Vietnam. The Third World had become the preeminent Cold War battleground. The American Friends of Vietnam group stated: "A free Vietnam means a greater guarantee of freedom in the world . . . there is a little bit of all of us in that faraway country."

In October of 1959, the Repressive Law went into effect in South Vietnam. It allowed military tribunals and summary executions without trial.[5] Democracy was only a fig leaf in Diem's South Vietnam. From 1955 to 1961, the United States put over $1 billion in economic and military aid into South Vietnam (78 percent of the aid was military). By the late 1950s, American aid prevented the collapse of the Saigon government and increased the standard of living for

---

Ngo Dinh Nhu

Ngo Dinh Nhu was born in 1910 and was the younger brother and chief political advisor to South Vietnamese president Ngo Dinh Diem. He was trained as an archivist but found that his real talent was as a behind-the-scenes political strategist. Nhu ran his brother's regime of secret political movements, the Can Lao. Nhu's wife, Madame Ngo Dinh Nhu, or Madame Nhu, was also influential on government policy and, since her brother-in-law was unmarried, was regarded as the First Lady of Vietnam.

As head of the secret police, Nhu was brutally efficient in dealing with any group that did not support the Diem regime (including the Buddhists). It was said that he was working on a compromise with the Communists prior to his assassination. Nhu was assassinated, along with his brother, during the 2 November 1963 coup.

those Vietnamese living in Saigon, but did little to promote economic development or improve living conditions for the people in villages, who constituted 90 percent of the population. Preoccupation with security precluded meaningful rural development and furthered dependency on the United States. Little concern was given to preserving democracy in South Vietnam. Diem was brutal with the Buddhists and other critics of his regime, but the U.S. government judged him mainly by his level of anti-Communism.

Diem did not listen to his U.S. advisors who said that the Saigon government should target villages for attention. The National Liberation Front (NLF, or the Viet Cong as Diem called them)[6] did not ignore the peasantry. Diem's heavy-handed treatment of the villages was met with resentment. The Viet Cong (VC) had been organized in the South in 1960, but they did not get full support from the North until later. Ho Chi Minh hid his support of the VC. Because the NLF operated far from Hanoi, they had a great degree of operational latitude. Many of the Viet Minh in the South became NLF fighters and enjoyed the same latitude in their war against the French. Eisenhower tried to convince Diem to change his ways and institute democratic reforms. Nation building was clearly failing in South Vietnam.[7]

The NLF was made up of over a dozen different political and religious groups. Although the leader of the NLF, Hua Tho, was a non-Marxist Saigon lawyer, many members of the movement were Communists.

The strategy and tactics of the NLF were very much based on those used by Mao Zedong in China. This became known as Guerrilla Warfare. The NLF was organized into small groups of between three to ten soldiers. These groups were called cells. These cells worked together, but the knowledge they had of each other was kept to the bare minimum. Therefore, when a guerrilla was captured and tortured, his confessions did not do too much damage to the NLF.

In early 1961, the Laotian crisis prompted by the U.S.-backed right-wing coup put Vietnam on the back burner. Eisenhower even contemplated sending troops to Laos. The Eisenhower administration's advisory program in Vietnam clearly laid the foundation for subsequent U.S. decisions to escalate American commitment in Vietnam. When Eisenhower briefed the young John F. Kennedy in 1961, he mentioned only Laos, not South Vietnam. Eisenhower believed

---

Bernard Fall

Born in 1926 in Austria, and professor at Howard University, Fall was an internationally known Vietnam War scholar. Fall, who was a French citizen, first went to Vietnam in 1953. He authored seven books about the French and American experiences in Vietnam: *Street without Joy* (1961), *The Two Viet-Nams* (1963), *Viet-Nam Witness: 1953–1966* (1966), and *Hell in a Very Small Place: The Siege of Dien Bien Phu* (1967). Fall was a critic of both U.S. and French policies in Vietnam. He was killed by a Viet Cong booby trap in Hue in 1967.

Laos could be another Korea. He did not take notice of the deteriorating situation in South Vietnam. This inattention may have come from greater concerns in Berlin, the U2 crisis, and the power transfer to JFK.

Americans did not want to become colonialists like the French, so we attempted nation building. The problem was that South Vietnam lacked the ingredients necessary to build a strong nation. Then there is the factor of time. It takes a long time to build a nation as well. Our own experience in the United States attests to this fact. A crisis was raging in Laos when Kennedy took the

---

Edward Lansdale

Edward Lansdale was born in Detroit, Michigan, on 6 February 1908. During the Second World War, Lansdale was a member of the Office of Strategic Services (OSS), an organization that was given the responsibility for espionage and for helping the resistance movement in Europe.

In 1953 Lansdale was sent to Vietnam to advise the French in their struggle against the Viet Minh. The following year Lansdale and a team of twelve intelligence agents were sent to Saigon. The plan was to mount a propaganda campaign to persuade the Vietnamese people in the south not to vote for the Communists in the forthcoming elections. In the months that followed they distributed targeted documents that claimed that the Viet Minh and Chinese Communists had entered South Vietnam and were killing innocent civilians. The Ho Chi Minh government was also accused of slaying thousands of political opponents in North Vietnam.

Colonel Lansdale also recruited mercenaries from the Philippines to carry out acts of sabotage in North Vietnam. This was unsuccessful and most of the mercenaries were arrested and put on trial in Hanoi. Finally, Lansdale set about training the South Vietnamese army (ARVN) in modem fighting methods.

After the 1955 election, Ngo Dinh Diem informed his American advisors that he had achieved 98.2 percent of the vote. Lansdale warned him that these figures would not be believed and suggested that he publish a figure of around 70 percent. Diem refused, and as the Americans predicted, the election undermined his authority.

Lansdale left Vietnam in 1957 and went to work for the secretary of defense in Washington. Posts held included deputy assistant secretary for special operations (1957–1959), staff member of the President's Committee on Military Assistance (1959–1961), and assistant secretary of defense for special operations (1961–1963).

In 1963 Lansdale was awarded the Distinguished Service Medal for counter-insurgency work and became consultant to the Food for Peace program. Lansdale returned to Vietnam in 1965 and became senior liaison officer of the U.S. mission to South Vietnam. Two years later he became an assistant to Ambassador Ellsworth Bunker. Lansdale retired in 1968 and his book, *The Midst of Wars*, was published in 1972. Characters in two novels, *The Quiet American* and *The Ugly American*, were patterned after him. Edward Lansdale died in McLean, Virginia, on 23 February 1987.

reins of government from Eisenhower in 1961 and inherited the groundwork for the Vietnam War.[8]

KENNEDY AND VIETNAM

The Cold War was raging when Kennedy took over the helm of the nation. Kennedy was in office only a few months when the United States was humiliated in Cuba at the Bay of Pigs. Fidel Castro prevailed in a CIA-led attack against his regime. The invasion planning started under Eisenhower, but JFK took the blame. The Cold War was the most pressing issue.

Kennedy came to office with flair. He offered a new vision and a new frontier for America. He also inherited a secret war in Cuba, a Cold War with the Soviet Union and China, and an emerging crisis in Southeast Asia. He preferred a flexible security strategy to Eisenhower's heavy-handed nuclear threats. Kennedy expanded conventional military forces and nuclear forces, and instituted the concept of counterinsurgency using his elite group of Special Forces. The world came to the brink of nuclear war over the placement of Soviet intermediate range missiles in Cuba in October 1962. Kennedy brought us back from that crisis only to be assassinated a year later. Controversy still surrounds the JFK assassination.

The Cuban Missile Crisis had a tremendous impact on Kennedy and on the Soviet Union. Shortly after the crisis subsided, a hotline was installed between Moscow and Washington to aid in communication. A Test Ban Treaty was also in the works. Despite all of this, Cuba remained a flashpoint and Vietnam was still not in the forefront of policy thinking.

John F. Kennedy

John Fitzgerald Kennedy was born in Brookline, Massachusetts, on 29 May 1917. Kennedy's father was a highly successful businessman who later served as ambassador to Great Britain (1937–1940). In 1940 Kennedy graduated from Harvard University with a science degree and published his first book, *Why England Slept* (1940). He joined the U.S. Navy in 1941 and became an intelligence officer.

After the United States entered the Second World War, Kennedy was transferred to the Motor Torpedo Boat Squadron, where he was given command of a PT boat. Sent to the South Pacific, in August 1943, his boat was hit by a Japanese destroyer. Two of his crew were killed but the other six men managed to cling on to what remained of the boat. After a five-hour struggle, Kennedy, and what was left of his crew, managed to get to an island five miles from where the original incident took place.

A member of the Democratic Party, Kennedy won in the election to the House of Representatives in 1946. He took a strong interest in foreign policy and in 1951 toured Europe, visiting Britain, France, Italy, Spain, Yugoslavia, and West Germany. On his return he told the Senate Committee on Foreign Relations that the United States should maintain its policy of helping to defend western Europe. However, he argued that the countries concerned should contribute more to the costs of the operation.

In 1960 Kennedy entered the race to become the Democratic Party presidential candidate. Kennedy won Democratic primaries in New Hampshire, Wisconsin, Indiana, Ohio, Oregon, Maryland, Nebraska, and West Virginia. At the national convention in July 1960, Kennedy was nominated on the first ballot. He selected Lyndon B. Johnson as his running mate.

At his inaugural address on 20 January 1961, Kennedy challenged the people of the United States with the statement, "Ask not what your country can do for you, but rather what you can do for your country." Kennedy also wanted the young people of the country to help the undeveloped world. He announced the establishment of the Peace Corps, a scheme that intended to send 10,000 young people to serve in Africa, Asia, and Latin America. Kennedy argued that this "practical, inexpensive, person-to-person program will plant trust, good will and a capacity for self-help" in the underdeveloped world.

In the first speech he made to the American public as their president, Kennedy made it clear that he intended to continue Eisenhower's policy of supporting the South Vietnamese government of Ngo Dinh Diem. He argued that if South Vietnam became a Communist state, the whole of the non-Communist world would be at risk. If South Vietnam fell, Laos, Cambodia, Burma, Philippines, New Zealand, and Australia would follow. If Communism was not halted in Vietnam it would gradually spread throughout the world. This view was essentially the Domino Theory. Kennedy went on to argue that America would be willing to "pay any price, bear any burden, meet any hardship, support any friend, oppose any foe to assure the survival and success of liberty." Kennedy's speech had a considerable impact on many young Americans.

The Cuban Missile Crisis in October 1962 was the first and only nuclear confrontation between the United States and the Soviet Union. The event appeared to frighten both sides and it marked a change in the development of the Cold War. It also galvanized the JFK leadership style in a crisis.

President Charles De Gaulle of France warned him that if he was not careful, Vietnam would trap the United States in "a bottomless military and political swamp." However, most of his advisors argued that with a fairly small increase in military aid, the United States could prevent an NLF victory in South Vietnam.

Kennedy had a good relationship with Ngo Dinh Diem, the leader of the South Vietnamese government, and in 1961 he arranged for him to receive the money necessary to increase his army from 150,000 to 170,000. He also agreed to send another 100 military advisors to Vietnam to help train the South Vietnamese army. As this decision broke the terms of the Geneva agreement, it was kept from the American public.

Kennedy gradually became convinced that Ngo Dinh Diem would never be able to unite the South Vietnamese against Communism. Several attempts had already been made to overthrow Diem, but Kennedy had always instructed the CIA and the U.S. military forces in Vietnam to protect him. In order to obtain a more popular leader of South Vietnam, Kennedy agreed to support the coup. As a result, at the beginning of November 1963, President Diem was overthrown by a military coup and killed.

Only a few weeks later, on 22 November 1963, John Fitzgerald Kennedy was assassinated in Dallas, Texas. Within two hours of the killing, a suspect, Lee Harvey Oswald, was arrested. Throughout the time Oswald was in custody, he stuck to his story that he had not been involved in the assassination. On 24 November, while being transported by the Dallas police from the city to the county jail, Oswald was shot dead by Jack Ruby. Diem, who had resisted the escalation of the war by adding U.S. military forces, was dead. JFK, who resisted a full-scale war in Vietnam, and, according to evidence now available, was planning a withdrawal of U.S. forces after the 1964 election, was dead as well.

John F. Kennedy's thinking on Vietnam evolved over time. As a young congressman, JFK went to Southeast Asia and came away with the opinion that

we have allied ourselves to the desperate effort of a French regime to hang on to the remnants of empire ... to check the southern drive of communism makes sense, but not only through reliance on the force of arms. The task is rather to build strong native non-Communist sentiment within these areas and rely on that as a spearhead of defense ... to do this apart from and in defiance of innately nationalistic aims spells foredoomed failure.[9]

In a *Meet the Press* interview in 1951, Kennedy said, "Without the support of the native population, there is no hope of success in any of the countries of Southeast Asia." Kennedy closely tied a victory for democracy in Vietnam contingent upon France's granting the Vietnamese their independence. "No amount of military aid could conquer an enemy of the people which has the support and covert appeal of the people," and victory could not be obtained in Indochina as long as the French remained there.[10]

In 1956, he spoke of Vietnam as "the cornerstone of the Free World in Southeast Asia, the keystone in the arch, the finger in the dike, and should the red tide of communism pour into it ... much of Asia would be threatened."[11] Kennedy spoke of Vietnam being vital to the regional economy of Southeast Asia and said that the United States had special obligations to Vietnam, which were even greater than simple national interests.

When Kennedy took office in 1961, he had many issues concerning him. One of the first orders of business for JFK was the Communist infiltration into Laos (following Eisenhower's advice). Kennedy received conflicting opinions on Laos from military advisors. Ho Chi Minh decided to back off on Laos and concentrate his efforts on South Vietnam. Like the question of Kennedy's continued actions in Vietnam, his commitment to the use of force to prevent a Communist victory in Laos also remains a mystery. Only Kennedy himself knew the exact mixture of bluff and determination.

Kennedy did feel a need to stand firm against Communism and restore public confidence. He felt that his credibility was slipping. He felt that Vietnam would be the best place to stand and fight with U.S. forces if necessary. He listed several reasons why Vietnam was better suited fo U.S. intervention than Laos:

1. Vietnam was more unified than Laos
2. South Vietnamese armed forces were larger and better trained
3. Vietnam provided direct access to the sea
4. Vietnam's geography complemented U.S. air and naval power
5. North Vietnam could serve as a buffer between South Vietnam and China.

Vice President Johnson put it more bluntly: The only alternative to standing by our allies was to "throw in the towel . . . and pull our defenses back to San Francisco."[12]

Kennedy sought an answer to a key question: Could the South Vietnamese build an anti-Communist base strong enough to survive on their own? But it seemed as if the U.S. government had already thrown in their lot with Diem. A popular refrain, reported in the *New York Times*, was, "Sink or swim with Ngo Dinh Diem." Or, as Arthur Schlesinger said in *A Thousand Days*, "By 1961 the United States had already supported the Diem government for seven years. Whether we were right in 1954 to undertake this commitment will long be a matter of interest to historians, but it had ceased by 1961 to be of interest to policy-makers."[13]

Although Kennedy was worried about overcommitment in Southeast Asia, U.S. policy was firmly entrenched, the U.S. government was strong, and the U.S. Army was willing to fight, which seemed to leave Kennedy with no option but to continue the effort begun in 1954. Kennedy sent General Maxwell Taylor and White House aide Walt Rostow to Vietnam in October 1961 in order to deter-

---

Robert McNamara

Robert Strange McNamara was born on 9 June 1916 in Oakland, California. He attended University of California at Berkeley, majoring in economics. He enrolled in the Harvard Business School in 1937, where he took to the concept of management based on the accumulation and analysis of quantitative data.

He applied this management style in the military during World War II, and in private industry (Ford Motor Company) after the war. The aggressive new management techniques earned McNamara and his colleagues the nickname "Whiz Kids." In November 1960 McNamara was named president of Ford Motor Company. But after only one month in this position, McNamara was called to the new Kennedy administration to serve as secretary of defense, with a mandate to bring the military under control through the application of efficient management.

The Vietnam War claimed much of McNamara's time and energy at the Defense Department, and over the years he began to feel that victory in this war was impossible. His thinking on the war gradually diverged from that of President Johnson.

McNamara supported the liberal policies of both JFK and LBJ: (1) continuation of the New Deal reforms, which ultimately became the Great Society, (2) exercising American power in the world to overcome Communism, and (3) the pursuit of civil rights for all Americans. But more than anything else, McNamara is associated with what went wrong in Vietnam. McNamara now feels that there was a basic misunderstanding of the threat to American security represented by the North Vietnamese pressure on South Vietnam. The Domino Theory presented during Eisenhower's time led Ike in 1954 to say that if Vietnam were lost, the dominoes would fall. Many in government believed in that concept. The threat may have been very real from Russia and China, but with respect to Southeast Asia, McNamara now believes that the U.S. government exaggerated the threat. Vietnam falling to Communism did not endanger the United States at all. Here are a few of McNamara's "lessons learned from Vietnam":

1. We misjudged the geopolitical intentions of our adversaries and we exaggerated the dangers to the United States of their actions.
2. We viewed the people and leaders of South Vietnam in terms of our own experience. We totally misjudged the political forces within the country.
3. We underestimated the power of nationalism to motivate a people to fight and die for their beliefs and values.
4. We failed to recognize the limitations of modern, high-technology military equipment, forces, and doctrine.
5. We failed to draw Congress and the American people into a full and frank discussion and debate of the pros and cons of a large-scale military involvement before we initiated the action.
6. We did not recognize that neither our people nor our leaders are omniscient. Our judgment of what is in another people's or country's best interest should be put to the test of open discussion in international forums. We do not have the God-given right to shape every nation in our image or as we choose.
7. We failed to recognize that in international affairs, as in other aspects of life, there may be problems for which there are no immediate solutions. At times, we may have to live with an imperfect, untidy world.[*]

*Interview with Robert McNamara, 5 February 2004. http://www.berkeley.edu/news/media/releases/2004/02/05_fogofwar.shtml.

mine whether Vice President Johnson's plan of increased stabilization in South Vietnam was feasible. JFK favored Secretary of Defense Robert McNamara and Taylor over State Department officials. Vietnam policy began to fall increasingly into the hands of the military. This was due to the following reasons:

1. Vietnam was a low-level crisis in relation to Cuba, Latin America, and Berlin
2. The military advisory system seemed to be working
3. The Strategic Hamlet program was apparently successful.

Maxwell Taylor

Maxwell Taylor was born in Keystesville, Missouri, on 26 August 1901. A West Point graduate (1922), he was among those who set up the first airborne units. In World War II, he commanded the 101st Airborne Division and was the first general to land in Normandy on D day. He was superintendent of West Point (1945–1949) and served as military governor of Berlin (1949–1951). He commanded the U.S. Eighth Army in the Korean War (1953–1955) before taking over as commander of the U.S. and UN Far East commands. He was army chief of staff (1955–1959) before retiring, but President John F Kennedy called him out of retirement in 1961 and appointed him chairman of the Joint Chiefs of Staff (1962–1964). He took an active role under presidents Kennedy and Johnson in escalating the U.S. commitment to South Vietnam and served as ambassador to South Vietnam (1964–1965).

Kennedy adopted Taylor's Flexible Response strategy that was designed to meet challenges presented in the Cold War struggle, increasingly focused on the developing world. Kennedy sent Taylor and Walt Rostow to Vietnam in 1961 to assess the situation and they produced the Taylor-Rostow report that severely downplayed the dangers of massive military intervention in Vietnam. General Taylor believed that counterinsurgency warfare could prevent a takeover by the Communists in South Vietnam. He returned to Vietnam in 1963, this time with Robert McNamara, and their report, the Taylor-McNamara report, noted progress in the war effort but recommended alternative leadership to Diem (the South Vietnamese president).

Taylor always supported the war but believed more in bombing North Vietnam than committing massive numbers of U.S. combat troops. As one of Johnson's "wise men," Taylor advised the president to not disengage from South Vietnam. Taylor was fluent in several languages and was the author of four books on military issues. General Taylor died on 19 April 1987.

Kennedy continued to get glowing reports of success for his policies in Vietnam, and because he was preoccupied with other matters, he accepted these. Taylor and Rostow made the following recommendations:

1. American aid must be significantly expanded to stop the deterioration of South Vietnam
2. The South Vietnamese must win the war themselves
3. The United States should work closely with South Vietnam
4. The United States should send an 8,000-man task force of engineers, medical personnel, and infantry, ostensibly to provide flood-fighting help for the South Vietnamese government.[14]

But Diem refused to accept U.S. military personnel in South Vietnam. On that point, he was most insistent. In November 1961, Undersecretary of State

Chester Bowles and veteran diplomat W. Averell Harriman concluded that Diem would not survive even with U.S. help. He was a dictator, was unpopular, and the "United States should not stake its prestige in Vietnam." JFK was worried about the Taylor-Rostow plan. He said that "it's like taking a drink, the effect wears off, and you have to take another." Choosing neither to send in combat troops nor negotiate out of Vietnam, JFK dramatically increased aid to South Vietnam and the number of military advisors. This was called the "limited partnership approach." Kennedy ultimately believed that it did not matter whether Diem was a good leader or not; Communist aggression had to be stopped in Vietnam. Kennedy felt compelled to keep the pressure on Khrushchev. When Kennedy announced that the United States would "pay any price and bear any burden" in fighting for freedom in the world, he seemed to be applying this in Vietnam.[15]

Kennedy was reluctant to send ground troops to Vietnam, but he wanted to appear to be tough. He felt the answer was counterinsurgency. Special forces, like the Green Berets, were sent to train the troops of threatened countries. They went in small numbers, but they brought with them the best of American military technology.

The VC in the South had made big gains in 1961. With increased U.S. aid and the new counterinsurgency program, Kennedy extended the American commitment. But one of the main problems was the instability of the South Vietnamese government. In early 1962, two of Diem's own air force officers bombed the government palace. The VC had assassinated 500 civilians and Diem officials and killed 1,500 of his troops in the first half of 1961. VC influence was growing. The Americans were trying to be optimistic, but there was rising opposition to Diem's government, especially to his brother Nhu, who controlled the secret police.

The United States and North Vietnam were working at two very different levels in the early 1960s. The U.S. government was committed to stopping Communist insurgency by the NLF and the North Vietnamese Army (NVA). The North Vietnamese were fighting against illegitimate government in the South and imperialism by the United States. JFK had a broad set of Third World policies, including aid to the Third World, the Alliance for Progress in Latin America, and the Peace Corps. The military had to change its strategy to fight wars in the Third World—counterinsurgency. But Kennedy and his counterinsurgency advisors did not understand the nature of the people's war strategy for the peasantry.

In 1962, Strategic Hamlets were being built in South Vietnam to keep the peasants safe from the VC. The spiked-perimeter hamlets resembled prison camps more than villages. Defense Secretary McNamara toured some hamlets with Ambassador Nolting in May 1962. Though American officials had private reservations about the program, McNamara publicly praised it. The peasants also became more of a target for the VC in such strategic hamlets. Early reports from journalists seemed to be critical of U.S. policy in South Vietnam. Diem

Malcolm Browne

Born in 1931, Pulitzer Prize–winning journalist Malcolm Browne began his professional career as a chemist. Drafted at the tail end of the Korean War, Browne was assigned to write for a military newspaper, *Pacific Stars and Stripes*, thus launching his celebrated career as a war correspondent. He was among the first correspondents to cover the war in Vietnam and was working for the Associated Press in Saigon when his insightful reporting on civil unrest in South Vietnam earned him a Pulitzer. On the morning of 11 June 1963, a startling spectacle of protest occurred in downtown Saigon. Buddhist militants blocked off a busy intersection as an elderly monk sat in the middle of the street. Thich Quang Duc did not move as he was drenched in gasoline. He sat unflinching in a meditative posture when a supporter set him on fire. Quang Duc burned quickly in orange flame and fell over dead before an ambulance or fire truck could reach him. Malcolm Browne was there and captured the photo. This photo was on the front page of most newspapers around the world the next day. U.S. support for the Saigon regime and its mishandling of the Buddhist uprisings in 1963 seemed to be a signal of bad times ahead.

He joined the *New York Times* in 1968 and eventually switched to science writing. After a stint as an editor at *Discover* magazine, he returned to the battlefield once more to cover the 1991 Persian Gulf War.

was reported as corrupt, more interested in collecting U.S. aid than fighting Communism, and the ARVN were criticized as largely ineffective.

Kennedy had been concerned about Vietnam, but in the spring of 1963, it became a crisis. Buddhist groups, protesting that Diem's soldiers had killed eight worshippers while breaking up a gathering in Hue, began a series of demonstrations. Diem and his family did not take the Buddhists seriously. As the demonstrations grew, Diem rejected compromise and met the challengers with force. The Buddhist uprisings, especially the horrifying self-immolation of an elderly Buddhist monk named Thich Quang Duc on 11 June 1963, and Diem and Nhu's brutal retaliations, signaled to the Americans that Diem was losing control.[16] The photos of Thich Quang Duc were on the front page of most newspapers the next day. Saigon students joined the Buddhists, and the protests against Diem exploded. In the summer of 1963, events became beyond Washington's control. The Buddhists galvanized the opposition to Diem. Diem's senior army officers began to talk of a coup. U.S. ambassador Nolting stood by Diem and opposed a coup. But JFK advisor Roger Hilsman and others in Washington had decided that Diem and Nhu had to go. Ambassador Nolting, Diem's ally, left Vietnam and was replaced by Henry Cabot Lodge, a Republican. Kennedy wanted bipartisan support in the Vietnam crisis.

By 1963, the Kennedy government began to pressure Diem and his brother Nhu for reforms. That summer, they started to formulate a plan to settle with the

North Vietnamese and pull out of South Vietnam. Close aids Roger Hilsman and Ken O'Donnell claim that Kennedy saw the futility of fighting in South Vietnam and was ready to pull out right after the 1964 elections.

During this time South Vietnam was on the verge of collapse. Diem and Nhu's special forces raided the pagodas and arrested thousands of Buddhists. Diem's generals hatched their plot against the government. The United States was now spending a million and a half dollars a day on the war. There were 16,000 American soldiers in South Vietnam, still classified as military advisors. The generals secretly asked Lodge for American support in their plot to oust Diem. Diem and Nhu declared martial law after they learned of the plot. Lodge asked the Kennedy inner circle for direction. Four top advisors took the initiative, and cabled Lodge to tell Diem to get rid of Nhu. Lodge could tell the generals to go ahead with their plan if Diem refused to cooperate.

The Buddhists continued their protests, and the tensions in Saigon grew ever greater. Then, in a television interview with Walter Cronkite on 2 September 1963, Kennedy sent a subtle message to Diem:

> In the final analysis, it's their war. They're the ones who have to win it or lose it. We can help them, we can give them equipment, we can send our men out there as advisors, but they have to win it—the people of Vietnam against the Communists. We're prepared to continue to assist them, but I don't think that the war can be won unless the people support the effort, and in my opinion, in the last two months the government has gotten out of touch with the people.

Then Cronkite asked: "Do you think that this government still has time to regain the support of the people?" Kennedy responded:

"Yes, I do. With changes in policy and, perhaps, in personnel, I think it can. If it doesn't make those changes, I would think that the chances of winning it would not be very good."[17]

Duong Van Minh

Duong Van Minh was born in 1916 in the Mekong Delta Province of My Tho. He is best known for leading the coup that seized power from South Vietnamese president Ngo Dinh Diem and led to his assassination.

Minh's military career began in the 1940s when he was only one of fifty Vietnamese officers to be commissioned in the French colonial army. After French colonial rule ended in 1954, Minh ascended through the ranks of the new South Vietnamese military, where he was called "Big Minh," because fellow troops were dwarfed by his six-foot frame, and to distinguish him from other officers with the same name.

Minh helped lead a U.S.-backed coup in 1963 that overthrew the then South Vietnamese president Ngo Dinh Diem, who was killed along with his brother, police chief Ngo Dinh Nhu, while trying to escape. Minh, the second-highest ranking general at the time, took power under a military junta. Two months later, General Nguyen Khanh deposed the junta and took control of the country. Minh went into exile. He resurfaced in 1971 and challenged President Nguyen Van Thieu, who was supported by the United States. Minh eventually withdrew from the race after alleging that the election was rigged.

Minh himself kept a low political profile until 1975, when Hanoi's forces launched what would be the final offensive of their long struggle to take over the south. In the final days, as Thieu fled the country, Minh was named interim president on 28 April 1975, with a promise to seek reconciliation with the northerners. The attempt at settlement failed, and Saigon fell to the Communists on 30 April 1975. Big Minh died on 6 August 2001 in Pasadena, California.

Kennedy felt that U.S. prestige was at stake in Vietnam. Yet, he also realized the dangers of a U.S. overcommitment. This prestige factor became the overarching concern for U.S. policymakers in Vietnam and it was seen more in a military, rather than a political, dimension. Diem's mishandling of the Buddhist uprisings convinced Kennedy that Diem would never be able to unite the South Vietnamese against Communism. In order to obtain a more popular leader for South Vietnam, Kennedy agreed to the military coup. After the generals had promised Diem that he would be allowed to leave the country, they changed their minds and killed him and his brother Nhu on 2 November 1963. JFK was assassinated a few weeks later, on 22 November 1963, in Dallas.[18]

JFK assassination conspiracy theories abound.[19] There are more books in the Library of Congress about the JFK assassination than there are about Elvis. Nearly 80 percent of the American people believe that there was some sort of conspiracy involved with the assassination of JFK. Yet, even after a release of documents and a congressional investigation in the late 1970s, no definitive proof exists. Conspiracy theorists point to the fact that all principals and witnesses are dead and that the government has had many decades to clean up any "smoking gun" in the files. What we do know is that shortly after Kennedy's assassination, President Lyndon B. Johnson dramatically expanded the war in Vietnam. It is also interesting that Ngo Dinh Diem was assassinated just weeks before Kennedy was, and Diem was absolutely resistant to U.S. troops (other than advisors) being deployed in Vietnam. What would Kennedy have done in Vietnam? Kennedy told some of his inner circle that he would pull out the military advisors after the elections of 1964. To others he said that the United States must hold the line in Vietnam.

His supporters argue that JFK held the dual objectives in Vietnam of stopping Communism and relying on indigenous military support to do so. His detractors contend that those objectives were incompatible since the administration misread the nationalist political current in Vietnam and chose to support an unpopular and weak government that would eventually fall and lead to heavy U.S. military involvement in order to achieve the first objective. Kennedy's ad hoc style of leadership makes a prediction of his eventual course in Vietnam uncertain. Some say he would have found a way out, others say he would have done much the same as Lyndon Johnson did. Evidence seems to indicate that Kennedy was holding two different ideas at once. Earlier public comments reflect this duality:

We must face the fact that the United States is neither omnipotent nor omniscient—that we are only 6 percent of the world's population—that we cannot impose our will on the other 94 percent of mankind—that we cannot right every wrong or reverse every adversary—and that therefore, there cannot be an American solution to every world problem.

JFK's remarks as a senator still ring true today:

No amount of American military assistance in Indochina can conquer . . . an enemy of the people which has the sympathy and covert support of the peo-

---

McGeorge Bundy

McGeorge Bundy was born on 30 March 1919 in Boston, Massachusetts. After serving as an aide to Admiral Alan G. Kirk during World War II, he collaborated on the memoirs of former secretary of war Henry L. Stimson, worked briefly on the Marshall Plan, and helped to advise the Republican presidential candidate Thomas E. Dewey on foreign affairs. In 1949, after Dewey's defeat, he became a lecturer in government at Harvard. Four years later, at the age of thirty-four, he was named dean of arts and sciences. Although he was a Republican, he was strongly attracted to John F. Kennedy and became one of Kennedy's "wise men" and part of the group that came to be called the "best and the brightest." He moved into public life in 1961, becoming national security advisor to JFK. He played a crucial role in all of the major foreign policy and defense decisions of the Kennedy administration and part of the Johnson administration—the Bay of Pigs Invasion, the Cuban Missile Crisis, and the Vietnam War. He was a strong advocate of the war in Vietnam and supported escalating the American involvement and the bombing of North Vietnam. Yet he did have his moments of doubt regarding Vietnam policies according to David Halberstam. His brother William Bundy served in government at the same time and was member of the CIA and a foreign affairs advisor to Kennedy and Johnson. McGeorge later came to strongly regret those decisions, one of the first administration members to do so. He spent much of the rest of his career trying to understand how he and so many others had made such a terrible mistake.

Bundy was one of the few Kennedy loyalists to stay on under Lyndon Johnson and adjust to their volatile new boss. Bundy's job was to evaluate, compress, and

clarify the avalanche of foreign affairs information in the White House. Some
believe that he was a skilled adjudicator, not an advocate, of the war in Vietnam.
He often tolerated and even encouraged dissent from conventional wisdom, as
long as it was expressed with brevity and evidence. His loyalty was to the pres-
ident and to the nation's security more than to any party or ideological position.
From 1979 to 1989, he was professor of history at New York University.
McGeorge Bundy was working on a book about Vietnam when he died on 16
September 1996.

ple ... for the United States to send troops ... [would force a situation] more
difficult than Korea. It seems to me it would be a hopeless situation.

"Is it true," he asked fellow senators, that "all or part of Indochina is absolutely essential to the security of Asia and the free world?"[20]

NSC advisor McGeorge Bundy's amusing remark about U.S. policy in
Southeast Asia is telling: "At this point we are like the Harlem Globetrotters
passing forward, behind, sideways, and underneath, but nobody has made a
basket yet."

Yet, some recent scholarship reveals that Kennedy did indeed plan the
withdrawal of troops from Vietnam. According to McNamara, in the 2 November 1963 NSC meeting, Kennedy's action had three elements: (1) complete
withdrawal from Vietnam by 31 December 1965, (2) the first 1000 troops to be
out by the end of 1963, and (3) a public announcement to set these decisions in
concrete. In other words, had Kennedy not been assassinated, the Vietnam
War would not have started again—it would have died with a whimper.

Johnson went on to fall into the trap that Kennedy and even Johnson
himself had recognized. Johnson decided to allow covert action (OPLAN 34-
A), which precipitated the Tonkin Gulf incident and the Tonkin Gulf resolution that authorized the Vietnam War. Recent tapes released from the
Johnson Library indicate that LBJ was aware of the trap that Vietnam presented
very early in the war. The question remains, why did he then proceed with the
war? John Kenneth Galbraith heard Johnson say that "you may not like what I
am doing in Vietnam, Ken, but you would not believe what would happen if I
were not here." More than likely he was referring to plans to make a pre-
emptive strike on Russia. Such plans had been conceived and the target date
was the end of December 1963, since the Soviet Union had only three or four
nuclear missiles at that time. It could be that Johnson gave the defense establishment the war it wanted in Vietnam, but kept it limited, not daring to
cross the nuclear threshold.[21]

What is clear, however, is that the Kennedy administration left their suc-
cessors with a heavy burden. JFK had apparently ruled out a diplomatic solution in Vietnam, but did not have a clear vision of the military solution

either. As it turned out, we looked at the crisis in Vietnam in strictly military terms.[22] Kennedy's government had played a role in Diem's overthrow, and that act and complicity deepened America's involvement in Southeast Asia. Kennedy's assassination in Dallas only three weeks after Diem's signaled a turning point for the United States in Vietnam.

II
PACKS AND RIFLES, 1964–1967

So, when we marched into the rice paddies on that damp March afternoon, we carried, along with our packs and rifles, the implicit convictions that the Viet Cong would be quickly beaten and that we were doing something altogether noble and good. We kept the packs and rifles; the convictions, we lost.

—Philip Caputo, *A Rumor of War*

4

Escalation

Lyndon B. Johnson inherited the crisis in Southeast Asia from JFK and earlier U.S. presidents. But it was his decisions in 1964 that ultimately led to America's entry into the Vietnam War. Between November 1963 and July 1965, LBJ transformed a limited commitment to assist the South Vietnamese government into an open-ended commitment to preserve an independent non-Communist South Vietnam. He tended to follow the policies of JFK. Johnson even kept many of Kennedy's advisors and cabinet members: Secretary of State Dean Rusk, Secretary of Defense Robert McNamara, and NSC advisor McGeorge Bundy. As Johnson and his advisors would discover, the key problem in South Vietnam was a lack of proper leadership and national unity.

Lyndon B. Johnson

Lyndon Baines Johnson was born in Stonewall, Texas, on 27 August 1908. Although both his father and grandfather had served in the Texas legislature, his family was poor. After leaving school he did many jobs before studying at the Texas State Teachers College at San Marcos. In 1930 Johnson began teaching at the Sam Houston High School. A strong supporter of Franklin D. Roosevelt and the New Deal, in 1935 Johnson was appointed director of the National Youth Administration.

Johnson was elected to the House of Representatives in 1937. During his campaign Johnson had promised, "If the day ever comes when my vote was cast to send your boy to the trenches, that day Lyndon Johnson will leave his Senate seat and go with him." Johnson kept his pledge, and when the United States entered the Second World War in December 1941, Johnson immediately joined the U.S. Navy. Commissioned as a lieutenant commander, he served in the South Pacific. In 1948 Johnson was elected to the Senate. Since he won by only eighty-seven votes he took the nickname "Landslide Lyndon."

In 1960 the Democratic Party selected John F. Kennedy as its presidential candidate. Only forty-three years old, Kennedy was politically inexperienced and very unpopular with certain sections of the party. Richard Nixon, Kennedy's opponent, had a long career in politics and had served for eight years as vice president under Dwight Eisenhower. Party managers believed that Johnson would make an ideal running mate for Kennedy.

In the winter of 1963, Johnson invited John F. Kennedy to make a tour of Texas. While in Dallas on 22 November, Kennedy was assassinated and Johnson was immediately sworn in as president. Over the next few months Johnson concentrated on persuading Congress to pass Kennedy's proposed program of civil rights legislation.

Johnson was a strong supporter of the Domino Theory and believed that a non-Communist South Vietnam was vital to the defense of the United States: "If we quit Vietnam, tomorrow we'll be fighting in Hawaii and next week we'll have to fight in San Francisco."

Johnson, like Kennedy before him, came under pressure from his military advisors to take more forceful action against North Vietnam and the NLF. The Joint Chiefs of Staff advised Johnson to send U.S. combat troops to South Vietnam. The overthrow of President Ngo Dinh Diem had not resulted in preventing the growth of the NLF. The new leader of South Vietnam, General Khanh, was doubtful that his own army was strong enough to prevent a Communist victory.

Johnson told his Joint Chiefs of Staff that he would do all that was necessary to prevent the NLF from winning in South Vietnam but was unwilling to take unpopular measures like sending troops to fight in a foreign war, until after the 1964 presidential elections. "Just let me get elected," he told his military advisors at a Christmas reception in 1963, "and then you can have your war."*

In August 1964, Congress approved Johnson's decision to bomb North Vietnam and passed what has become known as the Gulf of Tonkin resolution. This resolution authorized the president to take all necessary measures against Communist aggression from North Vietnam and the NLF.

Johnson's belief that the bombing raid on North Vietnam in August 1964 would persuade Ho Chi Minh to cut off all aid to the NLF was unfounded. In the run-up to the November election, the NLF carried out a series of attacks, and only two days before the election, the U.S. air base near Saigon was mortared and four Americans were killed.

Three months after being elected president in his own right in 1964, Johnson launched Operation Rolling Thunder. Unlike the single bombing raid in August 1964, this time the raids were to take place on a regular basis. In economic terms, the bombing hurt the economy of the United States more than that of North Vietnam.

On 8 March 1965, 3,500 U.S. marines arrived in South Vietnam. They were the first official U.S. combat troops to be sent to the country. This dramatic escalation of the war was presented to the American public as being a short-term measure and did not cause much criticism at the time. A public opinion poll carried out that year indicated that nearly 80 percent of the American public supported the bombing raids and the sending of combat troops to Vietnam.

The Tet Offensive proved to be a turning point in the war. In military terms it was a victory for the U.S. forces. In March 1968, President Johnson was told by his secretary of defense that in his opinion the United States could not win the Vietnam War and recommended a negotiated withdrawal. Later that month, President Johnson told the American people on national television that he was reducing the air raids on North Vietnam and intended to seek a negotiated peace. By 1968, the Vietnam War was costing $66 million a day. As a result, President Johnson increased income taxes and cut back on his program to deal with poverty.

Public opinion polls suggested that Johnson would have difficulty winning the 1968 presidential election. On 31 March 1968, Johnson made an announcement on television that he was not a candidate for reelection. He also told the American people that he had ordered major reductions in the bombing of North Vietnam and that he was seeking peace talks with the North Vietnam government.

In January 1969, Johnson retired to his ranch in Texas, where he wrote his memoir, *The Vantage Point* (1971). Lyndon Baines Johnson died of a heart attack at San Antonio, Texas, on 22 January 1973, five days before the conclusion of the treaty by which the United States withdrew from Vietnam.

*Stanley Karnow, *Vietnam: A History*, New York: Viking, 1983, p. 326.

The U.S. government assumed that it would require only limited power to fight the war in Vietnam. Late in 1963, North Vietnam escalated their war effort. The assassination of Diem had been a mixed blessing for the Communists. It eliminated a powerful anti-Communist leader, and the hatred so many Vietnamese had for Diem's regime had been a useful recruiting tool for the NLF. North Vietnam figured that massive infiltration into South Vietnam, including NVA regulars, would force disintegration of South Vietnam and stop the U.S. resolve to help. But LBJ did not weaken his resolve. NSC Action Memo 273, dated 26 November 1963, pledged, "[T]he central objective of the U.S. is to assist the people and the government of South Vietnam to win their contest against the externally directed and supported communist conspiracy."[1]

In 1964, the military junta controlling South Vietnam was overthrown by General Nguyen Khanh with tacit U.S. approval. The Strategic Hamlet program was in ruins.[2] LBJ saw the Peking government as on the move in Southeast Asia and wanted to stop the progress of Communism in Asia: "We must not appease aggression," as he liked to say (recalling the Lessons of Munich in World War II). Johnson did not consider negotiating his way out of Vietnam, and in 1964 he named General William Westmoreland the MACV (Military Assistance Command—Vietnam) in South Vietnam, and increased the number of

William Westmoreland

William Westmoreland was born in Spartanburg County, South Carolina, on 26 March 1914. He graduated from West Point in 1936 and during the Second World War commanded artillery battalions in Sicily and North Africa. Later he became chief of staff of the 9th Infantry Division.

Westmoreland commanded the 187th Airborne Infantry in the Korean War. He was also commander of the 101st Airborne Division, and at the age of forty-two became the youngest major general in the U.S. Army.

In 1960, Westmoreland was appointed superintendent of West Point. Four years later, he became the senior military commander of the U.S. forces in Vietnam (MACV). He played a major role in increasing the number of U.S. soldiers fighting in the Vietnam War.

In 1965, Westmoreland developed the aggressive strategy of search and destroy. The objective was to find and kill VC and NVA soldiers. This was not easy since it was difficult to distinguish friend from foe. Innocent civilians were often killed by mistake. Westmoreland was determined to avoid the kind of disaster suffered by the French army at Dienbienphu, so he did not allow any military operations by units smaller than about 750 men.

In September 1967, the NLF launched a series of attacks on American garrisons. Westmoreland was encouraged because now the NLF was engaging in open combat. At the end of 1967, Westmoreland was able to report that the NLF had lost 90,000 men. He told President Johnson that the NLF would be unable to replace such numbers and that the end of the war was in sight.

The Tet Offensive proved to be a turning point in the war. In military terms it was a victory for the U.S. forces. An estimated 37,000 NLF soldiers were killed compared to 2,500 Americans. However, it illustrated that the NLF appeared to have inexhaustible supplies of men and women willing to fight for the overthrow of the South Vietnamese government.

Westmoreland was replaced by General Creighton W. Abrams in 1968. On his return to the United States he was appointed chief of staff of the U.S. Army and vigorously defended the war. He retired in 1972. A member of the Republican Party, Westmoreland was unsuccessful in 1974 in his attempt to become governor of South Carolina. His memoirs, *A Soldier Reports*, was published in 1980. William Westmoreland died on 18 July 2005.

advisors to 23,000. Vietnam was becoming a much larger problem for Johnson than he first imagined.

Intelligence reports in 1964, backed up by McNamara's observations from his trip to South Vietnam to promote General Khanh, showed that the VC held 40 percent of the countryside in South Vietnam and had the support of 50 percent of the people. Additionally, North Vietnam had upgraded the Ho Chi Minh trail and sped up infiltration into the South. Yet LBJ figured that a graduated use of power would work: "I'm going up old Ho Chi Minh's leg one inch at a time," he said. He often referred to North Vietnam as "that little piss ant country." LBJ and his advisors felt that overwhelming U.S. technological superiority would scare Ho Chi Minh into bargaining. Idealism-influenced U.S. policies based on JFK's vision were captured in his famous quotes: "[P]ay any price, bear any burden," and "ask not what your country can do for you, but what you can do for your country."[3]

The turning point for the United States was the Tonkin Gulf incident in early August 1964. Two U.S. destroyers, the USS *Maddox* and the USS *C. Turner Joy*, were conducting missions off the coast of North Vietnam in support of South Vietnamese patrol boat attacks on North Vietnamese island bases. The North Vietnamese attacked the *Maddox* on 2 August—a fact that was not disputed. But a second attack was reported on 4 August, an attack that both American and Vietnamese officials agree did not take place. General Phung The Tai of the NVA said that the U.S. government fabricated the incident.[4] Deputy CIA director Ray Cline, speaking of the second incident, said that the reports of the second incident were unsound.[5]

A recent article (2005) by NSA historian Robert Hanyok reports that signal intercepts were honest mistakes made during the Tonkin Gulf incident. But midlevel NSA officials covered up the errors by falsifying documents.[6] It is

---

Dean Rusk

Dean Rusk was born in Georgia in 1909. Educated at Davidson College, North Carolina, and at Oxford University, he was appointed associate professor of Government and dean of faculty at Mills College.

Rusk served in the U.S. Army during the Second World War. A member of the Democratic Party, Rusk was appointed by President Harry S Truman as special assistant to the secretary of war in 1946. He also served as special assistant for Far Eastern Affairs (1950–1951). Rusk supported providing military assistance to the French in the French-Viet Minh War.

Rusk left office when Dwight Eisenhower was elected president in 1951 and served as head of the Rockefeller Foundation until being appointed as secretary of state by President John F. Kennedy in 1961. In this post he had to deal with the Cuban Missile Crisis and the country's growing involvement in the Vietnam War. Rusk always maintained that U.S. global interests required the establishment of a non-Communist South Vietnam. He felt Vietnam was a test for our resolve in the war against Communism worldwide. He favored incremental military escalation in Vietnam so it would not cause "an orgasm of decision-making in Moscow." He remained as secretary of state under President Lyndon B. Johnson and remained in the post until Richard Nixon and the Republican Party gained power in 1969.

After his retirement Rusk published several books, including *Waging Peace and War: Dean Rusk in the Truman, Kennedy and Johnson Years* (1988), and *As I Saw It: A Secretary of State's Memoirs* (1990). Unlike his friend Robert McNamara, who admitted that he was wrong in supporting the war in Vietnam, Rusk never doubted its importance. Dean Rusk died in 1994

unclear whether Johnson would have sought broad authorization to use force anyway, even if the signal intelligence was not in error and covered up. The second attack prompted the president to bring the Tonkin Gulf resolution to Congress, which was quickly passed with only two dissenting votes (Senator Wayne Morse of Oregon and Senator Ernest Greuning of Alaska).[7] The language was very broad: "All necessary measures to repel any armed attacks against the forces of the United States and to prevent further aggression."

Retaliatory bombing against North Vietnam began shortly thereafter. The measure was not really questioned. One reason for the lack of debate was that it was the middle of a presidential campaign and LBJ had already painted himself as the moderate compared to Republican contender Barry Goldwater. It did not seem dangerous to give LBJ such broad authority. The message was that you can trust LBJ. Secondly, Congress had also passed similar resolutions for situations in the Middle East and the Formosa Straits, and those incidents did not lead to deep American involvement. Johnson skillfully played up the attacks and his ratings shot up from 42 percent to 72 percent overnight. By November 1964, the United States was carrying out a carefully orchestrated bombing campaign against North Vietnam. Undersecretary of State George Ball dissented. He said that bombing would lead to escalation of the war. It is bitterly ironic that the resolution that authorized the president to wage the Vietnam War hinged on an incident that in fact did not occur and was covered up through falsification of documents.

George Ball

George Wildman Ball was born in Des Moines, Iowa, in 1909. He grew up in Evanston, Illinois, and graduated from Northwestern University. He was U.S. undersecretary of state in the administrations of John F. Kennedy and Lyndon B. Johnson. He is best known as the voice against the Vietnam War during the escalation in the 1960s. In 1961 Ball predicted that if the United States engaged in a war in Vietnam there would be tragic consequences with more than 300,000 soldiers fighting in a hopeless war. He wrote many papers and memos in an attempt to convince the president not to escalate the war. He said that air power would not demoralize the North Vietnamese or strengthen the South Vietnamese government. "Once on the tiger's back," he warned, "we cannot be sure of picking the place to dismount."* Ball resigned from his position and went on to serve as U.S. ambassador to the United Nations from 26 June to 25 September 1968.

Ball's importance as undersecretary went unnoticed by the public. But his vital role points out the impact of sub-tier advisors in government. Ball was a founding member of the Bilderberg group, an international clique of powerful European and American leaders. Ball's phronesis (prudent statesmanship guided by practical wisdom within a moral framework) contrasted with the *realpolitik* model of statesmanship practiced by Henry Kissinger. George Ball died in 1994.

*Stanley Karnow, *Vietnam: A History*, New York: Viking, 1983, p. 395.

On the eve of the U.S. presidential election in November 1964, the VC attacked a U.S. air base near Saigon. American carriers were ready to launch retaliatory attacks against North Vietnam, but Johnson held off. On Christmas Eve, the VC attacked again, and again Johnson held off bombing the North. A few days later, the VC blew up the Brinks Hotel in Saigon, used by American forces. But it was not until 19 February, after a third attack that took place in Pleiku in the Central Highlands that injured 126 and killed 8, that Johnson authorized bombing.[8]

American strategists assumed that North Vietnam could be pressured into quitting the war, ending its aggression in the South, and accepting a divided Vietnam. They figured that in the face of American military power, the North Vietnamese would want to negotiate. This was the basic premise for the grand strategy of escalation. America had never lost a war up to this point, and it was generally believed that power would enable the United States to achieve its goals in Vietnam. Americans were very confident and were used to having their way internationally. They assumed it would be an easy victory because North Vietnam was a Third World country. But, by 1967, this attitude was more pessimistic as the United States had committed more than 500,000 troops and dropped more bombs than it did in World War II. By 1967, America had committed not only arms, men, and money, but also its prestige. The United States would be able to achieve a stalemate in Vietnam by 1968, but not a clear victory.

The United States used a "limited war strategy" in Vietnam. LBJ said that the United States could not invade North Vietnam because he did not want China or Russia to enter the war (it was bad enough that both were already supplying North Vietnam). So we sent our forces into South Vietnam to shore up its weak government and root out the NLF and the infiltrating NVA. We sent troops because South Vietnam was too weak to stand on its own. Ironically, this was the very same reason that kept our troops out originally. South Vietnam was supposed to be stronger before we would commit troops. The idea was that U.S. troops would merely assist, not play the primary role, in defense of South

---

Wallace M. Greene, Jr.

Wallace Martin Greene, Jr., was born in Waterbury, Vermont, on 27 December 1907. He was a descendant of Nathanael Greene, the Revolutionary War hero. He attended the University of Vermont for a year before entering the U.S. Naval Academy at Annapolis. He graduated in 1930 and was commissioned as second lieutenant in the Marine Corps.

In World War II, General Greene was a naval observer in London and then a staff officer in American Samoa. In 1944, he helped plan operations in the Marshall Islands and the invasions of Saipan and Tinian in the Mariana Islands.

In the postwar years, General Greene graduated from the National War College and had assignments at the Quantico Marine Corps Base, Marine Corps headquarters in Washington, Hawaii, and elsewhere, and on the staff of the Joint Chiefs of Staff.

In 1956, General Greene was ordered to the marine recruit depot at Parris Island, South Carolina. Greene was put in charge of recruit training at the base and later served as commanding general of the base itself. He ended the traditional mass punishments and physical abuse of recruits.

In 1958, General Greene was ordered to Marine Corps headquarters. In 1960, he was named chief of staff, the number two position in the corps at that time. In October 1963, he was nominated by President John F. Kennedy to be commandant of the Marine Corps. By the time he retired at the end of 1967, the number of marines and sailors in the Amphibious Force in Vietnam had approached 100,000, about a fifth of all American personnel engaged in the war. In public statements and congressional testimony, General Greene joined the call for broadening the already heavy air attacks on North Vietnam.

General Greene's legacy for the corps was an overhaul of its training and planning procedures. Advances that he outlined remain in today's manuals, among them those employing up-to-date guidance systems with which marines in the field spot targets and call in artillery or air support. In addition to meeting the requirements of the war in Vietnam, General Greene centralized and reorganized the management of personnel and equipment. He served until 31 December 1967. General Greene died on 8 March 2003.

Vietnam. American power was to be increased gradually, to find the North Vietnamese threshold of pain. U.S. military leaders developed strategies within these limitations. General Westmoreland's strategy was twofold: (1) secure U.S. air bases in South Vietnam and undermine VC control, and (2) shut down North Vietnamese supply lines to South Vietnam.

Nguyen Cao Ky

Nguyen Cao Ky was born on 8 September 1930 in Son Tay (northern Vietnam). He became a jet fighter pilot in the French air force and even attended Air Command and Staff College in the United States in 1958. Ky was commander of the South Vietnamese Air Force (VNAF) from 1964 to 1967. Ky became prime minister of South Vietnam in 1965 and served as vice president from 1967 to 1971.

Ky was never considered a politician, even by his own admission. He was yet another converted military commander who served in the government of South Vietnam who could not provide adequate leadership for the country.

Alienated from Thieu, Ky intended to oppose him in the 1971 elections, but was outmaneuvered and retired from politics. After the Communist takeover in 1975, he settled in the United States, where he published a book, *Twenty Years and Twenty Days* (1976), and lectured at various universities, and currently is a businessman in Los Angeles.

This led to the most massive use of military force ever concentrated on such a small area against such a small country. Meanwhile, LBJ wanted to appear tough on Communism, but not reckless like Goldwater. Nguyen Cao Ky took over in a coup in January 1965 in South Vietnam. LBJ was convinced that the instability in the South could be solved by bombing the North.[9]

American Strategies

AIR WAR

The basic premise of the U.S. air war strategy was to bomb North Vietnam until they were forced to negotiate. U.S. planes were launched from South Vietnam, Thailand, and aircraft carriers off the coast of Vietnam. Johnson restricted the bombing initially. The U.S. planes could not bomb Hanoi, Haiphong harbor, or anywhere near the Chinese border. Johnson boasted, "They can't even bomb a shithouse without my approval." But by 1967, he removed those restrictions. With the sustained bombing campaign, called Rolling Thunder, there was a gradual increase in sorties and tonnage from 1965 to 1967. The bombing hurt North Vietnamese industrial capacity, which was rather limited anyway, disabled agricultural production, and killed 1,000 civilians per month on average. There were 25,000 bombing missions in 1965 and 79,000 in 1966. But the North Vietnamese were still able to construct an air defense system, develop alternative transportation systems, quickly rebuild roads and bridges, and move factories underground. Soviet aid to North Vietnam increased dramatically after 1965 to include fighter planes, SAMs (surface-to-air missiles), and tanks. Infiltration kept increasing despite the bombing: 35,000 men in 1965 and 90,000 in 1966. Each B-52 bombing mission cost $30,000, and by 1966, the United States had lost $1.7 billion in aircraft (950 downed aircraft). Every dollar of damage to North Vietnam cost the United States nearly ten dollars. This cost does not include the psychological cost of North Vietnam capturing

---

Daniel "Chappy" James, Jr.

Born on 11 February 1920, in Pensacola, Florida, James learned to fly at the Tuskegee Institute. After graduation in 1942, he continued in civilian flight training until receiving an appointment as a cadet in the army air corps in January 1943. He was commissioned in July and, through the remainder of World War II, trained pilots for the all-black 99th Pursuit Squadron and worked in other assignments. During the Korean War he flew 101 combat missions in fighters.

From 1953 to 1956 he commanded the 437th and then the 60th Fighter Interception Squadron at Otis Air Force Base, Massachusetts. He later graduated from the Air Command and Staff College, and in 1957 was assigned to staff duty in Washington, D.C. James went to Vietnam during 1966–1967 and flew seventy-eight combat missions. In 1969 he was promoted to brigadier general and was named base commander of Wheelus Air Force Base, Libya. In March 1970 James became deputy assistant secretary of defense for public affairs, and in that post he advanced to major general. In September 1974, with the rank of lieutenant general, he became vice commander of the Military Airlift Command at Scott Air Force Base, Illinois.

In September 1975 James became the first black officer to obtain four-star rank in any service. He was at that time named commander of the North American Air Defense Command (NORAD), with responsibility for all aspects of the air defense of the United States and Canada. James was also a public speaker and devoted considerable time to addressing youth groups, particularly minority students. General James died of a heart attack shortly after retiring in 1978.

---

downed U.S. pilots and holding them as POWs. Most importantly, Rolling Thunder did not stop the infiltration into the South. Some of the reasons why the bombing campaign did not work were

1. Civilian morale was not broken, roads and bridges were quickly rebuilt, the Ho Chi Minh trail was expanded
2. The United States was unable to stop North Vietnam from getting aid from China and Russia
3. Increased air defense in North Vietnam
4. Resiliency of North Vietnamese and world sympathy based on their civilian casualties.

With Rolling Thunder came an increasing need for security in and around the airfields in South Vietnam being used by American aircraft. After a few incidents of sabotage, the U.S. government decided to send in American troops around Da Nang to secure the airfield for bombing operations. Westmoreland followed General Taylor's advice in instituting an "enclave approach" wherein the defenders would have their backs to the sea and would only venture fifty miles from base. The bombing and troop deployments were explained to the

---

James Stockdale

James B. Stockdale was born on 23 December 1923 in Abingdon, Illinois. Stockdale graduated from the naval academy in 1946. He went on to receive flight training in Pensacola and, later, test pilot training (attending with John Glenn). He shined in academics as well, earning a graduate degree in philosophy from Stanford.

Admiral Stockdale was present at the Tonkin Gulf incident that provoked the American war in Vietnam. He noted that no attack took place but was told to keep quiet. He held this terrible secret about the Vietnam War when he was shot and captured on 9 September 1965. Stockdale was held prisoner for over seven years in North Vietnam, where he was routinely tortured and beaten. He did not reveal any information and went as far as to mutilate himself in order to stop the Vietnamese from using him for propaganda purposes. His wife Sybil was instrumental in pressuring the government to expose the torture and mistreatment of American POWs in North Vietnam.

Stockdale was the highest-ranking naval officer held as a POW in Vietnam. He was released in 1973 and was awarded the Medal of Honor in 1976 in addition to four Silver Stars, making him one of the most highly decorated officers in the history of the navy. Stockdale retired as an admiral and became president of the Citadel in Charleston, South Carolina. In 1981 he left for Stanford University, where he served as a fellow at the Hoover Institution. He wrote a book, along with his wife, called *In Love and War*.

Admiral Stockdale became Ross Perot's running mate in the 1992 presidential election campaign. His amusing and very unpolished performance during the 1992 vice presidential debates highlighted his sense of humor and forthright honesty, but also his naivety in politics. Stockdale died on 5 July 2005 and is buried at the U.S. Naval Academy cemetery.

U.S. public as being in response to the Pleiku attack and North Vietnamese aggression, not to shore up the weak South Vietnamese government. Public criticism began with newspapers, senators, students, and teachers. The first marines who landed in Da Nang in March 1965 soon found that simply sitting in a defensive position was not advisable. The first ground troops were met by South Vietnamese government officials and pretty girls handing out flowers. Soon, more troops arrived with little fanfare to support a new emphasis on aggressive patrols to search out and destroy hostile VC forces. Each week, more troops were gradually deployed.

In 1965, the ARVN desertion rate reached 50 percent. Westmoreland asked for additional 150,000 U.S. troops, saying that the United States must take the offensive. Nearly everyone in the United States held the conviction that U.S. technology would win the day. A journalist on board an aircraft carrier in the Tonkin Gulf said: "They ought to show this ship to the VC, that would make them give up." LBJ refused to submit his policies to the public, because he felt the public was too stupid to understand, and did not coordinate with Congress because he felt they were too divided. He feared that an official declaration of war against North Vietnam would get the Chinese and Soviet Union involved or would increase pressure for an unlimited conflict. He feared privately: "[T]hat bitch of a war would destroy the woman I really loved—the Great Society."

Johnson said that the bombing would stop if Hanoi stopped their infiltration into South Vietnam, but he did not want to negotiate from a weak position and always held to the idea of a non-Communist South Vietnam. Bombing proved to be a difficult proposition since North Vietnam was a Third World country and did not offer many targets. An industrialized country is more vulnerable to bombing because of the numerous industrial and built-up target areas. LBJ asked Congress on 4 May 1965 for $700 million to support the U.S. troops. "How could they say no to troops already deployed?" he thought. The measure passed and Johnson used that and the Tonkin Gulf resolution to drag Congress along with him hand in hand into the Vietnam War.

In July 1965, Johnson deployed 50,000 troops, and secretly planned another 50,000 by the end of the year. He told Westmoreland that he would furnish more troops later as needed. He also authorized the general to use U.S. troops independent of ARVN troops. This meant that the U.S. forces were essentially taking over the war. These decisions were critical turning points in the history of the Vietnam War.

Earle Wheeler

Earle Wheeler was born on 13 January 1908 in Washington, D.C. Wheeler served as an enlisted man in the army and rose to the rank of sergeant before he entered the military academy of West Point in 1928. He served briefly in World War II but was mostly known for his staff talents. Generals with more combat experience trusted Wheeler and his organizational skills.

He attended the National War College in 1950 and then returned to Europe in various NATO staff positions until 1955, when he transferred to the General Staff at the Pentagon. He became director of the Joint Staff in 1960. In 1962 he was briefly deputy commander of the U.S. forces in Europe before being named chief of staff of the U.S. Army later that year. He impressed both President Kennedy and Secretary of Defense McNamara. In 1964 he succeeded General Maxwell D. Taylor as chairman of the Joint Chiefs of Staff and held that post until 1970.

In this position, he advocated rapid modernization of the armed forces during the Vietnam War. In 1973 Wheeler revealed that he had, on the personal orders of President Nixon, directed secret and (when made public) highly controversial bombing missions over Cambodia in 1969–1970.

General Wheeler died in Frederick, Maryland, on 18 December 1975. He had held the chairmanship of the Joint Chiefs longer than anyone else. He was buried in Arlington National Cemetery.

Gradual escalation with little fanfare and downplaying the war (no war bond rallies, for instance) was the style LBJ decided to employ because he did not want to overly excite the Russians or the Chinese. Johnson misled the public and Congress as to the seriousness of the steps they were taking in 1965. In June 1965, he responded to critics who called for us to pull out our troops: "If the United States pulled out of Vietnam, we might as well pull out of Berlin, Japan, and South America." The U.S. objective was not to defeat North Vietnam, but to inflict enough pain on them and the VC to force them to negotiate on terms acceptable to the United States. As LBJ explained it, we apply sufficient force until the enemy "sobers up and unloads his pistol." So, quietly and without formality, the United States entered into its longest war, where it underestimated its enemy and overestimated its own power. The administration never developed a strategy appropriate for the war America was fighting.

GROUND WAR: SEARCH AND DESTROY

"Search and destroy" was the term given to General Westmoreland's aggressive ground war strategy. The United States sent in heavily armed troops by helicopter against a largely guerrilla force. They also used defoliants (e.g., Agent Orange) to destroy ground cover used by the enemy. Key to this strategy was American firepower. From 1965 to 1967, the Americans dropped twice the tonnage of bombs on South Vietnam as it did on North Vietnam.

The air war against North Vietnam necessitated an insertion of ground troops. Search and destroy as a ground strategy relied on extensive use of air mobility—the helicopter. The UH-1 Huey was the workhorse of the war. Hueys could be configured for medical evacuation, troop insertion, and gunship missions. From bases, U.S. forces were sent out on patrols to search for VC and NVA forces. There were no clear enemy lines. Success was measured by the body count. Reports were made by each command daily as to how many enemy soldiers were killed. Back home in the United States, Americans watched the evening news, where body counts appeared like box scores on their TV screens. There were always more Communists killed than Americans or South Vietnamese forces. The problem was that the Communists did not measure their success by body counts. They were willing to take tremendous losses and continue to fight. The impact on the individual psyches of the soldiers cannot be underestimated either. Body counts were also routinely inflated, which made it appear that America was winning the war.[1]

U.S. commanders used B-52s for saturation bombing and sent in 30,000 troops for Operation Cedar Falls in 1967, in the Iron Triangle region north of Saigon. Rice fields were destroyed and the surrounding jungles defoliated by herbicides. This operation sent over 7,000 refugees fleeing to other parts of South Vietnam. After a few months, the NVA and VC slipped back into the area.[2] Over 700 VC were killed, but most of them escaped. In Operation Junction City, in February 1967, massive firepower was unleashed in support

Jonathan Schell

Jonathan Schell was born in New York in 1943 and graduated from Harvard University in 1965. He began his career at the *New Yorker* magazine, where he was a staff writer from 1967 until 1987. His 1967 book, *The Village of Ben Suc*, goes a long way in explaining what went wrong in Vietnam. The American military believed that the village of Ben Suc was very important to the enemy, and the village was targeted as part of Operation Cedar Falls in the Iron Triangle area. They planned its total evacuation and destruction. It was estimated that nearly 3,500 persons lived in Ben Suc and another 2,500 in the vicinity. A village that had existed for a thousand years was wiped out and its inhabitants forcibly removed in a misguided attempt to win the hearts and minds of the Vietnamese. Six months later, the Viet Cong returned to use the area as a base of operations. *The Village of Ben Suc* pointed out the failure of pacification in Vietnam and predicted the failure of Pentagon policies long before the last helicopter left Saigon.

Schell followed this book with *The Military Half* (1968), another story based on reporting in Vietnam. In 1973 Schell won the George Polk Award for his excellence in journalism. He wrote about President Richard Nixon in *The Time of Illusions* (1976) and *Observing the Nixon Years* (1989). His book on nuclear disarmament, *The Fate of the Earth* (1982), was an international best seller and an inspiration for antinuclear movements. It received the *Los Angeles Times* book prize, among other awards, and was nominated for the Pulitzer Prize, the National Book Award, and the National Critics Award. Schell's other books are *The Abolition* (1984), *History in Sherman Park* (1987), *The Real War* (1988), *The Gift of Time* (1998), *The Unfinished Twentieth Century* (2001), *The Unconquerable World: Power, Nonviolence, and the Will of the People* (2003), and *A Hole in the World: A Story of War, Protest and the New American Order* (2004). He is a frequent media commentator and currently serves as the 2005 Distinguished Visiting Fellow at the Yale Center for the Study of Globalization.

of U.S. and ARVN troops. The body count suggested victory (1,800 VC killed), but the area remained unsecured after the operation, and the VC came back. These two major operations demonstrated how effective U.S. firepower can be in support of ground troops in field operations, but also showed the inadequacy, in terms of numbers, of U.S. troops and ARVN troops in trying to secure areas once conquered.[3]

To evaluate the success of a search and destroy ground strategy, the U.S. military planners only had the body count. The objective was not to hold territory, like in a conventional war, but to kill as many enemy troops as possible, causing them to reconsider war as an option and push them to a negotiated settlement. U.S. and ARVN forces did kill many more Communists than were killed within their ranks, but the VC and NVA seemed to keep coming and not give up in spite of the horrendous kill ratios. A stalemate ensued by 1967, and war weariness in the United States began to work in the North Vietnamese government's favor.

The United States never lost a major battle in Vietnam, but it proved to be irrelevant since the VC and NVA did not quit and replaced their losses. Would a different strategy have resulted in U.S. victory? Some considered an all-out air war with little or no restrictions and an invasion of North Vietnam. This type of escalation of the war was tempered by the following considerations:

1. The United States obviously wanted to keep the Soviets and the Chinese out of the war and avoid a World War III scenario
2. Military power and success did little solve South Vietnam's internal political and economic problems
3. The war protesting at home was wearing on the public and the administration.

By 1967, disillusionment had already set in at home in the United States. The country used its superior technology to fight a guerrilla war. Americans were fighting a war of attrition; the Communists were fighting a war of national liberation. The U.S. use of technology often backfired. Take the use of a powerful defoliant called Agent Orange, for instance.[4] The chemical was thought to be a godsend for troops in the field since it eliminated jungles within twenty-four hours to deprive the enemy of cover and concealment. The problem was that the substance was highly toxic. Many veterans have suffered a variety of medical problems since their exposure in Vietnam. Vietnamese have suffered more significantly since they had to live with the chemical long after the war ended.

General William Depuy, one of the proponents of search and destroy, said: "The solution in Vietnam is more bombs, more shells, more napalm, until the other side cracks up and gives up." An Americanized war was dominated by technology. A network of firebases dotted South Vietnam, each one with artillery support to protect infantry patrols ferried to landing zones within enemy territory. Air force assets could be used to "pile on" the firepower if needed.[5]

The North Vietnamese strategy was to carefully pick the place of engagement and strike at the U.S. and ARVN forces in intensive guerrilla operations. They also sought to put maximum pressure on the weak South Vietnamese government and the ARVN. The greatest weakness for the United States was its own public opinion and the ARVN, according to the North Vietnamese.

Body counts were notoriously inflated. A popular refrain was, "If it's dead and Vietnamese, it's VC." Thirty percent of Communist body counts may have been inflated. The U.S. government used these figures to show the American public that we were winning the war. U.S. bombing was doing more harm than good. Although the bombing disrupted Communist supply lines, it also destroyed South Vietnamese agriculture, further creating dependency on the United States, and produced large numbers of refugees. The key question was, how could you build a nation that was in ruins? Because the ARVN were not trusted, the United States used them for mop-up operations. This hurt their already bad morale as they became more and more dependent on the Americans. U.S. casualties and increased draft call-ups in 1967 led to mounting opposition to the war at home. Another problem was that the villages that were taken away from the VC had to be secured by troops to prevent the VC from reestablishing control. The ARVN had great difficulty doing that mission. There were two wars going on at the same time: a shooting war and one of pacification of the villages.

In 1967, Johnson put the U.S. Army in charge of directing the operations of the ARVN, but this produced only marginal results. September 1967 elections in South Vietnam cemented Ky and Thieu into their respective positions of leadership, although 35 percent of the vote was suspect. More than 25 percent of the South Vietnamese villagers had been uprooted by the war and became easy targets for the VC. There was major corruption in the cities, and the black market undermined U.S. aid efforts. Tensions grew between U.S. and South Vietnamese government officials as information leaks became apparent and VC

Nguyen Van Thieu

Nguyen Van Thieu, the son of a small landowner, was born in Vietnam on 5 April 1923. He was educated at the National Military Academy in Hue. Originally a Buddhist, he converted to Roman Catholicism when he married a doctor's daughter. After the Second World War he joined the armed forces, and by 1963 he was chief of staff of the armed forces of South Vietnam.

When U.S. president John F. Kennedy became convinced that President Ngo Dinh Diem would never be able to unite the South Vietnamese against Communism, he authorized a military coup. In early November 1963, President Ngo Dinh Diem was overthrown. After the generals had promised Diem that he would be allowed to leave the country they changed their mind and killed him and his brother Nhu. Being part of the coup, Nguyen Van Thieu was appointed chairman of a ten-member military junta. He then went on to become minister of defense and in 1967 was elected as president of South Vietnam.

During the period of Vietnamization, Nguyen Van Thieu appealed to President Nixon for more financial aid. Nixon was sympathetic but the U.S. Congress was not, and the move was blocked. At its peak, U.S. aid to South Vietnam had reached $30 billion a year. Heading an unpopular and undemocratic government, Thieu's regime was beset by corruption and scandal. Running low on funds by 1974, Thieu had difficulty paying the wages of his large army, and desertion became a major problem.

After the Saigon regime fell to the Communists on 30 April 1975, Nguyen Van Thieu fled Vietnam and lived in exile in Taiwan, England, and later in the United States. Thieu died in Boston on 29 September 2001.

infiltration into the government apparatus was exposed. In the field, ARVN soldiers and villagers seemed to be able to avoid booby traps and mines that were killing and maiming U.S. soldiers and marines. By 1967, in response to international pressure, both the United States and North Vietnam moved away from their rigid negotiating positions in an attempt to establish serious discussions of peace. The Americans had previously demanded that all North Vietnamese leave the country, but now said that the infiltration must stop. The North Vietnamese delegation had previously demanded that all U.S. troops leave and bombing stop, now they conceded that U.S. troops could remain, but the bombing must stop. Johnson was trapped in his own position by 1967, and there was no quick and painless victory in sight. Johnson likened the situation to "being stuck in a hailstorm on a Texas highway—nowhere to run, nowhere to hide, and you can't make it stop."[6]

America was dividing into two camps—Hawks and Doves. This division broke apart relationships with neighbors, friends, family, and coworkers. Antiwar rallies drew huge crowds in 1966 and 1967. On 21 October 1967, over

---

Bob Dylan

Bob Dylan, an American icon and Folk/rock songwriter and singer, was born Robert Allen Zimmerman, on 24 May 1941, in Duluth, Minnesota. While attending the University of Minnesota in Minneapolis, he began performing folk and country songs at local cafés, taking the name "Bob Dylan," after the late Welsh poet Dylan Thomas.

In 1960, Dylan dropped out of college and moved to New York, where his idol, the legendary folk singer Woody Guthrie, was hospitalized with a rare hereditary disease of the nervous system. Dylan visited Guthrie regularly in his hospital room. He also became a regular in the folk clubs and coffeehouses of Greenwich Village, met a host of other musicians, and began writing songs at an astonishing pace, including "Song to Woody," a tribute to his ailing hero. In the fall of 1961, after one of his performances received a rave review in the *New York Times*, Dylan signed a recording contract with Columbia Records. Released early in 1962, *Bob Dylan* contained only two original songs, but showcased Dylan's gravelly-voiced singing style in a number of traditional folk songs and covers of blues songs.

In 1963, Dylan released two of the most memorable 1960s folk songs, "Blowin' in the Wind" (which later became a huge hit for the folk trio Peter, Paul, and Mary) and "A Hard Rain's A-Gonna Fall." Those songs, along with "Times They Are A-Changin'," firmly established Dylan as the icon of the 1960s. By 1964, Dylan was playing 200 concerts annually, but had become tired of his role as the folk singer-songwriter of the protest movement. *Another Side of Bob Dylan*, recorded in 1964, was a much more personal, introspective collection of songs, far less politically charged than Dylan's previous efforts. In recent books and interviews, Dylan has rejected the notion of his being the icon of the 1960s and the voice of a generation. As one reviewer said, "It doesn't matter what he thinks, he is anyway."

100,000 protesters gathered in Washington, D.C. Many people wondered if the war protesters were really helping the North Vietnamese Communists and contributing to their victory. Some people found the war protesters more repugnant than the war itself. The impact of the war protesting was subtler in terms of its impact on policy. It did not turn America away from the war as has been reported. It did, however, force the issue into the public consciousness, put anxiety into lawmakers and policymakers, and encouraged them to look for ways to end the war. The initial "rally around the flag" reaction in 1965 wore off by 1967. Support for the war was dropping fast—only 27 percent of Americans polled in October 1967 approved of LBJ's handling of the war.

By the end of 1967, the United States was spending more than $2 billion per month on the war. A credibility gap had developed. People simply did not believe LBJ or his administration any more. The Joint Chiefs of Staff criticized the administration for not calling up the reserves and for the restrictions put on the military by the so-called amateurs in Washington.

In the spring of 1967, General Westmoreland and the Joint Chiefs tried to secure an all-out war in Vietnam. They planned an additional 200,000 troops to step up ground operations, expansion into Laos and Cambodia, and an amphibious attack into North Vietnam. They claimed that the bombing had reached a saturation point. Civilian advisors, on the other hand, began to abandon the war effort entirely. Bill Moyers and other advisors resigned. Robert McNamara, who had been supremely confident before, began to have doubts about the war and was disturbed by protests and civilian casualties. He

---

Bill Moyers

Born in Texas in 1934, Bill Moyers has been a public official and a television journalist/producer. Working for Senator Lyndon Johnson when Johnson became vice president, Moyers became his top assistant. But after a month he resigned to become an associate director of the new Peace Corps, becoming its deputy director in 1962. As president, Johnson appointed Moyers special assistant (1964–1965), then press secretary (1965–1967). Moyers left to become the publisher of *Newsday* (1967–1970). In 1971 he hosted WNET's (New York City's public television station) *This Week*, followed by *Bill Moyers Journal* (1971–1976, 1978–1981), with a break to serve as a correspondent for CBS Reports (1976–1978). He returned to CBS to do news analysis (1981–1986). Moyers returned to public television, where he began to produce a series of shows based on interviewing leading thinkers from various fields. Two of his series, *Joseph Campbell and the Power of the Myth* (1988) and *A World of Ideas* (1989–1990), were also converted into best-selling books. His 1992 television series, *Healing and the Mind*, which examined alternatives to traditional medicine, showed his continued commitment to covering contemporary issues with an intelligent, caring, and holistic perspective.

admitted that escalation was not working, saying: "Ho Chi Minh is a tough SOB...the picture the world is getting of the world's greatest superpower killing 1000 noncombatants a week while trying to pound a tiny backward nation into submission on an issue whose merits are hotly disputed, is not a pretty one."

By the summer of 1967, Johnson was a deeply troubled man, physically exhausted, emotionally drained, frustrated with lack of success, and torn between conflicting advice. He told his generals, "Bomb, bomb, bomb, that's all you know...when we add divisions, can't the enemy add divisions? Where does it all end?" Even with these sentiments, he could not accept McNamara's turning against the war, so McNamara resigned under pressure and accepted a position at the World Bank in 1967. LBJ held the middle ground between his advisors. The Joint Chiefs threatened to quit en masse if he stopped the bombing. The bombing continued in 1967 not because it was working, but because it appeased the hawks and kept the United States from appearing to be weak. However, LBJ did not give Westmoreland the soldiers he wanted.

Richard Helms

Richard Helms was born in Philadelphia, Pennsylvania, on 30 March 1913. After graduating from Williams College, Massachusetts, he joined the United Press news agency and in 1936 was sent to Nazi Germany to cover the Berlin Olympic Games.

After the bombing of Pearl Harbor, Helms joined the U.S. Navy. In August 1943, he was transferred to the Office of Strategic Services (OSS). The OSS had responsibility for collecting and analyzing information about countries at war with the United States and helped to organize guerrilla fighting, sabotage, and espionage. After the surrender of Germany in 1945, Helms helped interview suspected Nazi war criminals. Helms joined the CIA in 1947.

In 1963, Johnson promoted Helms to become head of the CIA. He was the first director of the organization to have worked his way up from the ranks. Helms underestimated the size of enemy forces in Vietnam. Johnson was told in November 1967 that the North Vietnamese and Viet Cong forces had fallen to 248,000. In reality the true figure was close to 500,000, and as a result U.S. troops were totally unprepared for the Tet Offensive.

In 1975 the Senate Foreign Relations Committee began investigating the CIA. Frank Church and his Select Committee on Intelligence Activities showed that Helms had lied to the Senate Foreign Relations Committee. They also discovered that Helms had been involved in illegal domestic surveillance and the murders of Patrice Lumumba, General Abd al-Karim Kassem, and Ngo Dinh Diem. In 1977 Helms was found guilty of lying to Congress and received a suspended two-year prison sentence.

Richard Helms died on 22 October 2002. He went to his grave holding many of our nation's most closely guarded secrets. His autobiography, Look Over My Shoulder: A Life in the CIA, was published in 2003.

Late in 1967, Johnson was disturbed by defections in his staff and did not listen to critics or to the protesters, whom he considered naïve. "The weakest chink in our armor is public opinion," he lamented. Oddly, in the early years of the war, he feared the hawks, now he feared the doves. Thinking that the peace movement was turning the public against the war, LBJ set out to destroy it. The CIA got involved in surveillance of antiwar leaders. George Ball's haunting advice on the problems associated with mounting escalation probably rang in Johnson's ears: "You know, once on the tiger's back, we can't pick the time to dismount. You're going to lose control of this situation, and this could be very serious."[7]

—————— 6 ——————

Leadership in North Vietnam

The two primary tasks of the North Vietnamese leadership were to wage war, and mobilize, and prepare for reunification of the nation. The war, from a North Vietnamese perspective, was a struggle for survival. From 1965 to 1967, the United States dropped 800 tons of bombs a day. The damage was obviously extensive. It disrupted North Vietnam's economy and the everyday lives of its citizens. The Big Three who ruled in North Vietnam—Ho Chi Minh, Vo Nguyen Giap, and Pham Van Dong—were the same leaders who had defeated France. Within the North Vietnamese communist party (*Lao Dang Party*), decisions grew collectively from Ho Chi Minh, Giap, Dong, and the southerner, Le Duan. Ho was the inspirational nationalist leader, but not a dictator. Giap wrote many books about the war against the United States and against France.

Pham Van Dong

Pham Van Dong was born on 1 March 1906 in Quang Ngai Province in the central part of Vietnam. His father was a member of the elite Mandarin class and a private secretary to one of Vietnam's last emperors.

The year 1925 was a turning point in Dong's life when he joined a student strike in Hanoi that was subsequently put down by the ruling French. Dong fled to China, where Ho Chi Minh was organizing covert opposition to the French. Dong joined Ho Chi Minh's Vietnamese Revolutionary Youth Association and learned of the tenets of Marxism and Leninist party organization.

In 1929, Pham Van Dong returned to Vietnam to organize Communist cells, but was caught by the French and sent to prison, where he was confined for seven years. This experience only made him a more committed Communist, and after his release he resumed his operations underground in Hanoi.

In 1939, Dong fled to South China again and joined his mentor, Ho Chi Minh, who had established a guerrilla base there, recruiting and training soldiers and cadres to cross into northern Vietnam. In 1941, Dong became a founding member of the Viet Minh.

At the end of World War II, in August 1945, as the French were trying to reestablish control of their colony in Vietnam, the Viet Minh formed a provisional government with Pham Van Dong as finance minister and Ho Chi Minh as president.

After the French-Viet Minh War, Dong was chosen to head the Viet Minh delegation to the Geneva Conference in 1954. Dong was upset that the Chinese forced the Vietnamese Communists to accept a division of Vietnam as part of the Geneva agreement. This disagreement between China and Vietnam would carry throughout the American War in Vietnam and result in direct conflict between the two countries after the Americans were defeated. Dong served as Vietnam's prime minister until 1987. He died on 29 April 2000, a day before the twenty-fifth anniversary of the fall of Saigon.

The North Vietnamese were very clever at propaganda filmmaking. Themes used in their propaganda were

1. Praise for all Vietnamese people
2. Certainty of victory
3. Hatred for U.S. weapons and military, but not for American people
4. History of struggle for independence used to inspire the people. The message was that the moral weak could defeat the immoral strong (kind of like the message of the story of David and Goliath in Judeo-Christian world).

The North Vietnamese infiltrated into South Vietnam throughout the 1960s. Between 1965 and 1967, more than 150,000 NVA troops infiltrated. The journey down the Ho Chi Minh trail was arduous. It could take between two to six months to complete. Many died from malaria, and one in five infiltrators did not make it. To adequately fight in South Vietnam, the North had to increase its army tremendously: from 250,000 in 1965 to 400,000 in 1967. They had to institute a draft because enlistments were not high enough. As the war dragged on, more and more soldiers stayed on for the duration. The North Vietnamese government was very concerned with desertion and put a lot of effort into preventing it. They held controlled, but not totally rigged, elections during the war. Women's roles changed as they were forced to take on jobs left behind by the men. Civilians were mobilized to capture downed pilots, and these pilots were used for propaganda purposes.

North Vietnam invested a lot of energy into sustaining the morale of the NVA soldiers. They were reminded that they were fighting for their fatherland. North Vietnamese resisted aerial bombardment and built underground facto-

Jane Fonda

Jane Seymour Fonda was born on 21 December 1937 in New York City. She is the daughter of Henry Fonda and the sister of actor Peter Fonda. The Oscar-winning actress is as noteworthy for her diverse film career as for her exercise franchise and political activism. In the 1971 film *Klute*, also starring Donald Sutherland, Fonda received her first Academy Award. She won her second Oscar for Best Actress in Hal Ashby's Vietnam War drama *Coming Home* (1978), cost-arring Jon Voight (who won a Best Actor Oscar for his performance).

In 1968, Jane was expecting her first child when she came down with a case of the mumps and was confined to bed. She began watching television coverage of race riots and the war and also spent much of her time reading. At first she defended America's presence in Vietnam, but slowly she was convinced that the war portrayed in the media was different from the actual war happening in Vietnam. She met military deserters who confirmed this and also met with antiwar student activists, with whom she was very impressed. Jane began to donate money to antiwar causes.

Jane joined an antiwar traveling theatre, called Free the Army or Free Theatre Association (FTA), along with Dick Gregory, Donald Sutherland, Peter Boyle, and others, using their fame to make a stand against the war. They would perform antimilitary skits, songs, and scripts in GI coffeehouses situated near military bases.

In July of 1972, Jane visited Hanoi and witnessed the effects of American bombing in North Vietnam firsthand. She filmed evidence of Nixon's increased bombing and used Radio Hanoi to appeal directly to the Americans dropping the bombs, accusing them of "betraying everything that American people have at heart, betraying the long tradition of freedom and democracy." Jane's presence in Hanoi angered Americans at home. Many, including congressmen Fletcher Thompson, argued that charges of treason should be brought against Jane. She welcomed this, thinking she would have a chance to testify and make permanent congressional records of what she had learned in Hanoi. Consequently, her political activism hindered her acting career and Nixon placed her on his "enemies list" to be monitored by the FBI. She was called names, such as "Hanoi Jane," and was accused of being a "Commie slut." Jane was unaffected. She continued to be an outspoken critic of the war, making television appearances and granting interviews to denounce the Nixon administration.

Jane and Tom Hayden established the Indochina Peace Campaign (IPC) to raise funds for medical aid to North Vietnam, to pressure Congress to cut off support to the South Vietnamese government, and to demand the release of political prisoners in South Vietnam. In 1973, Jane and Hayden married and that year they concentrated on persuading the government to a cease-fire agreement and withdrawing all American forces from Vietnam. In 1974, Jane and her family returned to Hanoi, to film a documentary entitled *Introduction to the Enemy*, which documented the rebuilding of Vietnam. Unfortunately, the film was not widely distributed.

Fonda championed political causes throughout her life, from supporting the Black Panthers and protesting the United States' involvement in the Vietnam War, to speaking out on equal rights for women. Her actions have sometimes been perceived as unpatriotic, such as when, in 1972, she broadcast antiwar sentiments from Hanoi, Vietnam. During this trip, she also posed in an antiaircraft gun so that it appeared as though she was shooting at American planes—a political stunt for which she earned the nickname "Hanoi Jane" and received enormous criticism from conservative nationalists. She apologized many years later, remorsefully telling *O* magazine in June 2000 that "it was the most horrible thing I could possibly have done."

In March 2001, Fonda donated $12.5 million to Harvard University's School of Education, the largest donation in the school's history. Fonda designated the money to create a center on gender and education studies. In a statement she said, "We still have a culture that teaches girls and boys a distorted view of what it takes to be women and men."

In her recent memoir, *My Life So Far*, Fonda reveals more about her political experiences during the Vietnam War. She had previously apologized for offering harsh rebuttals to American POW claims that her visit to Hanoi prompted more torturing of prisoners. The anti-Fonda movement, or Hanoi Jane movement, has no basis in reality. She was antiwar, not anti-GI. As she says in the close to her chapter on the war, "The U.S. loss represented our nation's chance for redemption. But we did not learn the lesson, and then we tried to rewrite history to blame it all on the very people who tried to stop it."

ries and other facilities. They could repair roads and bridges and other things very quickly and keep their society going. Surface-to-air missiles (SAMs) were introduced in 1965. The SAMs were not the highest quality and they did not affect the number of sorties, but did force U.S. pilots to fly higher and change their bombing patterns. By the end of 1967, the United States still had air superiority, but North Vietnam was reducing it somewhat. North Vietnam was afraid that the Americans would invade and that their Communist brethren would not help them.

The story of the Vietnam War has been told by the losers. This is contrary to conventional wisdom that holds that only the winners write the history. Precious little is known of the winners outside of Vietnam. Americans see the war as their personal tragedy and their loss. But this perspective ignores the suffering of the Vietnamese people. The Vietnamese suffered more than 1 million casualties. Americans always ask why they lost the war. But perhaps more productive questions are (1) Why did the Communists win? (2) Who was Ho Chi Minh and what role did he play? (3) How did the North Vietnamese and VC leaders outsmart the best and the brightest America had to offer and defeat a global hegemonic superpower? The Cold War changed everything for America. The Cold War forced Americans to see Vietnam differently. American strategists are not skilled in grasping internal subversion, infiltration, and civil war. They tend to focus on straightforward, massive cross-border invasions. The North Vietnamese and the VC were faced with massive American firepower and adapted a strategy whereby they fought only bit by bit over time. They also focused mostly on the Americans' weakest link, the ARVN and the South Vietnamese government.[1]

Muhammad Ali

Muhammad Ali, arguably the greatest boxer of all time, was born Cassius Clay in Louisville, Kentucky, on 17 January 1942. In addition to his boxing prowess and worldwide fame, Ali is also well known for his refusal to join the U.S. Army during the Vietnam War. Ali became a member of the Nation of Islam in 1964. He was friends with Malcolm X until Malcolm was driven out of the Nation of Islam by Elijah Muhammad.

In 1967, as the Vietnam War was continuing to escalate and antiwar protesting was rising, Ali was drafted into the armed services. Ali refused induction on the grounds of religious beliefs. He was in fact a practicing Muslim minister. He stated publicly, "I ain't got no quarrel with them Viet Cong." His simple explanation offered more than an excuse; to the contrary, his statement revealed insight and wisdom about a war that would forever change America. The government prosecuted him for draft dodging, and the boxing commissions took away his license. He was not allowed to fight for more than three years at the peak of his career. He was stripped of his championship title, and his passport taken, in addition to all of his boxing licenses being canceled. He lost an initial court battle and faced a five-year prison term. Ali made money during his exile by speaking to colleges. He was the first national figure to speak out against the war in Vietnam.

In 1970, after nearly a three-year layoff, and with the mood of the country changing, Ali had his comeback, his first match against undefeated champ Joe Frazier at Madison Square Garden on 8 March 1971.

Ali fought bravely, but lost. The exile had cost Ali; he could no longer dance in the ring. He lost in the Garden, but a few months later he won his legal battle. The Supreme Court reversed his conviction and upheld his conscientious objector claim. Ali was free from possible jail time, and was free to travel to box anywhere in the world.

Although Ali is disabled by Parkinson's disease, he still moves slowly through the crowds and signs autographs. He has probably signed more autographs than any other athlete in history. It is his main activity at home as he works at his desk. He was once denied an autograph by his idol, Sugar Ray Robinson, and Ali vowed that he would never turn anyone down. Even though the volume of mail is great, he continues to keep that promise. The 3 billion television viewers who saw Ali open the Atlanta Olympics in 1996 will never forget him light the Olympic flame.

Moreover, the U.S. understanding of the seamlessness of their enemy was mistaken. The VC (or NLF as they prefer) and North Vietnamese Communist leadership were quite different in style and orientation. The VC were a conglomerate of different groups, some of whom were not even Communists. The NLF was an umbrella group for various religious, political, professional, and ethnic groups that had suffered under Diem's regime.[2]

Studying the NLF, one can discover that a shared government solution would have neutralized Vietnam early on, as early as 1963. In fact, General Minh (Big Minh), who overthrew Diem, was in favor of such neutralization until he was overthrown by General Khanh, who followed U.S. policy that forbade any type of neutral settlement. This episode caused leaders in Hanoi to try to rein in the NLF leadership in the South whom they considered too independent. All of this subtlety was lost on the U.S. leaders and policymakers. At the time of the peace settlement with the United States in late 1972, Hanoi was quick to give up on the idea of shared government in Saigon, as they knew that the South Vietnamese government would not survive without U.S. support and that the North Vietnamese could easily take the whole country and unify under their Communist leadership without NLF interference.[3]

Escalation led to further escalation, and by the end of 1967, the United States had nearly 500,000 troops in Vietnam. Support for the war was beginning to

---

Oliver Stone

Oliver Stone is a very influential film director and has directed some important Vietnam War films. Stone wrote, cowrote, and directed such movies as *Platoon*, *Born on the Fourth of July*, *JFK*, *Salvador*, *Nixon*, *Natural Born Killers*, *The Doors*, *Wall Street*, *Heaven and Earth*, and *Talk Radio*. He also has screenwriting credits for *Midnight Express* and *Scarface*.

Oliver Stone was born in New York City in 1946. His mother was French and his father, American. He dropped out of Yale University in 1965 to teach history and English in Vietnam. He left Vietnam but returned in 1967 to serve for a tour of duty as a combat soldier in the 25th Infantry Division. He was wounded in combat. He also worked in the Merchant Marines and several other jobs prior to completing his film studies program at New York University Film School in 1971. He wrote many unfilmed scripts before he made his directorial debut with the Canadian horror film *Seizure* (1973). He then went on to win a 1978 Oscar for *Midnight Express*. Next, Oliver wrote and directed two highly regarded movies, *Salvador* (1986) and *Platoon* (1987). *Platoon* incorporated his experiences from the Vietnam War. The film won him Oscars for best director and best picture. He received another Directing Oscar for *Born on the Fourth of July* (1989). Other films as director include *The Doors* (1991), *JFK* (1991), and *Nixon* (1995), and he produced *The People vs Larry Flynt* (1996).

JFK was Stone's most controversial film. This film of the JFK assassination systematically picked apart the Warren Commission finding to develop, as Stone has said, "an alternative myth to the Warren Commission myth." Not surprisingly, he was attacked by many from the power structure in government and academe. But none of these criticisms really mattered since nearly 80 percent of Americans believe that the government has not told the whole truth about the assassination. Stone had struck a responsive chord with the public and this created pressure that led to the release of thousands of documents related to the assassination. Not one to sit still, Stone's latest project is a film about 9/11. The film project is already stirring controversy.

waver at home. After almost three years, Americans had won major battles, but not the war. U.S. strategists and politicians had expected their massive firepower to force the enemy to quit. But despite the enormous casualties, the NVA increased their infiltration into South Vietnam as they and the VC prepared for the Tet Offensive.

III
FIGHTING FOR PEACE, 1968–1972

Jingle Bells, mortar shells, VC in the grass, take your merry Christmas tree and shove it up your ass.

—GI Christmas song in South Vietnam, 1971

The War at Home

A paradox is a seemingly contradictory statement that may nonetheless be true. President Nixon called the Vietnam War "a war for peace." GIs used to joke that "fighting for peace was like screwing for virginity." The horror of the war was coming home and 1968 was the time of reckoning.

The year 1968 was a terrible year in American history. Dr. Martin Luther King, Jr., and Robert F. Kennedy were gunned down, the cities were burning, seething with racial tensions, and America seemed to be literally coming apart. To add to this turmoil came the turning point in the war in Vietnam—the Tet Offensive. Most Americans did not believe President Johnson's calls for an increased effort to win the war. The will of the people was not behind the war effort, and it is hard to win when the people are not behind the war. The reasons for the public withdrawing their support for Johnson's policies came from both supporters of the war and antiwar activists. Those who supported the war up to that point believed that Johnson was not fighting to win the war. Those who were against the war said that we should not have entered war in the first place. The year 1968 was the moment of truth in Vietnam.[1]

At the end of 1967, American attention was focused on Khe Sanh. Reinforcements were sent in to help the beleaguered marines, and B-52s dropped more than 100,000 tons of ordnance on a five-square-mile battlefield. While the Americans were to save Khe Sanh, the VC and the NVA were hatching their plan to attack every major city and installation in South Vietnam. On 30 January 1968, VC shock troops penetrated the wall surrounding the U.S.

Wallace Terry

Born in 1938, Wallace Terry was an African American journalist who covered the civil rights movement and the Vietnam War for the *Washington Post* and *Time* magazine. In 1967 he became deputy bureau chief for *Time* in Saigon, where he covered the Tet Offensive. He flew along on many combat missions with American and South Vietnamese pilots and joined assault troops during major battles. His 1984 book, *Bloods: An Oral History of the Vietnam War by Black Veterans*, became a best seller and was named one of the best books of the year by *Time* magazine.

In 1996, Terry was featured in three BBC television documentaries: *The Camera at War*, on the History Channel; *Muhammad Ali*, on the Arts & Entertainment Channel; and *Divided We Stand: Race & the Media*. In 1995 Disney released the Hughes Brothers film *Dead Presidents*, based on a Terry story.

As a reporter and war correspondent, Terry's scoops have landed his picture on the front page of the *New York Times*, and his stories across the pages of the *Washington Post* and *Time* magazine. As a news analyst, he has appeared on the BBC, CBC, Agronsky & Co., *Meet the Press*, *Face the Nation*, and the CBS Evening News. Terry died on 29 May 2003.

---

embassy in Saigon. The VC made it to the outer courtyard and remained there until they were killed six hours later. The symbolism of this action was more important than the flawed tactics. The very symbol of U.S. power in Southeast Asia was penetrated. General Westmoreland called this attack and the entire Tet Offensive a military failure for the Communists, and rightly so. But the general missed the point. The fact that the VC and NVA were able to overrun all provincial capitals and attack every installation shocked U.S. leaders and the American public alike. The Tet Offensive was demoralizing for the Americans and the South Vietnamese. U.S. and ARVN forces pushed the Communists back and killed many VC and NVA in the process, but the political damage had already been done. The American will to fight was broken at home. The VC had lost militarily, but had won a political and psychological victory. The United States lost 1,100 troops and the ARVN lost 2,300 troops during the Tet Offensive. More than 125,000 civilians were killed, and the fighting created more than 1 million refugees.

The ill-fated U.S. strategy in Vietnam can be summed up in one offhand remark by a U.S. Army officer speaking about the village of Ben Tre during the Tet Offensive: "We had to destroy the village to save it." There are many misconceptions associated with the impact of the Tet Offensive on the United States. The Tet Offensive took place during the weeks surrounding the New Year celebrations in Vietnam. By the beginning of February 1968, the NVA and the VC had attacked almost every major U.S. and South Vietnamese military installation. As devastating as this was to the morale of the American and South

Vietnamese soldiers, they struck back swiftly and took back every installation from the enemy. In the retaliatory fighting, the VC were no longer considered as much of a threat to the U.S. or South Vietnamese forces as they were prior to the Tet Offensive. As one U.S. official said, "The VC were effectively defanged." The war thereafter was fought largely as a conventional one, the type of war the United States was trained for and experienced with fighting. The bitter irony for U.S. war planners was that public support turned against the war just as it appeared that the war would be fought against the NVA as a much more conventional war. But none of this mattered since U.S. public opinion changed dramatically after Tet. Please see Table 7.1 below:

As one can see from the table, 61 percent of the U.S. public believed that we were either losing the war or stalemated after the Tet Offensive. The United States won the battle, but lost the war for public opinion. In March 1968, LBJ announced that he was not seeking reelection. Negotiations began with North Vietnam in May 1968. Ironically, U.S. forces held the military initiative after Tet and had noticed a marked deterioration in the quality of NVA troops. But there was also a growing rift between U.S. and ARVN forces. American forces were increasingly less tolerant of their allies. As many GIs joked at the time, "What you do is take all the Friendlies on to ships and take them out to the South China Sea. Then you bomb the country flat. Then you sink the ship." U.S. morale was lagging. Not surprisingly, the My Lai massacre occurred in March 1968.[2]

On 27 February 1968, Walter Cronkite might have summed up the American mood best:

> To say that we are closer to victory today is to believe, in the face of the evidence, the optimists who have been wrong in the past. To suggest that we are on the edge of defeat is to yield to unreasonable pessimism. To say that we are mired in a stalemate seems the only reasonable, yet unsatisfactory conclusion.[3]

In March 1968, General Westmoreland was sent home to be chief of staff of the army. LBJ policy advisor Clark Clifford begged for deescalation in March 1968, and on 31 March 1968 Johnson announced that he was not seeking

TABLE 7-1.   U.S. Public Opinion after the Tet Offensive

Gallup Poll	November 1967	February 1968
Losing	8%	23%
Standing still	33%	38%
Making progress	50%	33%
No opinion	9%	6%

Source: Steven Cohen, *Vietnam: Anthology and Guide to a Television History.* New York: Alfred A. Knopf, 1983, p. 219.

Walter Cronkite

Hailed as "the most trusted man in America" during his eighteen years as anchor of the CBS Evening News, Walter Cronkite first gained national recognition for his reporting from the battlefields of World War II. As a United Press correspondent, Cronkite covered the landings in North Africa and Sicily, the Allied invasion of Normandy, and the subsequent battles across France and Germany. He was also a member of the "Writing 69th," a group of intrepid reporters that accompanied Allied bombers on missions over Germany. Cronkite got his training in broadcast journalism at Midwestern radio stations, and during World War II he covered the European theater for United Press. After the war, he served as chief United Press correspondent at the Nuremberg trials.

Cronkite joined CBS News in 1950, worked on a variety of programs, and covered national political conventions and elections from 1952 to 1981. He was one of the original creators of the CBS Evening News in 1962. He anchored that broadcast until his 1981 retirement. The public's perception of him as honest, objective, and level headed led to his popular title. In 1968, Cronkite journeyed to Vietnam to report on the aftermath of the Tet Offensive. In a dramatic departure from the traditions of "objective" journalism, Cronkite concluded his reports with a personal commentary, in which he voiced his strong belief that the war would end in stalemate. Cronkite's editorial captured what many Americans were thinking already about the Vietnam War. Cronkite's influence was so great that LBJ once said: "If I have lost Walter Cronkite, I have lost Mr. Average Citizen." His nightly sign-off, "and that's the way it is," was his trademark. His voice enthusiastically narrated the U.S. manned space program and was one of calm reason during the Vietnam War and the Watergate Scandal.

reelection. Negotiations with North Vietnam began in earnest on 13 May 1968. U.S. planners started thinking about Vietnamization (the handing over of the war to the South Vietnamese) even though the VC were decimated as an effective fighting force.

Meanwhile, Paris peace talks stalled over table size, shape, and other arrangements. The U.S. delegation wanted two long tables, the South Vietnamese wanted one large round table, and the North Vietnamese wanted square tables with North Vietnam, South Vietnam, the NLF, and the United States seated on respective sides. A compromise was reached when it was suggested that two rectangular tables be placed at opposite ends of a round table. By that time, LBJ was on his way out.[4]

U.S. policy planners did not realize the impact of the Tet Offensive immediately. All they noticed was that VC and NVA gains were erased quickly and Americans were able to maintain their initiative even with a maximum effort by the enemy. This assessment failed to take into consideration the fact that Americans were tired of the war and the Tet Offensive really revealed the extent of the stalemate.

Clark Clifford

Clark Clifford was born in Fort Scott, Kansas, on 25 December 1906. He attended college and law school at Washington University, and built a solid reputation practicing law in St. Louis, Missouri, between 1928 and 1943. He served as an officer with the U.S. Navy from 1944 to 1946, reaching the rank of captain and serving as assistant naval aide to President Truman.

Few people in government were as familiar with as many of the nation's problems as Clark Clifford. He helped articulate the policies for the reconstruction of Europe after World War II. He wrote the basic legislation establishing the CIA and the Defense Department. On the domestic front, he wrote some of Truman's most important speeches and helped keep labor peace in the postwar period.

Johnson was hardly in office twenty-four hours when he called for Clifford. Faced with the sudden and enormous task of running the country after Kennedy's assassination, Johnson used to talk with Clifford. His warm relationship with Johnson became strained and almost broke over Vietnam in 1967, when Johnson asked him to be secretary of defense. Clifford's first assignment was to determine how to meet General William Westmoreland's request for 206,000 more U.S. troops in Vietnam. The special panel Clifford set up to study the issue soon became a forum for debating the rationale for the war.

Because he then had the complete confidence of the president, whom he had known for more than twenty years, and because he had the luxury of not being bound to previous official positions on Vietnam, Clifford was able to ask the difficult questions. He did not like the answers. No one could say whether the 206,000 troops would be enough. No one could say whether the war would take another six months, a year, two years, or more. Clifford finally came to the conclusion that there was no plan for military victory in Vietnam and that the United States was in what he called "a kind of bottomless pit."

When Clifford began to oppose Johnson on the war, a rift opened. Having persuaded Johnson to cut back the bombing and negotiate an end to the war, Clifford spent the next years trying to urge Nixon to end the war. Clark Clifford died on 10 October 1998 at the age of ninety-one at his home in Bethesda, Maryland.

American television showed how awful and endless the war seemed. The shooting of a VC prisoner on the streets of Saigon by the South Vietnamese General Nguyen Ngoc Loan horrified American viewers. Vietnam was history's first television war. Never was this more apparent than during the Tet Offensive. And nothing dramatized the VC's drive more vividly to Americans than the scene inside the U.S. embassy compound in Saigon, the South Vietnamese capital. The center of American power in Vietnam had come under fire.[5]

U.S. combat troops had been in Vietnam since 1965. The war was deadlocked even with superior American firepower. Lyndon Johnson was forced to raise taxes to fight the war and pay for war on poverty. To maintain domestic support, he had to show progress on both fronts. The Tet Offensive undermined Johnson's efforts to show progress in Vietnam.

Of all the battles of the Tet Offensive, none was more destructive for both sides than the battle for Hue. The NVA set up a command post in the Palace of Perfect Peace in what was known as the Citadel. Led by U.S. Marines, and after twenty-four days of fighting, South Vietnamese army units entered the Citadel and raised the South Vietnamese flag. Hue had been saved but it was virtually destroyed. Seventy-five percent of its people were homeless. More than 8,000 soldiers and civilians on both sides had been killed in the fighting.[6]

General Giap claimed that the Tet Offensive had both military and political objectives. The military operation had failed because the VC were killed and captured in large numbers. The Communists were also unable to force President Thieu to accept a coalition government. But Secretary of State Dean Rusk explained, "[I]t became very clear after the Tet offensive that many people at the grass roots, such as my cousins in Cherokee County, finally came to the conclusion that if we could not tell them when this war was going to end, and we couldn't in any good faith, then we might as well chuck it."[7]

President Johnson had to consider whether or not the United States could win without expanding the war and committing more troops. Johnson promised to send 206,000 more troops to Westmoreland, but Vietnam was draining America's overall military and economic strength. So, after the Tet Offensive was over and Khe Sanh was secured, Johnson quietly put aside the request for 206,000 troops. But the request had encouraged Secretary of Defense Clark Clifford to look at withdrawal as an option. The *New York Times* revealed the Pentagon's request for additional troops as Secretary of State Dean Rusk was questioned before Congress on live television. The administration could no longer escalate the war. As Senator Wayne Morse said in the Senate Foreign Relations Committee hearing on 10 March 1968, "There is incipient uprising in this country in opposition to this war and it's going to get worse. This talk about sending over 100,000, 200,000 more troops, you're going to create a very serious difficulty in this country if you people in the administration go through with that."[8]

Seymour Hersh

Born in 1937, Seymour Hersh published his book *Chemical and Biological Warfare: America's Hidden Arsenal* in 1968. The book detailed the use of such weapons in the American war in Vietnam. In 1969 he achieved worldwide fame for reporting on the My Lai massacre. The story earned him the 1970 Pulitzer Prize. Hersh exposed the CIA's surveillance of antiwar activists during the Vietnam War as well. Continuing his work as an investigative reporter, Hersh's latest book, *Against All Enemies*, details the extent of Gulf War Syndrome and the government's attempts to pretend it does not exist.

Senator Mike Mansfield, in the same hearing, asked Dean Rusk if they had stopped the infiltration of men and material into outh Vietnam through the Ho Chi Minh trail. Estimates were that the rate of infiltration in 1965 was about 1,500 a month, and had risen to 20,000 in January 1968. In addition, there had been no progress in peace talks with the Communists. The situation presented in full view of the American public was one of failure.

Johnson had more problems. Senator Eugene McCarthy nearly beat Johnson in the New Hampshire primary, and Robert Kennedy joined the presidential race as a peace candidate. LBJ's approval ratings dropped to 36 percent. His council of "wise men" gathered at the White House and most advocated withdrawal from Vietnam. Johnson's closest advisors were still divided on Vietnam. Feeling abandoned by his advisors and top policy consultants, on 31 March 1968, Johnson shocked them all when he announced at the end of a speech that he would not seek reelection in 1968.[9]

LBJ decided to suspend the bombing of North Vietnam as U.S. troop morale was beginning to slip. The My Lai massacre took place on 16 March 1968, but would not be reported until 1969. Upward of 400 innocent men, women, and children were killed by the men of Charlie Company, 1st Battalion, 20th Infantry, while on a search and destroy mission led by their commander, Lieutenant William Calley. Chief Warrant Officer Hugh Thompson intervened once he realized what was happening and saved many villagers.

William Calley

William Calley was born on 8 June 1943. His name will forever be associated with what went wrong in Vietnam—the lost convictions, the brutality, and the futility of that war.

Calley was not liked by his senior officers or by his men. He began his military career as an enlisted man. After basic training, he was transferred to Fort Lewis, Washington, where he trained as a clerk-typist. He then successfully applied to Officer Candidacy School and began six months of junior officer training in the middle of March 1967. Training was accelerated in the summer when the battalion was to be deployed earlier than had been expected. Upon arrival in Vietnam, Calley's Charlie Company did not encounter much action. Calley spent much of his time trying to keep his men from playing with and giving candy to the Vietnamese children. He said he was afraid of the Vietnamese children and that he hated them.

On 16 March 1968 the angry and frustrated men of Charlie Company, 11th Brigade, American Division, entered the village of My Lai. A short time later, the killing began. My Lai was in the South Vietnamese district of Son My, known to be a VC base. Many members of Charlie Company had been wounded or killed in the area during the preceding weeks. Calley and his men entered the village ready for a fight.

The routine search and destroy mission soon turned into the massacre of over 300 unarmed civilians, including women, children, and the elderly. Word of the massacre did not reach the American public until March of 1969, when journalist Seymour Hersh published a story detailing his conversations with an ex-GI and Vietnam veteran, Ron Ridenhour. Ridenhour learned of the events at My Lai from members of Charlie Company. As a result of the military investigation, Calley was charged with murder in September 1969.

At his trial, Calley testified that he was ordered by Captain Ernest Medina to kill everyone in the village of My Lai. Still, there was only enough photographic and recorded evidence to convict Calley, alone, of murder. He was sentenced to life in prison, but was released in 1974, following many appeals. After being issued a dishonorable discharge, Calley began managing his father-in-law's jewelry store. He has refused to give interviews.

On 4 April 1968, Dr. Martin Luther King, Jr., was assassinated in Memphis by James Earl Ray. Violent race riots broke out in over 100 U.S. cities in addition to massive antiwar protests. With the FBI hounding Dr. King, and with his recent antiwar position, no one is surprised that he was killed. Suspicions abound about the motive and the possibility of a conspiracy, not unlike the JFK assassination. A few days later, Defense Secretary Clark Clifford

Martin Luther King, Jr.

Dr. Martin Luther King, Jr., was the most famous and influential civil rights leader and peace activist in American history. His antiwar position and more controversial views would have had a greater impact had he not been gunned down in April 1968. King was born in Atlanta, Georgia, on 15 January 1929. Both his father and grandfather were Baptist preachers and civil rights leaders. King graduated from Morehouse College in 1948. He chose ministry as his career field, and while studying at Crozer Theological Seminary in Pennsylvania, King heard a lecture on Mahatma Gandhi and nonviolent civil disobedience. He read many of Gandhi's writings on nonviolence and became convinced that the same methods could be used in America. King was struck by Gandhi's belief that only love could turn the hearts of his oppressors.

After he finished his studies, King married Coretta Scott and became pastor of the Dexter Avenue Baptist Church in Montgomery, Alabama. Montgomery would become the focus point of the civil rights struggle when, on 1 December 1955, Rosa Parks, a middle-aged woman, who was tired after a hard day's work, refused to give up her seat to a white man. At the time, segregation was common in the south.

In 1957 King joined with the Reverend Ralph David Abernathy and Bayard Rustin to form the Southern Christian Leadership Conference (SCLC). The new organization was committed to using nonviolence in the struggle for civil rights. The importance of the SCLC was that it brought the traditional power of the black church together with the momentum of the modern civil rights activism.

In an attempt to persuade Congress to pass Kennedy's proposed legislation, King and other civil rights leaders organized the famous March on Washington for Jobs and Freedom in 1963. King was the final speaker and made his famous "I Have a Dream" speech.

Kennedy's Civil Rights bill was still being debated by Congress when he was assassinated in November 1963. The new president, Lyndon Baines Johnson, who had a poor record on civil rights issues, took up the cause. Using his considerable influence in Congress, Johnson was able to get the legislation passed.

J. Edgar Hoover became concerned about King's political development, especially when in 1966 he became a strong opponent of the Vietnam War. Hoover arranged for FBI agents to bug the telephones and hotel rooms where King stayed. Details of his private life were leaked to the press and the FBI sent King an anonymous blackmail letter in an attempt to force him to retire from political life.

King increasingly became involved in trade union struggles. In March 1968, James Lawson asked King to visit Memphis, Tennessee, to support a strike by the city's sanitation workers. On 3 April, King made his "I've Been to the Mountaintop" speech that seemed to predict his impending death. The following day, Martin Luther King was killed by a sniper's bullet while standing on the balcony of the motel where he was staying. His death was followed by rioting in 125 cities and resulted in forty-six people being killed.

On 10 March 1969, James Earl Ray pleaded guilty to the murder and was sentenced to ninety-nine years in prison. Ray later claimed that he was innocent of the killing, even convincing the King family who tried to reopen the case. The case has not been reopened and Ray died in prison in April 1998, thirty years after King's assassination.

announced that General Westmoreland's request for 206,000 more U.S. soldiers would not be granted.

On 10 May 1968, North Vietnamese diplomats arrived in Paris to negotiate for the first time. The United States demanded that North Vietnam remove all of the NVA from South Vietnam. North Vietnam demanded that the VC be allowed to participate in a coalition government in South Vietnam. Neither side would budge.

Robert F. Kennedy was assassinated in Los Angeles after winning the California Democratic primary on 5 June 1968. The assassin, Sirhan Sirhan, was an Arab who had emigrated to the United States in the 1950s and was reportedly disturbed by Kennedy's pro-Israel position. After a 1969 trial lasting nearly four months, Sirhan was convicted and sentenced to death. That sentence was commuted to life in prison and Sirhan has been in prison in California ever since. His repeated applications for parole have been denied.

In July 1968, General Creighton Abrams replaced General Westmoreland as the MACV commander. On 1 July 1968, America's Central Intelligence Agency started the Phoenix program. CIA teams searched the countryside and rounded up VC suspects. It was part of the overarching pacification program in

Robert F. Kennedy

Robert F. Kennedy was born on 20 November 1925 in Brookline, Massachusetts. Kennedy graduated from Milton Academy before entering Harvard. His college career was interrupted by World War II. Robert joined the navy and was commissioned a lieutenant. In 1946, he returned to Harvard and earned his degree in 1948. He went on to earn his law degree from the University of Virginia Law School and was admitted to the Massachusetts bar in 1951. Kennedy joined the Criminal Division of the U.S. Department of Justice. He resigned the following year to run his older brother John F. Kennedy's successful campaign for U.S. Senator.

In 1960, Kennedy managed his brother's successful presidential campaign. President Kennedy appointed Robert U.S. attorney general, amid cries of nepotism. Robert's role in his brother's Cabinet was unique. The brothers worked very closely and stood together through the Cuban Missile Crisis, the civil rights cases, and the growing war in Vietnam. Soon after President Kennedy's assassination in 1963, Robert resigned from Lyndon Johnson's administration to run successfully for New York State Senator in 1964.

Kennedy entered the presidential campaign in 1968, taking on a position against the war in Vietnam. He seemed to be able to reach and unite young people, revolutionaries, alienated African Americans, and blue-collar Roman Catholics. But the white South hated him, big business distrusted him, and middle-class, reform Democrats were generally skeptical.

On the night of 4 June 1968, following a hard-fought, narrow victory in the California primaries, Kennedy was shot by Sirhan Sirhan, a Palestinian immigrant. Kennedy died shortly thereafter in a Los Angeles hospital at the age of forty-two. Mystery still surrounds Sirhan Sirhan's motives. He claims to have no memory of shooting Kennedy. Some believe that he might have been subjected to hypnotic brainwashing under the CIA's MK-ULTRA program.* Robert Kennedy was different from his brother John. In some ways he was more intense, more committed than John had been, yet he shared John's ironic sense of himself and his conviction that one man could make a difference. America lost a great leader.

*http://en.wikipedia.org/wiki/MK-Ultra. *Jacob's Ladder* is perhaps the MK-ULTRA horror and redemption film that most reflects historical reality.

South Vietnam. CIA Director William Colby defended the program by saying it was not a program of assassination and torture. But the Phoenix program was managed by South Vietnamese operating with CIA advisors, and thousands of civilians—men, women, and even children—were classified as VC suspects. The system relied on a network of informants and secret agents. Communist officials later conceded its effectiveness as more than 20,000 VC were killed. Criticism of the program came as reports of extortion, blackmail, private revenge, and political assassination persisted. Prisoners were held without trial in hundreds of jails and internment camps throughout South Vietnam.[10]

At the Republican national convention on 8 August 1968, Richard Nixon was nominated as the Republican presidential candidate. He promised an

---

Creighton Abrams

Creighton Abrams was born in Springfield, Massachusetts, on 15 September 1914. A 1936 graduate of the U.S. Military Academy at West Point, Abrams was a veteran of three wars. Abrams was one of the heroes of the Battle of the Bulge.

In 1967, he became deputy commander of the U.S. Military Assistance Command, Vietnam (MACV). A year later he succeeded Westmoreland. As MACV commander he implemented Vietnamization. This was supposed to bring a gradual end to U.S. involvement in Vietnam and enable the South Vietnamese to become increasingly responsible for running the war. After returning to the United States, he served from 1972 to 1974 as army chief of staff. In that position, General Abrams was to rebuild the U.S. Army that had been alienated from American society and was transitioning to an all-volunteer force after the end of the draft in 1973.

He died in Washington, D.C., of lung cancer, on 4 September 1974, the first army chief of staff to die in office. He was buried in Arlington National Cemetery.

---

honorable end to the Vietnam War. Hubert Humphrey was nominated by the Democrats in the end of August amid riots in Chicago. Over 26,000 police and National Guardsmen confronted more than 10,000 protesters. More than 800 police, guardsmen, and protesters were injured.

On 31 October 1968, LBJ announced the end of Operation Rolling Thunder, a bombing campaign that had been going on for nearly four years. His hope

---

William E. Colby

William E. Colby was born in St. Paul, Minnesota, on 4 January 1920. He attended Princeton University, from where he graduated in 1940. In 1941 Colby joined the U.S. Army, and in 1943 the Office of Strategic Services (OSS). The OSS trained him for special missions, and he served behind enemy lines in France and Norway. He obtained a law degree from Columbia University in 1947, the same year that Congress approved the formation of the CIA. After working for a short time in a law firm, Colby joined the new agency in 1949.

Colby was CIA station chief in Saigon from 1959 to 1962 and headed the agency's Far East division from 1962 to 1967. Then, from 1968 to 1971, he directed the Phoenix Program in South Vietnam, which sought to identify and eliminate VC at the village level. Colby felt that the program was superior to the use of military force, which he believed was too blunt an instrument and alienated the Vietnamese. Nevertheless, estimates of the number of people killed under Phoenix range as high as 60,000. Critics of the Phoenix Program labeled it an assassination program and a crime against humanity, even though accounts written by VC at that time admit that the program was effective against them.

Colby rose within the CIA's Washington bureaucracy, and on 4 September 1973 President Richard Nixon appointed him director of the agency. During his tenure, the press and Congress turned on the CIA, accusing it of crimes ranging from assassination plots to espionage against Americans at home. When in 1975 both houses of Congress set up inquiries into the activities of the intelligence community, Colby offered limited, yet significant, cooperation.

Colby's candor in the Senate investigations on intelligence operations shocked colleagues in the CIA, some of whom never forgave him for opening up the activities of a secret agency. Colby may have wanted to atone for his part in the Phoenix Program. It is also clear that he disapproved of certain of the CIA's activities, which he called "deplorable" and "wrong," and wanted them stopped. In any case, he realized that a display of flexibility in his dealings with Congress would increase the agency's chances of survival. Attacked by both the left and the right, Colby had become politically vulnerable, and on 30 January 1976 President Gerald Ford replaced him with George H. W. Bush. Colby had introduced some significant reforms, such as the prohibition of assassination as an instrument of national policy and the practice of informing select members of Congress about the CIA's activities, but his intelligence career was over.

Colby's life continued to be eventful. In 1978, he published his memoir, *Honorable Men*, in which he defended himself against the Left over the Phoenix Program and against the Right over his decision to clear the air while director of the CIA. In 1982, following the enactment of secrecy legislation under President Ronald Reagan, the U.S. government began proceedings against Colby for making unauthorized disclosures in his memoir.

In 1984, Colby resumed legal practice and lectured widely, taking up a new cause—the campaign for a freeze on nuclear arms. In April 1996, Colby went down to the waterfront near his weekend home in Rock Point, Maryland, and launched his canoe. He was found dead a few days later with no evident signs of foul play, but many feel that his death is nonetheless suspicious.

was to push the peace negotiations along. On 5 November 1968, Nixon won a narrow election over Vice President Humphrey. Humphrey had trouble distinguishing himself from Johnson and his failed policies in Vietnam. Nixon asked Harvard Professor Henry Kissinger to be his national security advisor. At the end of 1968, the U.S. troop level in Vietnam stood at 495,000 and more than 30,000 Americans had died in the war.

8

Peace with Honor

President Richard M. Nixon and national security advisor Henry Kissinger[1] were quite different in terms of their backgrounds, but their destinies were inexorably linked. Nixon was from a poor family in California and had clawed and scratched his way to the top with hard-nosed determination. Henry Kissinger was a German-born, East Coast–educated intellectual from Harvard. Both men were loners, and perhaps that was what drew them together. They were sometimes brilliant together, other times bungling, but they alone controlled U.S. policies. Kissinger remarked that perhaps the United States overestimated the importance of South Vietnam, but having 500,000 soldiers in that country settled the issue of its importance. "It is a war for peace," as Nixon said. The Nixon Doctrine held that Asians should rely on themselves to supply a fighting force with U.S. aid and supplies. Nixon was committed to ending the war in Vietnam. He initially thought that he could get Russia or China to help broker a peace and end the war, but neither country was interested in that mission. So Nixon and Kissinger devised their "Peace with Honor" plan.[2]

Just as the French had done, the Americans began handing their war over to the non-Communist South Vietnamese after 1968. Lack of popular support at home had forced the French to abandon their war efforts, and the same may be said for America's efforts as well. The peace talks in Paris continued as Nixon announced his secret plan to end the war. But all would not go well for the Americans at home or abroad. The increased fighting on the part of the ARVN

Richard M. Nixon

Richard M. Nixon, the son of a grocer, was born on 9 January 1913. His father owned a small lemon ranch in Yorba Linda, California. A good student, Nixon graduated from Whittier College in 1934.

After obtaining a degree at Duke University Law School, Nixon returned to Whittier, where he practiced law. In 1937 he moved to Washington, where he served in the Office of Price Administration. Nixon joined the U.S. Navy in August 1942 and was assigned as an operations officer with the South Pacific Combat Air Transport Command. He left the navy in January 1946 and soon thereafter ran for Congress. During the campaign he attacked the New Deal and accused his Democratic Party opponent as an enemy of free enterprise.

Elected to the House of Representative, Nixon was invited to join the House of Un-American Activities Committee (HUAC), where he became involved in its campaign against subversion. J. Edgar Hoover and the Federal Bureau of Investigation provided Nixon with information on members of the Communist Party. Nixon soon emerged as the most skillful member of the HUAC. These cases brought Nixon to the attention of the public and Dwight Eisenhower chose him as his running mate in the presidential election of 1952.

In 1960 Nixon won the Republican presidential nomination. After his eight years as Eisenhower's deputy, Nixon was expected to win. However, the Democratic candidate, John F. Kennedy, ran a successful campaign and won by just 100,000 votes out of the 68 million cast. Nixon became a lawyer in Los Angeles, and after losing the race for governor of California in 1962, claimed he was retiring from politics.

Nixon changed his mind and in 1968 won his party's presidential nomination. Nixon picked Spiro T. Agnew as his running mate. This time Nixon won and, in his inaugural address on 20 January 1969, he promised to bring the nation together again.

During the presidential campaign Nixon promised to negotiate the end of the Vietnam War. However, negotiations with North Vietnam at the Paris peace talks were unproductive, and Nixon decided to escalate the war by bombing Communist bases in Cambodia. In an effort to avoid international protests at this action, it was decided to keep this information hidden. Pilots were sworn to secrecy and operational logs were falsified.

The bombing failed to destroy the Communist bases, and so in April 1970 Nixon decided to send in troops to finish off the job. The invasion of Cambodia provoked a wave of demonstrations in the United States culminating in the killing of four students by National Guardsmen at Kent State University.

Nixon won the 1972 presidential election against antiwar candidate Senator George McGovern (D-South Dakota). During the election campaign there was a break-in at the headquarters of the Democratic Party at the Watergate complex in Washington. Reports by Bob Woodward and Carl Bernstein of the *Washington Post* began to claim that some of Nixon's top officials were involved in organizing the Watergate break-in.

Nixon continued to insist that he knew nothing about the case or the payment of "hush-money" to the burglars. However, in April 1973, Nixon forced two of his principal advisors, H. R. Haldeman and John Ehrlichman, to resign. A third advisor, John Dean, refused to go and was fired. Nixon's vice president, Spiro T. Agnew, was also forced to resign after being charged with tax evasion.

When Dean testified on 25 June 1973 before the senate committee investigating Watergate, he claimed that Nixon participated in the cover-up. He also confirmed that Nixon had tape recordings of meetings where these issues were discussed. Under extreme pressure, Nixon supplied transcripts of the missing tapes. It was now clear that Nixon had been involved in the cover-up, and members of the Senate began to call for his impeachment. On 9 August 1974, Nixon became the first president of the United States to resign from office.

On 8 September 1974, the new president, Gerald Ford, controversially granted Nixon a full pardon and brought an end to all criminal prosecutions that Nixon might have had to face concerning the Watergate Scandal. However, other members of his staff involved in helping in his deception were imprisoned. Richard M. Nixon died of a stroke on 22 April 1994.

dramatically increased their casualties (which were much higher than for the Americans at any time).

Peace with Honor involved five elements:

1. Gradual withdrawal of U.S. troops
2. Handing over war fighting operations to the South Vietnamese (Vietnamization)
3. Increase in bombing over North Vietnam
4. Invasion of Communist strongholds in Cambodia and Laos
5. Increased efforts to negotiate a peace agreement.[3]

The Paris peace negotiations had stalled on two points:

1. The political status of South Vietnam
2. The status of military forces in South Vietnam.

The United States wanted South Vietnam to remain a nation-state, whereas North Vietnam wanted a coalition government, and a unified Vietnam. The Americans wanted North Vietnamese armed forces out of South Vietnam, and North Vietnam wanted the American troops out. The North Vietnamese never officially acknowledged that NVA troops were even in South Vietnam. The issues were difficult and the talks seemed to go nowhere.

Peace talks opened in Paris on 25 January 1969 with the United States, North Vietnam, South Vietnam, and the Viet Cong in attendance. However, in March, the VC launched new offensives and Nixon threatened to resume the bombing in retaliation. U.S. forces began their own offensive inside the DMZ. Also, in March, the My Lai massacre was exposed to authorities through letters from army veteran Ronald Ridenhour, and Nixon authorized the secret bombing of Cambodia by B-52s that targeted North Vietnamese supply lines located near the Vietnam border. In April of 1969, war protesters at Harvard took over the administration building, while the number of troops in Vietnam peaked at 543,000.

In May 1969, the *New York Times* reported the secret bombing of Cambodia, and Nixon ordered the FBI to wiretap the journalists involved and other government officials to find out who leaked the information. In the middle of May, the 101st Airborne Division fought in the A Shau Valley near Hue, the famed battle of Hamburger Hill. More than 400 Americans were wounded and 46 killed taking the hill, only to hand it back to the NVA shortly thereafter. Many Americans complained that lives were being wasted in a nearly pointless war. As a result, MACV commander General Abrams said that he would no longer order large unit missions.

On 8 June, Nixon met with Thieu and formalized the Vietnamization plan and announced withdrawal of 25,000 U.S. troops. Shortly thereafter, *Life* magazine published the photos of the 242 U.S. troops who had been killed within one week that June. The photo story psychologically impacted many Americans and made them question the purpose of the war and weigh the costs versus the gains. Nixon's diplomatic moves, some covert, some public, were all stalled over the same conditions: Americans refused to accept VC representatives in the South Vietnamese government and the North Vietnamese refused to acknowledge that they have NVA troops in South Vietnam.[4]

The American secretary of state, William Rogers, accused the North Vietnamese of mistreating American POWs in July of 1969. The issue was a sore point for the administration and a diplomatic lever for the Communists. Around the same time, Nixon made his Nixon Doctrine public. He advocated military and economic assistance to any nation that was fighting Communism, but did not include Vietnam-style ground wars. The strategy would promote military self-sufficiency, U.S. air power, and technical assistance. In many ways, this was an extension of the Truman Doctrine with more elaborate qualifications. The Nixon Doctrine was part of the overall Containment Strategy designed to stop the spread of Communism around the world. At the end of July, Nixon visited American troops in South Vietnam, his only trip to the country. As the Nixon Doctrine was announced, Kissinger was planning his secret peace negotiations with the North Vietnamese.

The Woodstock music festival took place in New York State in August 1969. More than 450,000 people showed up, many without tickets. The festival was a combination of youthful spirit, music, and antiwar sentiment—the very pinnacle of the 1960s hippie movement. One of the many highlights of the festival was Jimi Hendrix's performance of the Star Spangled Banner on his guitar. That stirring rendition told the story of the Vietnam War with his guitar alone—not uttering a word. Another highlight was Country Joe McDonald's "I feel-like-I'm-Fixin'-to-Die-Rag." This song became an anthem for the enlisted soldiers in Vietnam.[5]

Ho Chi Minh died on 3 September 1969. Le Duan succeeded him and vowed to drive the Yankees out of his country in accordance with Ho's last wishes. The My Lai massacre trial began, highlighting the frustration and brutality of the war in Vietnam. In order to make the draft more equitable, Nixon announced his draft lottery system based on birthdays, a draft reduction, and also announced a troop reduction of 35,000. As a result, a poll revealed that 71 percent of Americans approved of Nixon's handling of the war.

Massive antiwar rallies were held in major U.S. cities, and over 250,000 attended one Washington, D.C., rally. The Vietnam moratorium drew praises from world leaders including North Vietnamese prime minister Pham Van Dong. To further galvanize antiwar activists, the army finally admitted and discussed the My Lai massacre. By December 1969, negotiations were not going well in Paris, and Nixon ordered 50,000 more troops out of Vietnam.[6]

In February 1970, Nixon ordered B-52 strikes along the Ho Chi Minh trail as VC attacks continued relentlessly throughout South Vietnam. Peace negotiations were deadlocked, but Kissinger's secret negotiations with North Vietnamese negotiator Le Duc Tho continued. Americans were shocked by the breakup of the Beatles in April 1970. The cultural impact of the Beatles cannot

---

Henry Kissinger

Henry Kissinger, the son of a grocer, was born in Furth, Germany, on 27 May 1923. His family was Jewish and became concerned about the emergence of Adolf Hitler and the Nazi Party. In 1938 the family immigrated to the United States. During the Second World War Kissinger served in the U.S. Army Counter-Intelligence Corps.

Educated at Harvard University he obtained a doctorate in 1954. He taught in the Department of Government at Harvard and served on the Council of Foreign Relations (1955–1956), as associate director of Center for International Affairs (1957–1960), and as director of the Harvard Defense Studies Program (1958–1971).

In 1969 Richard Nixon appointed Kissinger as his advisor on national security affairs and he played an important role in the improved relations with both China and the Soviet Union in the early 1970s. He also arranged peace talks between the Arabs and the Israelis.

In 1972 Nixon was warned that a victory in Vietnam was unobtainable. Kissinger was put in charge of peace talks, and in October 1972, he came close to agreeing to a formula to end the war. The plan was that U.S. troops would withdraw from Vietnam in exchange for a cease-fire and the return of 566 American prisoners held in Hanoi. It was also agreed that the governments in North and South Vietnam would remain in power until new elections could be arranged to unite the whole country.

The North Vietnamese refused to change the terms of the agreement and so, in January 1973, Nixon agreed to sign the peace plan that had been proposed in

October. However, the bombing had proved to be popular with the American public as they had the impression that North Vietnam had been bombed into submission. Kissinger was awarded the Nobel Peace Prize for his role in ending the American War in Vietnam, but not without controversy.

Kissinger became secretary of state in 1973, and continued to serve under Gerald Ford. Books by Kissinger include *A World Restored: Metternich, Castlereagh and the Problems of Peace, 1812–22* (1957), *Nuclear Weapons and Foreign Policy* (1957), *The White House Years* (1979), *Years of Upheaval* (1982), and *Diplomacy* (1994).

be underestimated. The British invasion seemed to recall a happier and simpler time. The reality of the music business, and creative and personal differences, broke up the McCartney-Lennon team.

At the end of April 1969, Nixon announced U.S. incursion into Cambodia in an attempt to help a pro-American regime stay in power and to weaken Communist infiltration and supply areas in Cambodia. As a result, antiwar activists dramatically increased their protesting efforts, and Nixon called them all "bums." Most major college campuses were hit with waves of protests.

Vietnamization (1969–1971) allowed for a 50 percent U.S. troop reduction, and an increase in U.S. bombing over North Vietnam. Nixon thought that this strategy would buy time. He also employed the "Mad Man" strategy. With this strategy, Nixon appeared to be bombing out of irrational anger, even hinting that he would "bomb them [North Vietnamese] into the Stone Age." The insertion of troops into Cambodia and Laos to attack the Ho Chi Minh trail infiltration route effectively brought Cambodia into the war and the Khmer Rouge to power. At Kent State and Jackson State University campuses, innocent students were shot by U.S. National Guardsmen. Four protesters were killed at Kent State. More than 400 colleges and universities shut down across America due to protesting. As 100,000 antiwar protesters arrived in Washington, D.C., Nixon impulsively decided to meet with them one night at the Lincoln Memorial. This surreal scene was captured in Oliver Stone's brilliant movie, *Nixon* (1995). Crosby, Stills, Nash, and Young captured the spirit of the Kent State shootings with their song, "Ohio."[7]

In June 1970, massive air strikes were ordered in Cambodia to support American ally Lon Nol. Americans began to withdraw from Cambodia as the U.S. Senate repealed the Tonkin Gulf resolution. Recently declassified documents show that Nixon ordered his administration and top military leaders to say that Cambodian operations were strictly South Vietnamese operations. He went on to say, "Publicly, we say one thing. Actually, we do another." Nixon did not want America to be a "pitiful, helpless giant. "I want you to put the air in there and not spare the horses," he told his military leaders. "Just do it," Nixon added. "Don't come back and ask permission each time." Quietly, the military stopped using Agent Orange and other defoliants in Vietnam. Agent Orange made by Dow

Chemical was one of the more contentious issues from the Vietnam War. By the end of 1970, the U.S. troop level in Vietnam had been reduced to 280,000, ARVN forces had begun operations in Cambodia, and it was reported that drug abuse by American GIs was widespread in Vietnam and that at least 200 incidents of "fragging" had occurred that year (American soldiers killing their officers).[8]

In the beginning of 1971, Nixon announced that the end was in sight in Vietnam as U.S. bombers hit NVA supply camps inside of Cambodia and Laos, and the ARVN launched the Lam Son 719 offensive into Laos in an effort to cut off NVA supply lines along the Ho Chi Minh trail. Opinion polls were slipping for Nixon as his approval rating in March was down to 50 percent. By March, Lieutenant Calley was convicted of murder and was sentenced to life in prison. The decision divided the nation. Many Americans felt that Calley was a scapegoat for a war gone wrong. Others felt that he deserved what he got. In April, the VVAW staged protests in Washington, D.C., and were joined by 200,000 more protesters. More than 12,000 protesters were arrested.

To make matters worse for the Nixon administration, the *New York Times* began publishing the Pentagon Papers. The papers were a series of top-secret memos and other documents from previous administrations that revealed that the American government had lied about the war to the American public. The Pentagon Papers released in 1971 revealed to Americans that the war was never really fought to be won. As McNamara said in a secret memo discussing the reasons for escalation, escalation was 70 percent to avoid a humiliating defeat, 20 percent to keep South Vietnam from Communist domination, and 10 percent to allow South Vietnam to enjoy freedom and democracy.[9]

Nixon was furious with the release of the Pentagon Papers and organized the "Plumbers" with aides John Ehrlichman and Charles Colson. They focused on Pentagon Papers source Daniel Ellsberg, a former government official. They wanted to discredit him and fix leaks in the administration. Colson created an enemies list of 200 prominent Americans who were against Nixon. By the end of 1971, U.S. troop level in Vietnam was down to 156,800.[10]

9

Exit America

The American public was upset about the widening of the war even as more American soldiers were coming home. In 1972, Nixon decided to mine Haiphong harbor in order to curtail shipment of military hardware to North Vietnam by other Communist nations. A peace settlement was finally reached in late 1972, not so much due to Nixon's strategy as war weariness on all sides. The settlement spelled defeat for the United States since they unilaterally withdrew troops and the NVA stayed in South Vietnam. In exchange, North Vietnam gave up on the coalition government idea. The North Vietnamese figured they would win anyway once the Americans were gone. South Vietnam did not want to have anything to do with the settlement. But they were forced to sign by the Americans. Ironically, the same settlement could have been reached in 1969, saving an estimated 20,000 American and countless Vietnamese lives.

In January of 1972, Nixon revealed that Henry Kissinger had been secretly negotiating an end to the Vietnam War. Nixon followed this up with his historic trip to Communist China on 21 February. Nixon met with Mao Zedong and Zhou Enlai in order to forge new diplomatic relations. The North Vietnamese were concerned that Nixon would be able to convince China to force North Vietnam to accept an unfavorable peace settlement in exchange for better relations with the United States. Emboldened by his new relationship with the Chinese, Nixon boycotted the Paris peace talks in March 1972 in order to pressure the North Vietnamese.

On 4 April 1972, Nixon ordered a massive bombing of all NVA positions in both North and South Vietnam, including Haiphong harbor. This led to increased war protesting in the United States, but Communists returned to the bargaining table in Paris. There were only 69,000 U.S. troops in Vietnam as the ARVN abandoned Quang Tri to the Communists.

In May, Nixon ordered the mining of Haiphong harbor and intense bombing of roads, bridges, and oil facilities in an operation called Linebacker I. This bombardment and mining ignited an international condemnation and fueled the war protests at home. Nixon leveraged the Soviets in a meeting to try to pressure the North Vietnamese into an unfavorable peace agreement.[1]

In June 1972, five burglars were caught inside the Democratic National Headquarters at the Watergate building in Washington, D.C. It was considered a third-rate burglary until later it was discovered that the White House was behind the action. George McGovern was nominated as the Democratic challenger to Richard Nixon in the upcoming presidential elections. McGovern was a total peace candidate advocating immediate withdrawal of all U.S. forces. Actress Jane Fonda made her ill-fated trip to Hanoi in July and was photographed on a North Vietnamese antiaircraft gun and was duped by the Communists after meeting with U.S. POWs, who she believed were treated well. Fonda would become a scapegoat for many American veterans.

In early October, the stalemate between Henry Kissinger and Le Duc Tho finally ended as both sides agreed to major concessions. The United States would allow North Vietnamese troops already in South Vietnam to remain there, while North Vietnam agreed to leave South Vietnam's president Thieu and his government in power. Kissinger was desperate for a settlement in spite of the obvious problem of allowing NVA troops to remain in the South. He wanted to end the war before the election in November. President Thieu would not sign such an agreement that allowed North Vietnamese troops to remain indefinitely in South Vietnam. Nixon threatened Thieu with a total cut-off of all American aid.

Operation Linebacker I ended on 22 October 1972. The North suffered an estimated 100,000 military casualties and lost half its tanks and artillery. General Vo Nguyen Giap was quietly replaced as a result. More than 40,000 South Vietnamese soldiers died in the heaviest fighting of the entire war.

John Paul Vann

John Paul Vann was born in Norfolk, Virginia, on 2 July 1924. In 1943, he enlisted in the Army Air Corps. Vann went through pilot training, and graduated as a second lieutenant in 1945. The war ended before he could see action.

Vann served in the army in the Korean War, and in 1957 returned to the United States to attend the Command and General Staff College, and was promoted to lieutenant colonel in 1961. Vann was assigned to South Vietnam in 1962 as an advisor to the ARVN 7th Division. Fighting an antiguerrilla war against the Viet Cong, Vann became aware of how badly the war was going. He earned the Distinguished Flying Cross for his bravery while serving as an advisor. He drew public attention to the problems the United States was having in Vietnam, through press contacts such as *New York Times* reporter David Halberstam. Vann focused much of his criticism at the U.S. commander in the country, MACV General Paul D. Harkins. He felt that Harkins was covering up the fact that the ARVN did not have the will to fight. Not surprisingly, Vann lost his advisor position in March 1963 and left the army within a few months.

Vann returned to Vietnam in March 1965 as an official of the Agency for International Development (AID). He then was assigned as the senior American advisor in II Corps Military Region, which put him in charge of all U.S. personnel in his region, in addition to advising the ARVN Commander in the region. He was killed in battle in June 1972. He received the Medal of Freedom, the nation's highest civilian citation, posthumously, for his ten years of service in South Vietnam. He was the only civilian to be awarded a Distinguished Service Cross in Vietnam.

Neil Sheehan's book *The Bright Shining Lie: John Paul Vann and America in Vietnam* (1989), is not only the definitive account of the experiences of John Paul Vann, but is also a damning indictment of the Vietnam War itself. According to Sheehan, one of the many tragedies of Vietnam was that the Saigon regime had no will of its own to survive.*

*Harry G. Summers, Jr., "Troubled Apostle of Victory," *Vietnam*, vol. 12 (Spring 1989), pp. 26–32.

On 24 October, President Thieu publicly denounced Kissinger's peace proposal. Hanoi went public with the terms of the peace proposal and accused the United States of attempting to sabotage the settlement. In Washington, Henry Kissinger declared that peace was at hand. Two weeks later, Nixon won the presidential elections in the biggest landslide in American history. By the end of November, the American troop withdrawal from Vietnam was completed, although there were still 16,000 army advisors and administrators remaining to assist South Vietnam's military forces.

In December, in Paris, Kissinger presented a list of changes demanded by President Thieu to Le Duc Tho, and the peace talks collapsed. President Nixon issued an ultimatum to North Vietnam to negotiate within seventy-two hours. Hanoi did not respond, so Nixon ordered Operation Linebacker II (Christmas bombings), eleven days and nights of maximum force bombing against military targets in Hanoi by B-52 bombers. The Christmas bombing was the most intensive bombing campaign of the entire war, with over 100,000 bombs dropped on Hanoi and Haiphong. Fifteen of the 121 B-52s participating were shot down by the North Vietnamese who fired 1,200 SAMs. Hanoi propaganda reported 1,318 civilian deaths.

The bombing was denounced by many American politicians, the media, and various world leaders including the Pope. But, as a result, North Vietnam agreed to resume peace negotiations within five days of the end of bombing.

On 23 January 1973, President Nixon announced that an agreement has been reached that would "end the war and bring peace with honor." The Paris Peace Accords were signed on 27 January 1973. The United States agreed to immediately halt all military activities and withdraw all remaining military personnel within sixty days. The North Vietnamese agreed to an immediate cease-fire and the release of all American POWs within this period. More than 150,000 North Vietnamese soldiers were allowed to remain in South Vietnam. Vietnam remained divided, and South Vietnam had two governments, one led by President Thieu, the other led by Viet Cong; an agreement would be reached upon reconciliation.

The draft ended on 27 January 1973, and Lieutenant Colonel William Nolde became the last American soldier to die in combat in Vietnam. On 12 February 1973, 591 American POWs were released from their Hanoi prison. And, by 29 March, the withdrawal of all American troops from South Vietnam was complete. The American war in Vietnam was over, and that left the North Vietnamese, the NLF, and the ARVN to fight it out. The war left over 58,000 Americans and 1 million Vietnamese dead, $150 billion spent, a nation that was torn apart politically and economically and alienated from the Third World that the United States was pledged to help.

Peace negotiations had begun under Johnson, and continued with Nixon. The demands by the North Vietnamese in 1968 were for the United States to leave. The Americans demanded that North Vietnamese forces return to North Vietnam. The North Vietnamese never acknowledged, officially that is, their infiltration into the South. It was under terms that could have been negotiated easily in 1968 that the Americans agreed to leave the war in the end of 1972. Many question why we continued to fight for terms that were no better in 1972 than they were in 1968. An additional 20,000 Americans died during these negotiations. One of the ironic twists was that popular support for the war waned just as the war became more conventional and the VC weakened considerably. Domestic politics influenced military policy, so the initiative could not be seized. The Kent State shootings and the My Lai massacre seemed to indicate that the war was destroying our society both at home and abroad. On 4 May 1970, American military forces were rapidly leaving Vietnam, and it was clear that the ARVN and its weak government could not withstand alone the onslaught by the North Vietnamese.

Nixon became embroiled in the Watergate Scandal after the 1972 election. As the peace talks in Paris came to a close at the end of 1972, the Americans were ready to pull out and leave the war to the South Vietnamese, and the president was about to face his biggest challenge yet, the threat of impeachment and a constitutional crisis that still affects America to this day. Increasingly paranoid and worried about political enemies and leaks within the administration, Nixon ordered special operations against the Democrats and other enemies. Much of this activity was prompted by the release of the Pentagon Papers in 1971. Although the secret documents released to the press did not deal directly with Nixon's presidency, they damaged American political credibility. The public had been lied to about the conduct and strategy of the war. Nixon was worried about the 1972 election even though it was very clear that he would win. A group of White House "plumbers" broke into the Democratic National Headquarters at the Watergate Hotel in June 1972 and were caught. As the truth came out and the Nixon cover-up was exposed, the Watergate Senate Trial began. Nixon was ultimately forced to resign from office in 1974—the only U.S. president ever to resign from office. The Vietnam War had nearly destroyed American society.

IV
BACK IN THE WORLD, 1973–1975

There's an ancient idea that when a man travels, he doesn't go anywhere. Instead, he performs a series of actions that, if done in the proper sequence, will bring his destination to him.

—Robert Mason, *Chickenhawk: Back in the World*

———— 10 ————

Home Front

President Johnson's Great Society domestic programs, built with bipartisan support, were threatened by an ever-widening war in Vietnam. In
1964 and early 1965, Johnson's commitment to South Vietnam was taken at
face value by most Americans. Early antiwar groups and opponents of the war
were small and little noticed. They included civil rights activists, members of
old left, women's organizations, pacifists, students, and clergymen. The draft
seemed inherently unfair. College students could avoid military service if they
remained in school. Prior to 1968, it was clear that African Americans were
doing more than their share of the fighting. As Dr. Martin Luther King, Jr., said
on 15 April 1967,

> Despite feeble protestations to the contrary, the promises of the Great Society
> have been shot down on the battlefield of Vietnam. The pursuit of this widened
> war has narrowed the promised dimensions of the domestic welfare programs,
> making the poor white and negro bear the heaviest burdens, both at the front and
> at home.[1]

Statistics show that at the beginning of the war, blacks constituted 20 percent of the combat deaths (more than twice their percentage of the total population). But this percentage lowered during the course of the war, reaching
12.5 percent by the end, which was just slightly higher than the black percentage of the population. With college deferments readily available, anyone

who could afford to go to school could avoid the draft. As a result, much of the fighting force in Vietnam was from the working and poor classes. Estimates are that of the enlisted men in Vietnam, 25 percent were poor, 55 percent were working class, 20 percent middle class, and 5 percent upper income. To add to the sense of disenfranchisement, eighteen-year-old combat soldiers were not allowed to vote until 1971.[2]

As the war dragged on into 1967, criticism grew. Even Senator Fulbright, an early supporter of the war, was beginning to question America's involvement.

William Fulbright

J. William Fulbright was born on 9 April 1905 in Sumner, Missouri. He was educated at the University of Arkansas and attended Oxford University as a Rhodes scholar, and studied law at George Washington University in Washington, D.C. During the 1930s, he served in the Justice Department and was an instructor at the George Washington University Law School. In 1936 he returned to Arkansas, where he served as a lecturer in law and, from 1939 to 1941, as president of the University of Arkansas, at the time the youngest university president in the country.

He entered politics in 1942 and was elected to the U.S. House of Representatives, entering Congress in January 1943 and becoming a member of the Foreign Affairs Committee. In September of that year the House adopted the Fulbright Resolution supporting an international peace-keeping machinery encouraging U.S. participation in what became the United Nations, and this brought national attention to Fulbright.

In November 1944 he was elected to the U.S. Senate and served there from 1945 through 1974, becoming one of the most influential and best-known members of the Senate. His legislation establishing the Fulbright Program slipped through the Senate without debate in 1946. Its first participants went overseas in 1948, funded by war reparations and foreign loan repayments to the United States. This program has had extraordinary impact around the world. There have been more than 250,000 Fulbright grantees and many of them have made significant contributions to their countries as well as to the overall goal of advancing mutual understanding.

In 1949 Fulbright became a member of the Senate Foreign Relations Committee. From 1959 to 1974 he served as chairman, the longest serving chairman of that committee in history. His Senate career was highlighted by some notable cases of dissent. In 1954 he was the only senator to vote against an appropriation for the Permanent Subcommittee on Investigations, which was chaired by Senator Joseph R. McCarthy. He also objected to President Kennedy's Bay of Pigs invasion in 1961.

He was always in the spotlight as a powerful voice in the chaotic times of the war in Vietnam. Although he favored the passage of the Tonkin Gulf resolution in 1964, he later turned against the war and chaired the Senate hearings on U.S. policy and the conduct of the war.

After leaving the Senate, he remained active in support of the international exchange program that bears his name. In 1993 he was presented the Presidential Medal of Freedom by President Clinton. Senator J. William Fulbright died on 9 February 1995 at his home in Washington, D.C.

Johnson remained firm and Congress continued to fund the war. Troop levels continued to rise. Though most young men responded to their draft notices, some fled the country or otherwise evaded the draft. The war was already turning the economy sour by 1967 as Johnson was forced to raise taxes to pay for the war in Vietnam and his war on poverty. By late 1967, for the first time, a poll showed that a majority of Americans considered the war a mistake. Early in 1968, voters, shocked by a massive enemy offensive in Vietnam, the Tet Offensive, were persuaded by presidential challenger Eugene McCarthy's anti-war platform.[3]

Martin Luther King's assassination on 4 April 1968 rocked the nation and sparked riots in more than a hundred cities. Black power militancy increased. Unlike most political leaders, Robert F. Kennedy had sympathized with King's opposition to the war:[4]

He dedicated himself to justice and love between fellow human beings. He gave his life for that principle. And I think it's up to those of us who are here, as fellow citizens and public officials, and those of us in government, to carry out that dream, to try to end the divisions that exist so deeply within our country, and remove the stain of bloodshed from our land.[5]

Opposed to both Kennedy and McCarthy, President Johnson picked Vice President Hubert Humphrey to take over. Over the next two months, Kennedy and McCarthy continued their rivalry in the Democratic primaries. The contest reached a climax in California. Robert F. Kennedy was shot dead in June 1968. His assassination, two months after King's, seemed confirmation that the country was on the brink of self-destruction.[6]

The Democratic Party decided to hold its convention in Chicago in 1968. Torn by strikes and ripe for violence, thousands of protesters arrived in Chicago—militants, pacifists, and hippies. Some demonstrators were nonviolent. Others deliberately provoked the police.[7] Humphrey won the nomination easily but lost in a very close election to Nixon. Nixon promised law and order and peace with honor in Vietnam. But during the first six months of 1969, American casualties were high. Body counts were featured like box scores as viewers tuned in to the nightly news reports.

In 1969, the Vietnam moratorium drew 50,000 to the nation's capital. Over 1 million participated nationwide. Amid arguments whether peace protests lengthened or shortened the war in Vietnam, the war in America was a continuing story. If things were not bad enough, *Life* magazine published pictures of Vietnamese peasants massacred in 1968 by U.S. soldiers in a village called My Lai. The trial of Lieutenant William Calley and others implicated in the My Lai massacre dominated the news for months. Only Calley was convicted, amid controversy and a terrible national reckoning of the nature of the war in Vietnam. The American public wavered between labeling Calley a murderer and seeing him as a victim. The trial was carefully run by the military. The army deliberately chose very tall guards for Calley to make him seem even smaller and less significant (he was just over five feet tall). Nixon responded by reducing draft calls and instituting a lottery system.[8]

ANTI-WAR PROTESTING

LBJ was fighting two wars at once: the war in Vietnam and the war on poverty. His Great Society program sought to wipe out poverty in America. Johnson first came into political power during the Great Depression in the 1930s and was a part of President Franklin D. Roosevelt's New Deal strategy to combat the Depression. LBJ's two-front war efforts bankrupted the nation. The struggles at home were over civil rights and U.S. involvement in Vietnam. The country had not been so divided since the Civil War. Hawks and doves argued and fought over their views on the war. The media's coverage of the war and the antiwar movement was blamed by many for the failure to achieve victory in Vietnam (especially MACV commander General Westmoreland).

Abbie Hoffman

Flamboyant and outrageous political activist Abbie Hoffman was one of the most colorful counterculture figures in the 1960s and a leading antiwar figure. Abbot "Abbie" Hoffman was born on 30 November 1936 in Worcester, Massachusetts. He is also the founder of the Yippies (the Youth International Party). Though Hoffman was serious about his causes, he was not adverse to satire. One example was the demonstration march he led in 1967 to exorcise the Pentagon. One of his most clever protests was on 24 August 1967, when he led an antiestablishment group in the gallery of the New York Stock Exchange (NYSE). They threw fistfuls of dollar bills down to the traders below, who naturally began to scramble for the money and disrupted trading. The stock exchange installed barriers in the gallery to prevent this kind of protest from interfering with trading again.

In 1968, Hoffman, as part of the Chicago Seven, became infamous for attempting to disrupt that year's Democratic Convention with a riot (the group included Jerry Rubin, Tom Hayden, and Bobby Seale). Hoffman was acquitted of all charges. He disappeared from the scene in 1974 when he was charged with drug activities. In 1980, he came out of hiding and served a small jail term. Hoffman once said, "Revolution is not something fixed in ideology, nor is it something fashioned to a particular decade. It is a perpetual process embedded in the human spirit." Abbie continued his protest activities, but he had lost his audience since many of his followers had transformed themselves into Yuppies. Hoffman occasionally appeared in feature films and documentaries, beginning in 1970 with *Brand X*. In 1989, Hoffman played a strike organizer in *Born on the Fourth of July*.

Hoffman wrote many books, including *Steal This Book*, *Fuck the System*, and *Revolution for the Hell of It*. He once said of his books, "It's embarrassing when you try to overthrow the government and you wind up on the Best Seller's List." Abbie Hoffman's life is documented in the film *Steal this Movie*. Hoffman suffered from repeated bouts of clinical depression, and committed suicide on 12 April 1989.

War protesting began in 1964 in isolated college campuses. But by 1968, full-scale protests involving thousands were not uncommon in most cities as well as campuses around the United States. Most Americans did not sympathize with the protesters, but the protest movement succeeded in keeping the war in the limelight and causing people to take sides and question the war. It was not until veterans began protesting in great numbers that mainstream Americans began to really question the war. This came at about the same time as the Tet Offensive in February 1968. This brings to mind the impact of the media on domestic views on the war. Media coverage was largely patriotic and positive toward the military early on. There was very little, if any, negative coverage until 1968. After Tet, and Walter Cronkite's assessment (saying that it did not look like we were winning the war), coverage changed and became more critical.

The so-called counterculture emerged in the 1950s. Civil rights activists combined with the Beat Generation poets and writers, rock and roll music enthusiasts, and others to form an alternative to the mainstream, other-directed, consensus-driven masses of the 1950s. Sociologist David Riesman called that generation the "Quiet Generation." War protesting probably began as soon as the United States supported the French, but it did not get picked up and reported until 1964. There was a reform spirit in the air in the early 1960s. The antiwar movement picked up on that, and the concept of a "just war." As it turned out, the 1960s was one of the most divisive decades in American history, ironic since it started out in the spirit of reform. The focus was on social protest, civil rights, and the Vietnam War. The 1960s might have been a difficult decade anyway; the war made it even more difficult.

The civil rights protesting was focused on racial discrimination, segregation, and voting rights. Most of this activity was taking place in the south. With demographic shifts that began in the 1940s, more African Americans moved to the northern industrial cities from the south. Martin Luther King, Jr., emerged as a civil rights leader in 1956 during the Montgomery Bus Boycott and used Gandhian methods of nonviolent resistance. King forced the issue of racism into the American consciousness. The 1963 march on Washington led to the first significant lawmaking on civil rights since Reconstruction. By 1965, King was under fire from other black leaders, such as H. Rap Brown and Stokely Carmichael, who both advocated Black Power.[9]

Martin Luther King came to look at the Vietnam War as another example of racism and a waste of economic resources that kept the poor down. His antiwar

---

Stokely Carmichael (Kwame Ture)

Stokely Carmichael was born in the Port of Spain, Trinidad, on 29 June 1941. Carmichael moved to the United States in 1952 and attended high school in New York City. He entered Howard University in 1960 and soon afterward joined the Student Nonviolent Coordinating Committee (SNCC). In 1961 Carmichael became a member of the Freedom Riders. In Jackson, Mississippi, Carmichael was arrested and jailed, and in 1966 he became chairman of SNCC.

Carmichael and some of the other marchers were arrested by the police as they marched in support of James Meredith in 1966. After his release in June 1966, Carmichael made his famous "Black Power" speech, in which he called for "black people in this country to unite, to recognize their heritage, and to build a sense of community." He also advocated that African Americans should form and lead their own organizations and urged for a complete rejection of the values of American society.

The following year Carmichael joined with Charles Hamilton to write the book *Black Power* (1967). Some leaders of civil rights groups such as the National Association for the Advancement of Coloured People (NAACP) and Southern Christian Leadership Conference (SCLC) rejected Carmichael's ideas and accused him of black racism. In 1966 and 1967 Carmichael lectured at campuses around the United States and traveled abroad to several countries, including North Vietnam, China, and Cuba. He made perhaps his most provocative statement in Havana. "We are preparing groups of urban guerrillas for our defense in the cities," he said. "It is going to be a fight to the death."

Carmichael also adopted the slogan "Black is Beautiful" and advocated a mood of black pride and a rejection of white values of style and appearance. This included adopting Afro hairstyles and African forms of dress. Carmichael began to criticize Martin Luther King and his ideology of nonviolence. He eventually joined the Black Panther Party, where he became "honorary prime minister."

When Carmichael denounced United States' involvement in the Vietnam War, his passport was confiscated and held for ten months. When it was returned, he moved with his wife to Guinea, West Africa, where he wrote the book *Stokely Speaks: Black Power Back to Pan-Africanism* (1971).

Carmichael, who adopted the name Kwame Ture, also helped to establish the All-African People's Revolutionary Party and worked as an aide to Guinea's prime minister, Sekou Toure. After the death of Toure in 1984 Carmichael was arrested by the new military regime and charged with trying to overthrow the government. However, he only spent three days in prison before being released. Stokely Carmichael died of cancer on 15 November 1998.

message was more radical than his ideas on desegregation. King essentially called for an overturning of the capitalist system in America. His ideas were very radical, even though today they seem to have been homogenized in order for his image to have gained mainstream acceptance. He was warned by fellow civil rights leaders not to pursue antiwar pressure because it would distract him from civil rights. He saw the connection between the two. It also made him more dangerous to the establishment.[10]

There was a resurgence of feminism in the 1960s. For the first time, women voted independently from the dominant male in the household and formed their own voting bloc that politicians had to cater to in elections. Women also provided much of the support for the antiwar and civil rights movements. Sexism, however, was still alive and well in most movements (Stokely Carmichael once remarked that the prone position is the only position women hold in the Black Power movement). Betty Friedan's book *Feminine Mystique* provided a devastating critique of American society and its level of sexism. The National Organization for Women formed in 1966.

Student movements were at the heart of the antiwar movement nationwide. Most college campuses were affected. This was a big difference from the silent 1950s. The student movement can be traced to Port Huron, Michigan, in 1962, where students organized the Students for a Democratic Society (SDS). The Port Huron Statement formed the basis for the movement, and Tom Hayden emerged as an early antiwar leader. The first teach-in was held in 1965 shortly after the first U.S. combat soldiers were sent to Vietnam. Protesting was

---

Eldridge Cleaver

Leroy Eldridge Cleaver was born on 31 August 1935 in Wabbaseka, Arkansas. His family moved first to Phoenix and then to Los Angeles, where the teenaged Cleaver began running into trouble with the law, with arrests for theft and selling marijuana. In 1957, he was convicted of assault with intent to murder and did time in San Quentin and Folsom prisons. While there, he wrote a powerful set of essays outlining his views on racial issues and revolutionary violence. In 1968, they were published as the book *Soul on Ice*.

Cleaver went on to help found the militant group the Black Panthers in 1966 and became famous as the group's outspoken minister of information. *Soul on Ice* cemented Cleaver's reputation as a spokesman for black power and became the philosophical foundation of the Black Power movement. The same year he was wounded in a Panther shootout with Oakland police. Cleaver jumped jail, fled to Algeria, and lived in exile there and in Paris. He returned to America in 1975. Paradoxically, in later years Cleaver renounced his former radical views, became a born-again Christian, embraced conservative political causes, and even ran for political office as a Republican. He also suffered well-publicized struggles with drug addiction in the years before his death, in 1998.

Huey Newton

Huey Percy Newton was born on 17 February 1942 in New Orleans, Louisiana. Newton and fellow activist Bobby Seale founded the radical Black Panther Party in 1966. An illiterate high school graduate, Newton taught himself how to read before attending Merritt College in Oakland and the San Francisco School of Law, where he met Seale. In Oakland in 1966 they formed the Black Panther group in response to incidents of alleged police brutality and racism and as an illustration of the need for black self-reliance. At the height of its popularity during the late 1960s, the party had 2,000 members in various chapters in several cities.

In 1967 Newton was convicted of voluntary manslaughter in the death of a police officer, but his conviction was overturned twenty-two months later, and he was released from prison. In 1971 he announced that the party would adopt a nonviolent manifesto and dedicate itself to providing social services to the black community. In 1974 he was accused of another murder and fled to Cuba for three years before returning to face charges; two trials resulted in hung juries.

Newton received a Ph.D. in social philosophy from the University of California at Santa Cruz (1980). His dissertation was called "War against the Panthers: A Study of Repression in America." Succumbing to factionalism and pressure from government agencies, the party disbanded in 1982. In March 1989 Newton was sentenced to a six-month jail term for misappropriating public funds intended for a Panther-founded Oakland school. In August of that year he was found shot dead on a street in Oakland.

organized and supported by students, pacifists, civil rights groups, women, religious leaders, and others. The protests took the form of teach-ins, marches, civil disobedience, burning of draft cards, and some violence. The antiwar movement was diversified. Even former members of the establishment in Washington took part (e.g., George Kennan and Senator William Fulbright). The antiwar movement brought together many different groups, often for different reasons.[11] Among their grievances were

1. Vietnam was not in our national interest, and U.S. national security was not threatened
2. The costs were too high and loss of manpower was not justifiable
3. The French defeat provided an example and a warning of a negative outcome that was not being heeded
4. The Domino Theory was irrelevant
5. Americans were suffering from a government credibility loss and disapproval from other allies
6. It was a distant war, a civil war, we were being painted as imperialists and colonialist like the French
7. Our government was out of touch with the people, there was an arrogance of power, and senseless destruction of a Third World country.

Tom Hayden

Tom Hayden, a radical activist, state legislator, and author, was born on 11 December 1939 in Royal Oak, Michigan. One of the best-known student radical leaders of the 1960s, he was a cofounder of the Students for a Democratic Society (SDS) in 1961, president of SDS (1962–1963), cofounder of the Economic Research and Action Project (1964), and leader of the Newark Community Union Project (1964–1967). Hayden was married to actress Jane Fonda. He ran for U.S. Senate in California (1976), was founder of the Indochina Peace Campaign, founder and chairman of the California Campaign for Economic Democracy (1977), and chairman of the California SolarCal Council (1978–1982). He was elected to the California State Assembly (1982) and was author of several books, including *The American Future* (1980).

After the news leaked that Nixon had ordered troops into Cambodia to stop North Vietnamese infiltration and resupply, the Kent State University ROTC hall was burned down by an arsonist. On 4 May 1970, students confronted Ohio National Guardsmen. Some guardsmen fired into the crowd. Four students were killed. As a result, student protests erupted on hundreds of campuses, forcing many to shut down. Nixon's handling of student protests was heavy-handed and led to further polarization. He could have reached out to the more moderate antiwar groups to bridge differences, but Nixon chose not to.[12]

Many Americans were coming back from Vietnam with changed perspectives. One of them was John Kerry, who would become a U.S. Senator and presidential candidate. He was one of many decorated veterans who flung away their medals on the steps of the Capitol in protest of the war. The American war was winding down, casualties were decreasing, but those veterans who opposed the war were asking for something more than an end to hostilities.

John Kerry

Born on 11 December 1943, John Kerry is probably best known for losing the 2004 U.S. presidential election to George W. Bush. He was a man born of privilege and schooled in the best institutions of learning on the East Coast. But his life's ambition was politics. An early encounter with President John F. Kennedy was a highlight for the young John Kerry (not unlike President Clinton's experience).

Kerry entered the military in 1966 and served in the U.S. Navy as a lieutenant, operating on the rivers of South Vietnam as a swift boat commander. He earned three Purple Hearts for wounds suffered in combat and a Bronze Star and a Silver Star for valor. Kerry's wartime heroism was attacked in the 2004 election by a veteran's organization sponsored by the Bush campaign, even though George W. Bush never served in Vietnam and had a less-than-distinguished short career in the Air National Guard. The campaign revealed how the wounds of Vietnam have not healed. It also reflected the historical revisionism caused by Ronald Reagan's Conservative revolution. Many Americans no longer wanted to hear the ugly truth about the Vietnam War.

Kerry began his antiwar activism in 1970 as a member of the VVAW and testified before the Senate as well. Kerry was elected to the Senate in 1985 and has served as the junior senator from Massachusetts under Edward Kennedy.

Across America, thousands of families by now were visiting the gravesites of their children killed in Vietnam. And millions of Americans were sharing their losses. The war had hit home.

THE MEDIA, PUBLIC OPINION, AND THE WAR

The media covered the Vietnam War like no other war. The Vietnam War was called a television war. But the coverage evolved over time. The impact that the media had on the public and their perceptions of the war is an interesting and vital topic. U.S. policymakers claimed that their biggest problem, late in the war, was public opinion and lack of support.[13]

Benjamin Spock

Dr. Benjamin Spock was a world-renowned pediatrician who wrote a parental guide on how to raise a successfully adjusted and healthy child in modern society. He was born on 2 May 1903 in New Haven, Connecticut, to a prominent attorney at law and a stay-at-home mother who would eventually give birth to five more of his siblings. He helped raise his younger siblings, which was probably a factor in his decision to become a pediatric physician. He graduated from Yale with a degree in literature and history. Spock later graduated from Columbia's School of Physicians and Surgeons, majoring in Pediatrics.

He would go on to write *The Common Sense Book of Baby and Child Care*, with many revisions for the changing times. It is the second best-selling book in the world (the first being the Bible). But Dr. Spock also had a reputation later in his life as a social and political activist. He wanted to help children grow up in a world and environment free from dangerous distractions and unnecessary government interruption. He demonstrated against the Vietnam War because he believed that every child should grow up in a world without the threat of fear and with some security, and was willing to put his reputation on the line to show this. Unlike many doctors of the time, he believed in his thought and he lived his beliefs, which I believe made him stand out among pediatricians of his time. In 1972, Spock made a run for the White House as a Third Party candidate. Dr. Spock died at the age of ninety-five in 1998.

Gloria Emerson

Born in 1930, Gloria Emerson's work as a foreign correspondent took her to many war zones. Her moving reports about the civilian casualties in the Vietnam War earned her the George Polk Award in 1971 for excellence in international reporting. Emerson's book about Vietnam, *Winners and Losers*, won the National Book Award for nonfiction in 1978.

Winners and Losers presented America's reaction, and lack of reaction, to the Vietnam War, as well as her personal recollections. From 1965 to 1972, Emerson was a foreign correspondent for the *New York Times*, covering the Nigerian Civil War, northern Ireland, and Vietnam. She was in Vietnam from 1970 to 1972. Emerson went on to take magazine assignments in El Salvador and Nicaragua. Her essays on Vietnam, Central America, and a variety of other subjects have appeared in *Esquire, Harper's, Saturday Review, Vogue, Playboy, New Times, Rolling Stone*, and *Vanity Fair*.

The ancient Greek playwright Aeschylus said that "the first casualty in war, is the truth." Governments naturally seek to control information, especially during times of war. The Vietnam War was one of the best-reported but least understood wars in American history. By 1967, there were nearly 1,000 reporters in Vietnam. Reporters were typical of their generation. They believed that the United States needed to stop Communist aggression. We held a sacred mission to do so. Most reporters went to Vietnam believing that the United States was right in being there. The Tonkin Gulf incident that led to the Tonkin Gulf resolution was reported uncritically. Reporters in Vietnam lived alongside the soldiers, under similar conditions. Although there was no censorship, they felt pressure to report what was helpful to the U.S. military and the South Vietnamese government.

War is not easy to report on, and measures of success were difficult to gauge in Vietnam. With passage of time, reporters came to be critical of the ARVN, the South Vietnamese government, and finally the U.S. military and its measures of success. There grew a level of mistrust between the media and the military. Nevertheless, the reporters did not form a monolithic group: some were neutral, some became critical, some held to the Cold War ideology tightly. There were three basic models of coverage: (1) heroic, (2) detached or objective, and (3) critical.

Heroic coverage portrayed the United States as good, the NVA and VC as evil. Prior to 1967, most coverage was like this. Reporters had experience in other U.S. wars (Korea and World War II) and carried the heroic ideal with them. Those reporters who tried to remain neutral, detached, and objective were criticized as not supporting the U.S. cause in Vietnam. This type of coverage was mostly in print, and some on television. Critical coverage changed over time. TV networks did not like this kind of coverage, but it came to be more standard late in the war.[14]

In 1965, the U.S. military said that their air strikes had surgical precision. North Vietnam invited U.S. reporters to come and take a look for themselves. Harrison Salisbury (one of the first reporters in Vietnam) of the *New York Times* wrote a series of articles in December 1966 that were critical of the U.S. bombing campaign in North Vietnam. The military did not deny his reports, but he was widely criticized by other members of the media. Salisbury was nominated for, but did not win, the Pulitzer Prize.

Other reporters criticized the United States' use of defoliants and bombing in South Vietnam. In 1967, a reporter named Martha Gelchorn could not get her articles printed in U.S. newspapers. She had them printed outside of the United States and was promptly asked to leave Vietnam. One might ask, if the war was so well reported, why was it so poorly understood? Part of the explanation is that the war was very complex. Journalists deal best with daily events, not the underlying long-ranging complexities of world events. The haunting of the past, the United States falling in the same footsteps as France— that did not come across in daily reporting on the war. One exception was David Halberstam and his books *Fire in the Lake* and *Making of a Quagmire*.

Antiwar protesting did have an impact, but exactly how much and what is still in debate. Many people looked unfavorably on the antiwar movement and the protesters, especially the more radical factions. Despite that shortcoming

---

Harrison Salisbury

Born in 1908, American journalist Harrison E. Salisbury was well known for his reporting and books on the Soviet Union. A distinguished correspondent and editor for the *New York Times*, he was the first American reporter to visit Hanoi during the Vietnam War.

He worked in news bureaus in Chicago, Washington, D.C., and New York before being sent to Europe in 1942. It was in London that he became friends with Walter Cronkite.

In the spring of 1954 he traveled extensively through Siberia and wrote a fourteen-part report for the *New York Times*: "Russia Re-viewed." The series received the 1955 Pulitzer Prize for international reporting. By the end of the decade Salisbury was focusing on the growing civil rights movement. Sent to cover race relations in the South in 1960, his reports led to a $6 million libel suit against the *Times*, which was not resolved in the *Times*' favor until 1964.

In 1962 Salisbury was named national news editor of the *Times*. He supervised the paper's coverage of President Kennedy's assassination and in 1964 became assistant managing editor. In 1970 Salisbury became the editor of the *New York Times*' Op-ed page. At the end of 1973, he retired from the *New York Times*. Harrison died in 1993.

David Halberstam

Born in 1934, and one of America's most successful authors, David Halberstam began his career as a journalist in the 1950s, first as a reporter for the *Daily Times Leader* in West Point, Mississippi, and later for the *Nashville Tennessean.* In 1960 he joined the *New York Times* and shortly thereafter was assigned to the paper's bureau in Saigon. Halberstam was among a small group of reporters there who began to question the official optimism about the growing war in Vietnam. Halberstam's work from Vietnam so rankled officials in Washington that President Kennedy once asked the publisher of the *New York Times* to transfer Halberstam to another bureau. In 1964, at age thirty, Halberstam earned a Pulitzer Prize for his reporting from Vietnam. His best-selling book, *The Best and the Brightest*, chronicles America's deepening involvement in Vietnam through the Kennedy and Johnson administrations. His book *Vietnam: A History* is a standard text for most Vietnam War history courses.

---

and negative publicity, the antiwar movement framed the terms of the debate in America. The movement cast the war in terms of LBJ's policies versus Vietnam's liberation. If the debate was not as strong as it was, then perhaps the result would have been different for the United States in Vietnam—perhaps a larger war as the military and defense contractors wanted. Those who blame TV coverage for loss of popular support for the war give the war protesters more credit than they deserve.

1. Not that many people watched the evening news on a regular basis
2. People saw what they wanted to see in the coverage, and the TV news confirmed, but did not change minds
3. Most TV coverage did not show the worst of the death and destruction.

From 1965 to 1967, TV coverage did not have as much impact on public opinion as some people think. By late 1967, support and opposition to the war were about even and had shifted over time. Johnson then became a victim of the credibility gap, his leadership was in question, and his approval rating slipped to a dismal 38 percent.

Peter Arnett

Born on 13 November 1934 in New Zealand, Peter Arnett covered the war in Vietnam with the Associated Press. His candor established him as a high-profile reporter and almost got him expelled by Ngo Dinh Diem over his coverage of the Buddhist uprisings. Arnett was in hot water with the U.S. military as well. President Johnson was so angered that he had Arnett under surveillance. Arnett's gung ho reporting earned him a Pulitzer Prize in 1966. He recorded a young lieutenant with one of the most famous lines from the Vietnam War: "We had to destroy the village in order to save it."

Arnett went on to work for CNN for eighteen years ending in 1999. During the Gulf War he became a household name worldwide when he became the only reporter providing live coverage directly from Baghdad. Together with two other CNN journalists, Bernard Shaw and John Holliman, Arnett brought continuous coverage from Baghdad for the sixteen initial intense hours of the war (17 January 1991). Even though forty foreign journalists were present at the Al-Rashid Hotel in Baghdad at the time, only CNN possessed the means to communicate to the outside world. Very soon the other journalists left Iraq, including the two CNN colleagues, which left Peter Arnett as the sole reporter remaining there. His reports on civilian damages caused by the bombing were not received well by the coalition war administration, who by their constant use of terms like "smart bombs" and "surgical precision" had tried to project an image that civilan casualties would be at a minimum. On 25 January, the White House said Arnett was used as a tool for Iraqi disinformation, while CNN received a letter from thirty-four members of Congress accusing Arnett of unpatriotic journalism.

The week after the start of the war, Arnett was able to obtain an uncensored interview with Saddam Hussein. The Gulf War became the first war seen truly live on TV, and Arnett was in many ways the sole player reporting from the "other side" for a period of five weeks. In 1994, Arnett wrote *Live from the Battlefield: From Vietnam to Baghdad, 35 Years in the World's War Zones.*

In March 1997, Arnett was able to interview Osama bin Laden, being the first Western journalist to do so. On assignment for NBC and *National Geographic*, Arnett went to Iraq in 2003 to cover the U.S. invasion. After a press meeting there, he granted an interview to state-run Iraq TV on 31 March 2003, in which he criticized the American invasion as not well planned.

When Arnett's remarks sparked protest, NBC initially defended him, saying he had given the interview as a professional courtesy and that his remarks were "analytical in nature." A day later, though, NBC, MSNBC, and *National Geographic* all severed their relationships with Arnett.

The United States was divided into pro-war Hawks and antiwar Doves. The highly educated tended to oppose the war, but they were not a significant majority in the country. Religious affiliation seemed to cut across the spectrum of support for the war, and there was no strong correlation. In terms of regions, the western United States tended to be hawkish, the southern region not as much so. Women tended to be more critical of the war than men were, and a higher percentage of blacks were critical of the war than whites were. A typical critic of the Vietnam War was not a long-haired radical student, but a middle-aged black woman with a high school education.

Support shifted because people did not think the war was going the way it should. They became disillusioned. Support decreased as casualties increased. As the cost of the war escalated, support diminished. Even in World War II, there was war weariness and an ebbing of support. It appeared that LBJ and his

Neil Sheehan

Pulitzer Prize–winning reporter and writer Neil Sheehan was born in Holyoke, Massachusetts, on 27 October 1936. He was a UPI correspondent and Saigon bureau chief from 1962 to 1964. Later he was a *New York Times* reporter. Sheehan exposed problems with the U.S. war in Vietnam fairly early on. In 1968, Sheehan broke the story about a large troop request after the Tet Offensive, and Daniel Ellsberg later leaked the Pentagon Papers to Sheehan, who published them in the *New York Times*. His book *A Bright Shining Lie: John Paul Vann and America in Vietnam* (1978) won both a Pulitzer Prize and a National Book Award. Both South Vietnamese and U.S. government officials did not want Sheehan's stories of South Vietnamese corruption and U.S. military over-confidence to get out. He left UPI in 1964 to work for the *New York Times*, saying that the war was "a long way toward being lost." He returned to Vietnam only once before 1972 and covered the war from Washington. Sheehan's book *A Bright Shining Lie* eloquently documented the lost cause in Vietnam.

war were doomed even before Tet. By the time he announced his decision not to run for reelection in March, Johnson's approval rating was 35 percent. The war had destroyed Johnson's presidency, the War on Poverty was falling apart, and the very social structure of the country was off balance by the end of 1968.

A Decent Interval

By early 1968, America had dropped almost 3 million tons of bombs on Vietnam—twice the tonnage dropped on Germany and Japan in World War II. The bombing was supposed to stop North Vietnam from sending soldiers and supplies to the South and force the Communist leaders in Hanoi to give up their goal of a unified Vietnam. After the negative political impact of the 1968 Tet Offensive, President Johnson ordered a bombing cutback, and peace talks began with North Vietnam, the VC, South Vietnam, and the United States. The delegates spent a lot of time haggling over the political implications of the seating arrangements as President Johnson prepared to leave office—yet another casualty of the war. A few days before the American presidential elections in November 1968, Johnson halted all bombing of North Vietnam. Nixon won by a very narrow margin.

The 1968 Tet Offensive focused on South Vietnam's cities and towns, but the fighting after Tet shifted back to the countryside. More than half a million American soldiers were still in Vietnam at the end of 1968. Four years had passed since American combat troops had landed in Vietnam, and the densely populated Mekong Delta in the South was still not pacified.

In the beginning of 1969, more than 800 Americans were wounded and more than 200 Americans were killed each week. Each week, more than 450 South Vietnamese allied soldiers died alongside them. And each day, more than 500 NVA and VC soldiers were killed.

In July 1969, President Nixon announced that U.S. troops would soon be going home. Through a slow, phased withdrawal, America was leaving the fighting to the South Vietnamese. He called his policy Vietnamization. As the American troops began their phased withdrawal, Nixon stepped up air and artillery attacks.

Sadly, some of the American troops who had just returned from Vietnam in 1970 were deployed to Washington to protect the capital against antiwar demonstrators. Nixon, with his requisite paranoia, and claiming that antiwar activists were helping the Communists, ordered illegal wiretaps and drew up a domestic enemies list. In a single Washington demonstration in 1970, a quarter of a million Americans denounced the war.

By April 1970, Nixon had reduced the forces in Vietnam by more than 100,000. But Nixon had also resumed full-scale bombing of the North. American generals were asking for permission to launch a major offensive against Communist sanctuaries in Cambodia. Although it was not a full-scale invasion of Cambodia, the geographical broadening of the war further divided America and fueled the protests.

On 4 May 1970, four students had been shot dead by National Guardsmen during demonstrations at Kent State University in Ohio. Campus protests against the war and the Cambodian operations reached a peak. Polls showed that a majority of Americans supported administration policy, unconvinced and not sympathetic to the protesters. In Washington, impatient senators urged ending the war in nine months, contingent upon the release of U.S. prisoners of war. Antiwar sentiments grew among the intelligentsia as well. In June 1971, the *New York Times* published the stolen Pentagon Papers, a secret history of official war decisions. This damaged the government's credibility and fueled Nixon's paranoia.

On the diplomatic front, Henry Kissinger had been secretly meeting with the Communists since August 1969. South Vietnamese and American officials had been kept in the dark about the negotiations. Kissinger's counterpart was Le Duc Tho, a member of North Vietnam's ruling politbureau.

Le Duc Tho

Le Duc Tho was born in Nam Ha Province, Vietnam, on 14 October 1911. As a young man he became involved in radical politics and in 1930 helped establish the Indochinese Communist Party. He campaigned against French rule in Vietnam and was twice imprisoned for his political activities (1930–1936 and 1939–1944).

In 1945 Le Duc Tho returned to Hanoi and joined with Ho Chi Minh and Vo Nguyen Giap in establishing the Viet Minh. He was responsible for organizing the rebellion against the government of South Vietnam throughout the 1950s and 1960s.

Peace talks between representatives from United States, South Vietnam, North Vietnam, and the NLF began in Paris in January 1969. Le Duc Tho served as special advisor to the North Vietnamese delegation. He eventually became North Vietnamese leader in these talks.

In October 1972, the negotiators came close to agreeing to a formula to end the war. The plan was that U.S. troops would withdraw from Vietnam in exchange for a cease-fire and the return of 566 American prisoners held in Hanoi. It was also agreed that the governments in North and South Vietnam would remain in power until new elections could be arranged to unite the whole country.

The main problem with this formula was that whereas the U.S. troops would leave the country, the North Vietnamese troops could remain in their positions in the south. In an effort to put pressure on North Vietnam to withdraw its troops, U.S. president Richard Nixon ordered a new series of air raids on Hanoi and Haiphong. It was the most intense bombing attack in world history.

The North Vietnamese refused to change the terms of the agreement, and so in January 1973, Nixon agreed to sign the peace plan that had been proposed in October. However, the bombing had proved to be popular with many of the American public as they had the impression that North Vietnam had been "bombed into submission."

As a result of their role in these peace talks, Le Duc Tho and Henry Kissinger were jointly awarded the Nobel Peace Prize. However, Le Duc Tho refused to accept the prize on the grounds that his country was not yet at peace.

Le Duc Tho and Vo Nguyen Giap continued the war against South Vietnam. The Communists took Saigon on 30 April 1975 and claimed victory. Communist governments were also set up in Laos and Cambodia. Le Duc Tho remained a member of the ruling Politburo until retiring in 1986. Le Duc Tho died in Hanoi on 13 October 1990.

In February 1972, Nixon startled the world when he announced his plans to visit Communist China. Nixon offered the Chinese trade recognition, a counterweight to the Russians. China's isolation was coming to an end. Nixon played his "China card" in hopes of driving a negotiating wedge between Russia and China and using China's influence to negotiate a favorable settlement in Vietnam.[1]

In spite of these efforts, on 31 March 1972, the North Vietnamese launched a new offensive as they crossed over the 17th parallel into South Vietnam. Using large units and tanks, they quickly captured Quang Tri Province. Not wanting to engage U.S. troops, but wanting to respond, Nixon ordered the mining of Haiphong harbor and increased the bombing. Nearly a thousand American aircraft struck both North and South Vietnam. The North Vietnamese offensive was halted.

Nixon and Kissinger had forged an agreement with the Communists that allowed them to keep NVA troops in the South in exchange for the return of U.S. POWs. Nixon was unable to convince the South Vietnamese to sign, so the North Vietnamese made the agreement public.

Employing his Mad Man strategy to scare the North Vietnamese into a favorable agreement,[2] Nixon ordered massive bombings during Christmas 1972. The eleven-day Christmas bombings were widely criticized. In Hanoi, more than 1,300 people were killed.[3]

On 11 January 1973, Kissinger notified Nixon that the agreement was ready. The terms were almost the same as those presented in October. Le Duc Tho and the North Vietnamese were prepared to sign. The agreement affirmed that South Vietnam was one country with two governments. There were to be moves toward reconciliation, prisoners of war would be released, American troops would leave, and NVA forces could remain in the South. Lyndon Johnson, the president who had sent U.S. combat troops to Vietnam eight years earlier, died the day before the agreement was signed. Put bluntly, over 58,000 American troops had died in Vietnam to achieve this less-than-adequate agreement.

On 27 January 1973, all parties signed the peace agreement. Hanoi celebrated with fireworks, but Vietnam was still divided.

WATERGATE

The so-called third-rate burglary at the Democratic National Headquarters in June 1972 did not affect the reelection of Richard Nixon because his administration did everything they could to cover it up. Nixon had been obsessed with leaks since the release of the Pentagon Papers in 1971. Although none of the leaked documents related to the Nixon administration, they did reveal a pattern of deception as to the true purpose of the war in Vietnam. The public trust had been betrayed, and Nixon would pay the price. His paranoia led to his orders to bug the Democratic National Headquarters despite the fact that McGovern, the Democratic challenger, had no chance of winning.[4]

Former Nixon aides G. Gordon Liddy and James W. McCord, Jr., were convicted of conspiracy, burglary, and wiretapping in the Watergate incident on 30 January 1973. On 30 April 1973, Nixon's top White House staffers, H. R. Haldeman and John Ehrlichman, and Attorney General Richard Kleindienst resigned over the scandal, and White House counsel John Dean was fired. On 18 May 1973, the Senate Watergate Committee began its nationally televised hearings. Archibald Cox was picked as the Justice Department's special prosecutor for Watergate. As the Watergate hearings were televised, they revealed the depth of the scandal, linking it in a complex tangle to Vietnam, and to Nixon's covert actions against the antiwar movement.

As Nixon's power decreased with each passing day of the Watergate hearings, his ability to intimidate the Communists in Vietnam also diminished. Nixon ended the draft and the troops had come home, so to most Americans the war was over.

White House counsel John Dean told Watergate investigators on 3 June 1973 that he discussed the Watergate cover-up with President Nixon at least thirty-five times. Watergate prosecutors found a memo on 13 June 1973 addressed to John Ehrlichman, describing in detail the plans to burglarize the office of Pentagon Papers defendant Daniel Ellsberg's psychiatrist. In mid-July, Watergate investigators found out that Nixon had secretly recorded all White House conversations. Nixon later refused to turn over the presidential tape recordings to the Senate Watergate Committee or the special prosecutor. Nixon then fired Archibald Cox and abolished the office of the special prosecutor as pressure for impeachment mounted in Congress.

Matters got worse for the Nixon administration when Spiro T. Agnew was forced to resign because of charges of tax evasion and taking bribes, on 10 October 1973. Congressman Gerald R. Ford (R-Michigan) was nominated and confirmed as Vice President. As an interesting side note, Ford, at the time of this writing, is the only living member of the Warren Commission that investigated the assassination of JFK.

Nixon had made a secret pledge to Thieu. If the Communists broke the cease-fire agreement, America would reenter the war in full force. But Nixon could not back up his promise. He was in serious trouble over Watergate and was on his way out of power.

The House Judiciary Committee passed the first of three articles of impeachment, charging obstruction of justice, on 27 July 1974. On 8 August 1974, Richard Nixon became the first U.S. president to resign. Vice President Gerald R. Ford assumed the country's highest office, the only time America would have a president that no one elected. He will later pardon Nixon of all charges related to the Watergate case, an act of political suicide for Ford, as it turned out.

Gerald R. Ford

Gerald Ford was born in Omaha, Nebraska, on 14 July 1913. An outstanding sportsman, he won a football scholarship to the University of Michigan, before studying law at Yale University. Ford graduated in 1941, and after being admitted to the bar, he began work in Grand Rapids, Michigan.

During the Second World War Ford served in the U.S. Navy and, by the time he was discharged in 1946, had reached the rank of lieutenant commander. A member of the Republican Party, Ford was elected to the House of Representatives in 1946. He was reelected eleven times and in 1965 was appointed minority leader of the House of Representatives. Ford also served on the Warren Commission that investigated the assassination of President Kennedy.

When Spiro Agnew resigned in October 1973, President Richard Nixon appointed Ford as his new vice president. He became president when Nixon was forced to resign over the Watergate Scandal in August 1974. Ford therefore became the first man to become the president of the United States without having been elected as either president or vice president. On 8 September 1974, Ford granted Richard Nixon a full pardon.

President Ford offered amnesty to all draft evaders who would be willing to sign a statement of loyalty and perform community service. He tried to secure more money for the beleaguered South Vietnamese government but was unsuccessful. Ford arranged the airlift of more than two thousand South Vietnamese orphans in 1975 and bombed Cambodia when they seized the U.S. merchant ship *Mayaguez*. Ford was the last U.S. president to deal with the Vietnam War, serving as the Communists took Saigon to finally end the war.

Ford's ability to govern was handicapped by the way he had obtained power and the fact that he had to deal with a Congress controlled by the Democratic Party. On over fifty occasions Congress vetoed his proposed legislation. At the Republican National Convention in August 1976, Ford defeated Ronald Reagan and won the party's nomination. Ford, handicapped by his association with Richard Nixon and the Watergate Scandal, was defeated by Jimmy Carter, the Democratic Party candidate. After his defeat in 1976 Gerald Ford retired to his home in Palm Springs, California.

END OF THE WAR

A key vote on 19 June 1973 sealed the fate of South Vietnam. On that day, the U.S. Congress passed the Case Church Amendment that forbade any further U.S. military involvement in Southeast Asia. North Vietnam was now free to invade South Vietnam without fear of U.S. bombing retaliation. Later, in November 1973, Congress passed the War Powers Resolution that required the president to obtain the support of Congress within ninety days of sending American troops abroad. After Nixon resigned, Congress dramatically cut aid to South Vietnam. The ARVN were underfunded, demoralized, and lacking in leadership and support.[5]

The Communists welcomed the January 1973 agreement as recognition of their legitimacy. They did not see themselves as aggressors. They saw the Americans as the aggressors. In 1973, both sides knew the struggle was not over. Two huge armies, one equipped by America, the other by the Soviet Union, were prepared for the final battle for control of a devastated country.

Whether they were hawks or doves, by 1973 most Americans believed that the cost had been too great, and the greatest cost had been American lives. They came to the realization that no more Americans should die for Vietnam. After the agreement was signed, the American POWs began to come home from Hanoi. Their homecoming played and replayed on national television. The last American fighting men were out of Vietnam. But America was still committed to the South Vietnamese government.

As unrealistic as it seemed, Thieu, like many Vietnamese, could not believe the United States would abandon its enormous investment in Vietnam. They

TABLE 11-1. U.S. Casualties in the Vietnam War

Year	Total	Year	Total
1957	1	1969	11,614
1958	0	1970	6,083
1959	2	1971	2,357
1960	5	1972	640
1961	16	1973	168
1962	53	1974	178
1963	118	1975	160
1964	206	1976	77
1965	1,863	1977	96
1966	6,144	1978	447
1967	11,153	1979	148
1968	16,589	1980–1995	66
Total Deaths			58,178

Source: http://thewall-usa.com/stats/.

Note: The deaths tabulated above represent those given on the Vietnam War Memorial Wall, which includes service members who died after the war due to injuries and wounds from the war.

counted on a last-minute defense when the Communists reached Saigon. President Ford believed that America had a moral responsibility to South Vietnam, but there was little he could do. Funding had been cut off by Congress and the American people were done with Vietnam.

On the morning of 29 April 1975, Tan Son Nhut airport in Saigon was under fire, preventing passenger planes from taking off. Americans and their South Vietnamese allies were ordered to evacuate before being captured by the Communists. By late afternoon, most Americans and thousands of Vietnamese had reached the U.S. carriers offshore. But many more thousands of Vietnamese were stuck in Saigon. Communist forces entered Saigon from six different directions. The Communists had attained their goal: they had removed the Saigon regime and reunified Vietnam. But the cost of victory was high. Nearly a million and a half Vietnamese had been killed, and three million wounded. The Americans were gone. America had lost over 58,000 in the war, and more than 300,000 wounded. It was America's first defeat. (See Table 11.1)

THE DEBATED LEGACY OF VIETNAM

During the presidential campaign of 1976, former Georgia governor Jimmy Carter, Ford's principal rival, offered a strikingly different analysis of the Vietnam War's significance to the larger national story. Carter periodically called attention to the continuing relevance of the war, citing it as an instructive, if painful, illustration of how overreaching, arrogant, and insulated governmental leaders can produce disastrously counterproductive policies. The secrecy and deception in which the Vietnam intervention was enveloped from its inception led Americans to take actions "contrary to our basic character," he charged in one speech.[6]

Reagan took a different approach than Ford or Carter. In a speech to the VFW on 18 August 1980, he said: "It is time we recognized that [in Vietnam] ours, in truth, was a noble cause . . . We dishonor the memory of 50,000 young Americans who died in that cause when we give way to feelings of guilt."[7] His rhetoric continues to inspire the neo-conservative movement today.

George H. W. Bush and Bill Clinton each drew negative lessons from the Vietnam War. When Bush announced the successful completion of the Gulf War in 1991, he said that we had "kicked the Vietnam syndrome."[8] Clinton often brought up the Vietnam experience to help explain why we did not intervene militarily on a large scale in Somalia, Haiti, Bosnia, Kosovo, and other problem areas around the world.[9] Clinton announced the normalization of relations with Vietnam on 11 July 1995. To help stem the controversial nature of such a decision, he added that this was related to ongoing efforts to recover the remains of U.S. servicemen missing in action, saying we were honoring veterans while moving "beyond the haunting and painful past . . . the brave Americans who fought and died there had noble motives. They fought for the freedom and the independence of the Vietnamese people."[10]

Harry G. Summers, Jr.

Colonel Harry G. Summers, Jr., was a soldier, a scholar, and a military analyst. He was born in Covington, Kentucky, on 6 May 1932. He enlisted in the army at fifteen by falsifying his age, and served in the Korean War. In February 1966 he went to Vietnam. During his seventeen-month tour in Vietnam, Summers was decorated with the Silver Star and the Bronze Star with V device for valor.

Following Vietnam, Harry attended the Army Command and General Staff College, where one of his classmates was Colin Powell. After Harry completed the course, he remained at Fort Leavenworth for several more years as an instructor. It was during this period that Harry Summers first began to acquire a reputation within the army as a military writer and analyst.

Summers published *On Strategy* in 1982. This book criticized the American war of attrition in Vietnam. His main critic was that the United States should have focused on the NVA and have the ARVN deal with the VC. He criticized LBJ for failing to maintain public support for intervention.

Summers' strategic advice was not limited to merely military strategy. He felt that Americans have an emotional tie to the concept of citizen soldier. This is because Americans are often antimilitary, but not antisoldier. Summers believed that most of our civilian leaders did not really understand the limitations of our military power. The American military is really a people's military and cannot be committed to extended campaigns without popular support. This places a severe limitation on the use of American military might. Summers held that the founding fathers, after all, believed in a citizen army and this concept is built into the design of our government.

Summers said that the great tragedy of the Vietnam War was that all of the military effort, bravery, and sacrifice were not focused because of the lack of a clear and realistic goal. Summers wrote that Americans turned against the war in Vietnam because they did not think that the government was really trying to win. There was no real plan to win and to measure progress toward that victory.

His later books included the award-winning *Vietnam War Almanac, Korean War Almanac, The New World Strategy: A Military Policy for America's Future*, and the *Atlas of the Vietnam War*. During the Gulf War, Harry acted as a military analyst for NBC News. He made more than 250 appearances on network television, and he was a frequent guest commentator on Voice of America and National Public Radio. Immediately after the Gulf War he wrote *On Strategy II: A Critical Analysis of the Gulf War*.

In 1988 Harry Summers became the founding editor of *Vietnam* magazine. He died in the year 2000.

The United States suffered more of a psychological and political setback from the Vietnam War than a military one. This is unlike the experience of Japan or Germany in World War II or of the American South in the Civil War.[11] Public opinion polls have shown since 1969 that most Americans feel that the U.S. intervention in Vietnam was a terrible and tragic mistake. In 1982, 72 percent of the Americans polled considered the war wrong and immoral. In 2000, that number had dropped slightly to 69 percent.[12]

Personal History

PARIS OF THE EAST

For as long as I could remember, my dad told stories. As a sailor, he had been all around the world. Sitting on the living room carpet, by the foot of my father's well-worn green armchair, I would hold on to his ship-in-a-bottle in one hand while leafing through our world atlas with the other. Almost every spot on the world map that I would point to, my father had visited. And he would have a story to color the picture in my imagination. One time, I pointed to Vietnam, and the story began.

In the fall of 1939, the steamship *Storlenko* entered Saigon harbor from the South China Sea. The ship had come through the Suez Canal, loaded cargo in Mombassa, and was now ready to load rice in Saigon. The young sailors on board were itching to find out why Saigon was called the "Paris of the East." One of those sailors, my father, Asbjorn Solheim, toured the city with his fellow shipmates and marveled at the strange sights—beautiful and delicate women in white dresses, cyclos (human-powered taxis), the smells of outside cooking, and French people everywhere. Open cafes spilled over with French-speaking customers. Asbjorn had two of his teeth fixed in gold and rode in a cyclo. His cyclo driver was so old that he could not keep up with the others, and my father had to get out and help him push the vehicle up a hill. He left Saigon as the world order was beginning to crumble. The heyday of the French empire would not last—there was an industrialized Asian nation waiting in the wings with its own dreams of empire. My father could not have imagined that nearly thirty years later, his son, my brother Alf, would arrive in Saigon to fight his war—the Vietnam War.

Beginning in Manchuria, China, the Japanese empire extended its reach to Vietnam by 1940 and the Vietnamese people had new masters. By this time, Asbjorn had reached his home in Norway just in time for the European war. He had jumped ship in New York and signed on with an old coal-driven Greek ship in Pensacola. The ship was slow and in poor condition. The lifeboats had fist-sized holes in them. As my father's ship was en route to Europe with wartime supplies for the British, a German U-boat sank another freighter that was not far from their position. The distress call came and the hard-nosed Greek captain changed course to avoid the sinking ship. "Those German bastards are just waiting for another ship to come to the rescue so they can sink it too," he said. Hitler's armies invaded Norway on 9 April 1940, and Asbjorn and his young bride Olaug (my mother) were trapped for five years under the yoke of Nazi tyranny.[1]

THE NUCLEAR FAMILY

My parents immigrated to America after World War II. The 1950s found my family playing the role of the nuclear family. We lived in the countryside, north of Seattle, that was fast becoming suburban. And always, the Cold War was in the background. A Nike missile site was just above our house on the hill. We saw the army trucks come by every day with soldiers. We laughed and waved and they waved back. One day, an army jeep accidentally hit my brother on the side of the road as he was walking down to the Farmer's store. It was not our first brush with the military nor would it be our last. He was okay, but my mom was very upset with the military. She had had enough of war. We lived our lives like so many other Americans, blindly building the American dream in the middle of a nuclear nightmare.

In August 1962, my family made it back to Norway to visit. The plan was to spend the school year in Norway and live with Grandma on the island. My sister had already moved back to Norway and was working in a bank in Oslo. She had also just recently married a Norwegian. My mom's mom had died before we could get to Norway. My mom wanted so desperately to see her before she passed away. My grandmother raised my mom and her siblings almost by herself. My mom's father was known as the town drunk and died shortly after World War II. He did not provide for my mom's family, which included eight kids.

The World Fair was in Seattle when we left in 1962. We traveled across the United States in a two-tone blue 1958 Ford station wagon. Then we took a ship from New York to Oslo. I was only four years old during our trip across America, but I do remember the thunderstorms and hail in Montana and getting on the ship in New York. We had loaded our car and all of our belongings on board and stood on deck by the railing, waving to the crowd as the ship shoved off. My mom was so excited about returning to Norway that she dropped her sunglasses into the harbor. My dad said that there would now be some fish swimming around with my mom's sunglasses.

The eleven-day trip across the Atlantic was great except for two stormy days. The crew treated us kids very well. They called me Master Bruce. For two days while crossing the Atlantic we were not allowed to go on deck because of the weather. Everyone seemed worried, but I used the time to explore beneath the decks. The steward showed me the "mechanical cow" that made all of our milk on board the ship. I was very impressed.

When we reached Norway we got to see the house where my mom was born just before it was bulldozed to the ground. I remember my mom crying and holding some of the possessions that she had salvaged from the house. In October 1962, during the Cuban Missile Crisis, my parents worried a great deal. My mom called the U.S. embassy in Oslo and they told her to listen to the radio and stay in touch in case something happened. My mom was tired of war. Our Christmas at my grandma's house was great. There was so much snow and she had a tree with real candles on it. Unfortunately for my parents, my grandma was one to spoil children, especially me. One time I was doing something really bad and my dad wanted to spank me. My grandma grabbed me from my father and told him: "If you spank this child, then you are the next one to get spanked." She was a perfect grandma. She even liked to look at *MAD* magazine although sometimes she had the annoying habit of tearing the pages out to use as toilet paper in the outhouse.

The island in northern Norway was a winter paradise. I remember riding in the sleds Norwegians used, called a "spark." They looked like chairs with long runners. My grandma would put me in the spark and slide us down to the village market for food. One day I was playing out in the snow too long, and when I came home I could not move my neck. I had a high fever and everyone was worried. The old lady next door came over and told my grandma that her son had the same thing and now he was crippled with polio. My mom and grandma panicked and prayed. The next day I was fine though.

I had learned Norwegian quickly because my parents spoke the language at home. I became so proficient in it that I forgot my English. When we returned to America, I taught my little buddies Willy and Johnny to say some things in Norwegian. The first day they heard me speak Norwegian, they ran into their house and told their mom: "There is something wrong with him, he is speaking Spanish!"

My first major historical memory was when President John F. Kennedy was shot. My parents were JFK supporters and we even had a large picture of JFK on the wall in our den. My parents have never had any other pictures of presidents in the house. I used to sit and stare at the picture and wonder if he was in heaven looking down on us. I remember that my parents and my brother were very upset. My mom was crying. Even my brother seemed on the verge of tears. My dad left work early, which was unheard of in the construction business. It was as if the entire nation went into shock. My brother collected clippings from the newspaper. "This is something that we will never forget," he said as he neatly folded the clippings in his scrapbook. I did not know what would happen, but it seemed to me that everything changed after that young president was killed. My mom and dad never believed the Warren Commission's findings.

When the Beatles came to America in 1964, we all watched them sing on the Ed Sullivan show. My brother and I liked it, but Mom and Dad thought it was silly. My first-grade teacher, Mrs. Savik, said that we were not allowed to talk about the Beatles because they were "long-haired devils." My brother started to grow his hair longer, a fact that drove my dad crazy.

As a kid I remember lying on my back in the yard and looking up at the sky, thinking that we must be living in the belly of a giant. When he drank, it rained. Maybe, I thought, I am also a giant and a world is in my stomach, too. I think it was those thoughts that led me to believe that we were not alone in the universe. Strange things happened sometimes that did not seem to have any reasonable or logical explanation. One time in 1965, when we were camping at Deception Pass, we stopped on the tiny island that separated the mainland from Whidbey Island. The bridge that connected both sides was several hundred feet above the water. There were trails around the island and I ran around ahead of my parents. One trail headed directly to a viewpoint. There was no guardrail, and the trail ended at a sheer cliff that fell hundreds of feet to the water. I ran headlong for the cliff, not thinking. Luckily, my dad ran after me and grabbed me before I fell off. Sometimes I remember this event as if I fell off and died and that I was living a second life or something. Thoughts like that scared me, so I tried not to dwell on them.

WHERE IS VIETNAM?

My parents became more worried about a faraway place where a war was raging—a place called Vietnam. The United States seemed to be getting more and more involved, and they were afraid that my brother would have to go and fight. By 1966, it was clear that there was a big war in Southeast Asia with no end in sight. I sure was glad that my big brother was still home in September 1966 when the first episode of *Star Trek* aired. I was scared to death. The story involved a salt vampire that drew all the life out of people. The salt vampire appeared as a woman, but when it got ready to kill, it revealed its true form—a hideous creature with shaggy hair, rows of sharp teeth, and a giant suction-cup mouth and fingers. I hated vampires of any kind. My friend Willy was afraid of mummies, but I was not. Mummies were old, dumb, slow, and could not see through all those bandages. Why be afraid of them? U.S. troop strength at the end of 1966 stood at 385,300.

When my brother finished high school in 1967, the war was in full swing. My parents were really afraid by then. There was talk, whispers actually, of sending him to Norway or Canada. I sat and quietly played with my GI Joes and wondered if I could play army with my brother if he had to go. Playing army was my favorite game. I had a Johnny Seven rifle that had a drop-down pistol, a grenade launcher, a machine-gun, and a rocket launcher—all in one. My friends and I played army everyday in the woods by our house. The only problem was that we could never agree on who was dead in play battles. This would often lead to the war breaking up and all of us going home.

I could never get away from war. At school we had civil defense drills. The alarm would go off and we would drop beneath our desks as the teachers closed the blinds and turned off the lights.

"Don't look at the flash," we were told. I would sit under my little desk and look at the window anyway. Was this the real one? I often thought to myself. Would I have time to run home to my mom or would she pick me up? It really did not matter, I figured, the bombs would incinerate us all instantly. Then why were we under the desks? Because we were told to, that was why. That was why we did everything in those days.

The day finally came that my brother was going to be drafted into the army or make another decision. He decided to join the air force because he figured he would be safer and have less chance of going to the war in Vietnam. My dad said that he had been in Saigon in the 1930s and it was a beautiful city. My mom said that she did not care how beautiful it was, she did not want her boy going there. In 1967, my brother was leaving the sanctuary of our family. Our family that had survived only through my mom's love and my father's strong and caring hands.

WE GOTCHA NOW

In the fall of 1967, we went to the Armed Forces Induction Center on the waterfront in Seattle to pick up my brother after his physical and swearing in to the air force. When he came out of the building and got into the car, he told us that the officer who swore them in asked them to burn their draft cards because, as he said, "We gotcha now." The next day we drove him to Sea-Tac International Airport. He carried only a shaving bag. The recruiters told my brother that he did not need anything else. Mom cried as the Braniff jet pulled away from the gate. I cried too. Maybe it was because my mom was, and maybe because I would not have my brother to harass anymore. For instance, I would not be able to call his friend's house and tell him Mom wanted him home when she did not. I would not be able to follow him everywhere he went. Especially annoying to my brother was when I would follow him and his friends down to the Farmer's store to beg for candy. His friends would want to hang out and smoke, but I was always in the way. And I would not have anyone to play catch with. My dad could not throw a ball and was even worse at catching one. But

Norwegians are not known to be great baseball players anyway. This was going to be hard. Who would watch "Bonanza" with me on Sunday nights?

My brother went to basic training at Lackland Air Force Base (AFB) in Texas. He wrote home and told us about how the Technical Instructors (TIs) made them eat the laundry tags he found on their uniforms. His TI was a small Puerto Rican man with a loud voice and too much aftershave. After basic training they were loaded on buses, wearing their woolen dress blue uniforms, even though it was very hot. My brother was heading for Keesler AFB in Biloxi, Mississippi, to learn how to be a radio operator. As his bus was pulling away from the basic training barracks, one of the new airmen gave the TIs the finger. The bus stopped suddenly and the guy was dragged off the bus by the TIs. They continued on and no one saw the guy again.

In Biloxi, race segregation was in full effect. My brother and his friend Sparks went to get a haircut, and the barber said that he would cut my brother's hair but not Sparks', because he was black. There were "Whites Only" signs on drinking fountains and bathrooms. One Friday night, my brother and his friends were walking around downtown when they saw a fire by the high school. Some of the locals told them that the Ku Klux Klan was burning crosses to "scare the niggers." My brother called on Christmas Eve and told us that he had KP (Kitchen Police) duty. The United States had nearly 500,000 troops in Vietnam by the end of 1967.

In February 1968, all major U.S. installations in South Vietnam were attacked by the VC during the Tet lunar New Year celebration. We also saw on TV that the U.S. embassy was attacked. My mom and dad were so worried that my brother would end up in Vietnam. Walter Cronkite, my dad's favorite TV newsman, said on 27 February that it looked like the United States was not winning the war.

On 4 April 1968, just before my brother got his first assignment orders, we heard that Dr. Martin Luther King, Jr., had been assassinated. My parents were sad because they said he was a good man who wanted to help people. We talked about the assassination at school and some kids were laughing. It seemed to me that the war over there in Vietnam was killing people at home too.

At school we were playing a new game. When the duty teachers were not looking, we would divide the kids on the playground in two and have one group gather at the top of the hill above the playground while the other remained at the bottom. Then, with a great deal of clamor, we would descend down upon the kids at the bottom of the hill and run them over. We called this war. The duty teachers would put a stop to this game whenever they saw us massing for attacks, but we all seemed to accept it as part of what we should do at recess.

My sister took me to see *Planet of the Apes* at the Kenmore Drive-In. I was terrified, especially by the giant ape scarecrows and the music. I imagined apes taking over the world. Maybe they would not have wars like we did. The scene at the end of the movie, where Charleton Heston finds the half-buried Statue of Liberty, was very shocking to me. It frightened me to think that some day the United States, my home, my family, might be gone.

I SHALL RETURN

After he got his technical training in Mississippi, my brother Alf was sent to Clark AFB in the Philippines. It was May 1968 and I was ten years old. Mom was so glad that he was not sent to Vietnam. After Alf arrived in the Philippines, he wrote to us and said that a couple of soldiers had wandered into the wrong area off base and got their heads chopped off. Mom began worrying again. I wondered why the Filipinos did that. Did they not know we were the good guys? Later I would come to find out that the United States had a long history in the Philippines—replacing vile Spanish tyranny with apparently not-so-vile American tyranny—and many Filipinos did not care for Americans in spite of General MacArthur's carefully orchestrated heroics during World War II.

On 7 June 1968, John F. Kennedy's brother Robert was assassinated. Even though I was just a kid, it seemed kind of strange and suspicious that so many important people should be killed within such a short period of time. I wrote to my brother and sent him a picture of Robert F. Kennedy (RFK) that I had clipped from the *Seattle Times*. My parents were very upset when RFK was killed, and I thought my brother would want the clippings. It did not seem that long ago that JFK was killed.

Alf sent home pictures of the Philippines. It looked like a tropical paradise. His duty area looked very neat with lots of plywood desks and radios and typewriters and hotel room–like quarters. He wore heavily starched uniforms and his hair was kept very short unlike so many young people at home—hippies, as my parents called them. In fact, my parents used to drive through the University District (the Ave) on our way home from visiting my great uncle in Tacoma. My dad would slow down and point at all the "long-haired, drug addicted hippies." My parents were proud that their son was serving his country.

My parents and I watched a special on TV about the Philippines and could not believe what we saw. My brother confirmed for us that the Filipinos actually did nail themselves to crosses and beat themselves to a pulp at Easter. That was a little bit tougher than the Easter egg hunts at the Norwegian Lutheran church in Seattle.

Alf wrote to us fairly often throughout the rest of 1968 and told us about the different duty assignments he had and all the "hops" he took to travel to other AFB locations. He went to American Samoa and sent pictures of himself on the beach. The coral beach was so sharp that he needed shoes to walk on it. He also visited some friends of ours in Hawaii. To me, being in the military seemed pretty cool. He got to go to so many different places.

My brother came home for Christmas 1968 and we had a great time. We went skiing and he gave me some of his uniforms to play with. I showed Alf my comic book collection. He told me that most of the soldiers he knew liked comics and that the *Incredible Hulk* was one of their favorite comics. I liked the *Hulk*, but my favorite comic was the *Fantastic Four*. I was sad when Alf had to go back to the Philippines in January of 1969. He wrote to us in February and March and kept us abreast of his daily routine. Mom and Dad were very happy that he was still in the Philippines and not in the war.

Alf wrote home in April of 1969 and said that some of his friends were getting orders to go to Vietnam, but he thought that he would not go. He was pretty sure that he could get orders for the West Coast so he could be closer to home. "But, you never really know until you get the orders," he wrote. Just a few weeks after he wrote that letter, we got another one—he was going to have a ninety-day temporary duty assignment (TDY) at Tan Son Nhut Air Base near Saigon. He asked us not to be upset, but Mom was, anyway. That was exactly where my parents did not want him to go. Even though the Communists were attacking Saigon, he wrote, everything would be okay.

TDY

Alf went to the waterfront when he arrived in Saigon in April 1969 and remembered that dad had been there in the 1930s while in the Norwegian merchant marines. I wrote to my brother and asked him if there were any B-52 bombers at Tan Son Nhut. I really liked the B-52s. He told me that they flew out of bases in Thailand and Japan and other Pacific islands. He did say that he could sit in his bunk at night and listen to them bomb the enemy positions around Saigon.

According to Alf, it was almost the rainy season in Vietnam. Seattle had a rainy season too—from October through September. He also wrote in his letters that the local paper—the *Northshore Citizen*—we were sending him showed that most of his friends were getting married. Also, he was able to call home occasionally using a MARS station in Vietnam and one at McChord AFB.

My brother was extending his assignment in Vietnam to get more money. My mom was upset again. But to me $110 sounded like a lot of money for doing something that was fun anyway. He also wrote that VC terrorists threw a hand grenade into an air police jeep just down the street from his hotel. Two Americans were injured and a Vietnamese girl was killed. Another bomb exploded in the Saigon main post office and killed another Vietnamese. He urged us not to worry because he did not wander around the town much and there were four guards at the hotel where he was staying. My mom was not so sure about that and she kept calling them VDs instead of VCs. I wondered what kind of a war was it anyway. Didn't they know the rules?

In May of 1969, my brother wrote that they used a spent artillery shell buried in the ground as a urinal. It faced so that they pissed toward Hanoi in the North.

He also announced that he was going to get promoted to sergeant. But there was more trouble in the end of May 1969—Saigon was under attack but his station was not hit. Alf wrote that they eventually lifted the twenty-four-hour curfew, but one U.S. soldier was injured while unloading a truck full of C-rations. The case of rations exploded—booby-trapped by the VC, no doubt. When we played war at home, we also set up booby traps around our tree forts just in case the bad boys and girls came. The bad boys and girls were kids who lived on the hill above us. I am not sure why they always attacked our forts and stole stuff. I did not even know their names, but you do not have to know someone's name to have them be your enemy. The rainy season was in full force, my brother wrote. He got his orders to South Carolina and was not happy.

In May, Alf wrote about how neat the Apollo 10 mission was. He had helped set up communications for the Apollo 7 previously. He said that we were getting ready to set foot on the moon and that he was proud to be an American and got chills up and down his spine whenever he heard the National Anthem. I was proud too—proud of my brother serving his country. I also was excited about the moon shot. I would have my dad stop to fill gas at the Gulf Station so I could get the Lunar Lander model they gave away with a full tank of gas. Being an astronaut would be great, but it was a lot of hard work.

Later in June, Alf wrote to let us know that "all was quiet in Saigon except for the occasional VC rocket exploding in the densely populated areas." My mom was hysterical again, of course. "But," he continued, "the T-bones arrived finally, and all would be okay."

The Fourth of July 1969, and Alf was back at Clark AFB in the Philippines. He was assigned to guard duty for a solid week even though he thought he would not have to pull any more details. He would be coming home for leave before his assignment in South Carolina. It would be great to have my big brother back home to go camping with. We read that there were homecoming parades in Seattle for the soldiers, but war protesters ridiculed the veterans. My brother even heard about it in the Philippines. He thought that the protesters should have been arrested because they had no idea what was going on. I agreed. The Americans were the good guys, the VC were the bad guys. Couldn't they see that? It seemed so obvious to me.

In July 1969, my brother was sure that he would get orders for Vietnam after his assignment at Shaw AFB, South Carolina. He said that they had a glut of radio operators in the States and too few overseas, especially in Southeast Asia. He also said that two of the astronauts on the Apollo 11 moon shot were air force officers. He was proud that he was wearing the same uniform as them. It seemed unreal to him to watch (on the barracks TV) those astronauts walking on the moon. I thought that it was so cool, and I wanted to be an astronaut too.

Alf wrote about the increase in anti-American violence in Manila when President Nixon came to visit. He also said he was sorry that Edward Kennedy got into some trouble and that it might hurt his chances of being president someday. Kennedy had driven off a bridge on Chappaquiddick Island,

Massachusetts, and his young female companion had drowned. I did not really understand at the time, but I do remember thinking that Kennedy must have been a pretty bad driver. Probably because he did not drive very often, since the Kennedys were so rich and their butlers did most of the driving. My brother said that he was so short in the Philippines that he needed a parachute to get out of bed. My mom and dad did not get it. "I hope he is not going to be a paratrooper," my mom said nervously.

My brother sent an article in August 1969 about how U.S. soldiers were being attacked. A recent bombing attack left six soldiers and two Filipinos injured. The city outside of the Clark AFB, called Angeles City (population 150,000), was said to have 200 bars and nightclubs catering to U.S. service personnel. The suspects in the bombing were said to be hoodlums or Communist Huk terrorists. His rifle-range training had been cancelled twice because the Huks had stolen their ammunition.

My parents and I watched the news on TV in August 1969 and saw reports from the Woodstock music festival in New York. The festival was said to be peaceful. I cut out some pictures from the newspaper and sent them to my brother. I thought he would especially like the picture of Jimi Hendrix, since he was from Seattle.

It was reported in the paper that Ho Chi Minh, the leader of North Vietnam, died on 3 September 1969. I thought that was weird—he died on my birthday. In November 1969, Alf wrote about his friends in Vietnam and the Philippines. He said that there were more terrorist attacks in Saigon, where he was on TDY. Elections in the Philippines had also produced violence. He finally bought a car—a 1961 Rambler Classic for $250. Now he did not have to walk or bum rides anymore.

My brother came home for Christmas 1969. He sure had a lot of neat stories. I could hardly wait until I could be in the military. I wanted to be a sergeant just like Alf. I played army in the woods almost everyday with my friends Willy and Johnny. The cool thing about playing army was that you felt you were doing something important. Most kids did not get respect from their parents. But the soldiers in Vietnam were not that much older than we were, and they seemed to get respect, at least from their parents. One problem was that Willy and Johnny were brothers and would fight. Those fights ruined our wars sometimes.

There were 475,000 U.S. troops in Vietnam in December 1969. Alf put in his volunteer statement for Vietnam in February 1970. He would make $350 a month if he went to Vietnam. Alf called home in April and said that he was in the hospital with hepatitis. He said that he would be okay, but Mom got upset anyway. I remembered when he got sick several years earlier when he swam in Lake Washington and swallowed water. The water was bad because those rich dummies with waterfront property dumped their sewers into the lake. He was fine after a week or so. Anyway, he would still go to Vietnam even though Mom thought that the military could not possibly send him after he got hepatitis. He lost twenty pounds, but he would gain it all back if he could eat Mom's cookies every day. The base doctor checked my brother for needle marks when he was first admitted. They thought he got hepatitis from using drugs.

In May, when Alf was still recovering at the base hospital in South Carolina, four students were shot by National Guardsmen at Kent State University, while protesting the U.S. invasion of Cambodia in April. I could not figure out why we were shooting our own people. Was not it bad enough that the VC were killing Americans? Maybe those National Guard soldiers should have gone to Vietnam to shoot VC instead of doing something dumb like that. But what did I know? I was just a kid.

Alf felt bored in South Carolina, so he fixed his schedule so that he could play golf all the time. In fact, he and his friends played thirty-six holes of golf a day until Master Sergeant Muck, a savvy lifer, ruined it for them. He revised the schedule so that they could no longer play so much golf. One time, on the golf course, a group of golfers in front of my brother and his friends were playing very slowly. As was the custom in golf, slower golfers were supposed to let other golfers play through if they were faster. Well, this group refused. So my brother drove his ball right into the middle of their entourage, almost hitting a distinguished gray-haired gentleman. As it turned out, that distinguished gentleman was a general, the base commander. What was he going to do, send my brother to Vietnam? Great, that was where he wanted to go anyway.

On 20 October 1970, Alf got his orders to go to Vietnam. He would be going to Cam Ranh Bay around the beginning of February 1971. He had to extend for one year in order to get the assignment in Vietnam. My mom did not understand. I figured that he would be safer in the Vietnam War than with those southern sheriffs and their dumb rules. He was very worried that he would not get to drive when he was home for Christmas leave in 1970.

Mom was glad to hear on the news that on 11 November 1970, no U.S. soldiers were killed in Vietnam. That was the first day in five years that no Americans were killed. But, unfortunately, there were 365 days in a year. Late in November, my brother sent a copy of his orders for Vietnam. This time it was not just TDY for a couple months, but a full year in country. Alf would be with the 483rd Combat Support Group in Cam Ranh Bay. My big brother would be home on the 22nd of December. He would have forty-three days of leave before he went to Vietnam on 3 February 1971. U.S. troop strength in Vietnam stood at 325,000 when Alf came home on leave.

VIETNAMIZATION ON THE HALF SHELL

We read in the *Seattle Times* on 2 January 1971 that heavy fighting had broken out on the DMZ between South Vietnamese forces and the NVA. This all took place at the closing hours of a seventy-two-hour cease-fire. This was a cease-fire called by the Communists in observance of the Western New Year. Twelve Americans were killed and forty-nine wounded. I figured that a cease-fire was kind of like a time-out in football. My mom still thought it was crazy for Alf to volunteer to go to Vietnam. But my brother said that he wanted to do his duty like the rest of the guys. It was hard to argue with that.

The North Vietnamese said that the American prisoners of war (POWs) were not being mistreated. I did not believe it, even though I watched *Hogan's Heroes* regularly. The *Seattle Times* reported that the Calley trial was nearly completed on 12 January. One witness said that they killed everyone in the village because they were afraid—even the babies clinging to their mother's breasts might have been booby-trapped. I wondered what I would do. War did not seem as simple as I had once thought. Just when you thought you knew the rules, someone changed them.

The *Seattle Times* also reported that a hawk (war supporter) senator said that the war in Vietnam was a civil war, a fact that was not recognized by the United States at the beginning. The senator said that "the United States should not defend nations that did not have dedication to freedom and a willingness to defend their nation to the death." But my parents and I had seen the body counts on TV. Every night on the news they would show the number of soldiers killed, next to their respective flags. There were always more VC and North Vietnamese killed than Americans. But we also saw that the South Vietnamese were dying in greater numbers than Americans. Could the U.S. government be trying to blame its losses on the South Vietnamese? The Congress said that even though the North Vietnamese used the Ho Chi Minh trail, which ran through Cambodia and Laos, to supply its troops in South Vietnam, the United States could not send troops into Cambodia or Laos. I began to think that it was a dumb war.

The news on 17 January reported that drug use in the military was mainly occurring in the army. Alf said that some soldiers would have care packages (filled with cookies and other goodies) sent to them in Vietnam, and then they would dump the stuff out and fill the empty package with heroin, mark "Return–KIA" on it, and mail it back to the sender (KIA meant killed in action). The post office usually did not inspect or mess with a package that was sent to a dead soldier, and returned it.

My brother arrived at Cam Ranh Bay on 4 February. The process of Viet-namization was taking place according to the news. Later I found out that the French had a similar policy in their war with the Viet Minh (1946–1954). The French called it *le jaunissement*, or "the yellowing of the war." It took him two days to in-process. Alf said that his unit was really not the 483rd Combat Support Group—that was just his in-processing unit. He was assigned to the 21st Tactical Air Support Squadron (TASS). He would be going out to the field very often to many different locations throughout South Vietnam. His job would be to maintain communications with Forward Air Controllers (FACs) who flew O-2 aircraft.

The same day my brother arrived in Vietnam, the *Seattle Times* Letters to the Editor section was devoted to the issue of draft evasion. President Nixon said that young men should not refuse to sacrifice their lives so as not to dishonor those who have already died in the war. But, as my dad said, with all the information uncovered about how the U.S. government had set up the war and lied to its people, were it not the men who sent the U.S. soldiers to die the ones dishonoring fallen Americans? So many people argued about the war at home. But the soldiers still had to go and fight.

Alf got orders to go up country to Quang Tri. He sent home pictures of the walled-in, high security communications compound in which he worked. He explained in his letters that the place was safe because it was located inside of a graveyard. The VC did not want to disturb their ancestors. I could understand that, ghosts and stuff could be very scary. From the pictures my brother sent home, Vietnam looked like a beautiful country with mountains, jungles, wide, open plains, and oceans.

The *Seattle Times* also reported that the United States stepped up its use of B-52 bombers in Vietnam in anticipation of a Tet lunar New Year offensive by the NVA. The pilots said that they did not think they were hitting much, and assessment reports were sketchy. B-52s were my favorite planes because they were the biggest bombers and had eight engines.

On 19 February Alf was sent to Pleiku, about 200 miles north of Cam Ranh Bay and thirty or forty miles from the Cambodian border. He said that he was very busy with lots of radio work to do. They maintained four different radio circuits that were operated twenty-four hours a day. The main purpose was to act as a middleman between the aircraft in his control area and the command posts that gave the planes information on targets and where not to bomb. He was in support of the Second Corps Direct Air Support Center that covered 48 percent of the South Vietnamese landmass. He talked mainly to FACs, who were, as he wrote, "the brave souls who actually flew into enemy areas to check for targets and then recommended different kinds of missions." They would then fly back in to bombed areas and check for damage: number of soldiers killed, hootches blown up, bunkers destroyed, bridges destroyed, and any-thing else. The Vietnamese called the FACs "bringers of death" because they came in just before the bombers and the fighters. The pilots sat on their flak jackets and painted "rice hats" on their aircraft for every VC killed. Alf said that he did not know what we were being told at home, but many of the missions he directed were over the Cambodian border. He said that the radio room was safe and protected. With special field ration pay, he now made $450 a month. In the papers, we read that the South Vietnamese army was attacking North Viet-namese positions and supply lines within Laos, but that the operation was proving to be unsuccessful. What a strange war!

Alf wrote on 24 February that he had moved again, this time to Ninh Hoa, which was fifty miles north of Cam Ranh Bay and right on the coast. He said that there were only seventy Americans where he was, the rest were ROK (Republic of Korea) marines—the meanest soldiers in the world. The VC and NVA rarely messed with them. He sent us some pictures of the ROK marines.

From what I could see, he was in very good hands with them. In one picture there was an observation tower in which the ROK marine colonel stood all day and watched his men. One day, an ROK marine walked by and did not salute the colonel in the tower. The colonel barked some orders to other soldiers and they promptly subdued the soldier and beat him. My brother said they were not as busy there as in Pleiku. He had to fly into the base by helicopter—a UH-1 Huey. His mail had not really caught up with him yet.

Alf wrote that he could always tell the helicopter pilots from the jet pilots, on the radios. The helicopters made the pilots' voices warble. Too many times he heard them call out "Mayday" as they were going down. He wrote that those "warbled Maydays" kept playing through his head like a broken record. Each one probably meant that the pilot died or was captured as a POW. He got to ride on Hueys all the time, but he hated riding on the medevacs because sometimes the floor would be slick with blood and tissue from dead or wounded soldiers. I thought that you had to be pretty tough to be a helicopter pilot, especially a medevac (medical evacuation) pilot.

The Vietnam War was dangerous all right, but it was dangerous at home as well. My brother's best friend, Alfred, was our next-door neighbor. His parents were so happy that their son was not drafted and was attending the University of Washington, "where he was safe with his family and not in that war," as Mrs. Newman told my mother. I used to see Alfred once in a while, down at the Farmer's store, and driving down the driveway. He always used to ask about my brother. He was always pretty nice to me. But on a rainy spring evening in February 1971, his car collided with an abutment on the University bridge, ending his life. His family, who felt he was safe at home, never really recovered from his death.

On 1 March, a bomb went off in the U.S. Senate. It was linked to war protesters and their reaction to the expansion of the Vietnam War into Laos. I did not understand why the protesters would use bombs against their own people to stop war and bring peace somewhere else. Should not peace start at home? I thought. But then, my friends and I had our own problems going on. The other day we noticed that the bad boys and girls built a fort near our part of the woods. Now, there was not any clear boundary between our part of the woods and theirs, but we seemed to know somehow. Their fort seemed to be a little too close for comfort. Willy, Johnny, and I decided to break into their fort and conduct some sabotage. Once we got into the plywood and junk-ridden structure about ten feet up into a tree, we saw all sorts of stuff. There were dirty magazines, cigarettes, beer, a bottle of whiskey, and other naughty things. We took all of the stuff and put it in a bag and left. We gave it all to Willy and Johnny's father. He said he would smoke the cigarettes, drink the beer and whiskey, and burn up the magazines. Willy noticed that it took him a lot longer to get rid of those magazines than it took him to smoke and drink the other stuff.

We read in the paper that President Thieu of South Vietnam had threatened to invade North Vietnam again on 4 March. He could not do it without U.S.

support. But the United States was committed to its policy of Vietnamization and was worried about Communist China's reaction to such a move. My brother sure was in a mess over there.

Our community newspaper reported that a local boy had been killed in the war. He was a nineteen-year-old marine. The article said that he died when he jumped on a grenade to save his buddies. He was awarded a Silver Star medal. I thought about how brave he was and if I could be so brave. I thought maybe you do not know until the time comes if you could be that brave. I wrote to my brother that he was a hero to me already and did not have to do something like that boy did.

Alf was in Da Nang on 9 March, where he had spent six days directing air strikes on a hilltop camp in the Central Highlands. He was assigned to a group of Koreans again. He did not get to take a shower for six days. How cool. I hated taking showers and baths. The air force was so cool. He had been reassigned to the 20th TASS and would more than likely be sent to Quang Tri and then to Khe Sanh. He told Mom that he knew those names were in the news and that was where the action was. He said he would be working with Americans and South Vietnamese instead of Koreans. Quang Tri was only a few miles from the DMZ and Khe Sanh was also near the border, so action would be constant. He thought that his taking on these assignments would be appreciated at a later date, maybe by employers, so we were not supposed to worry.

The *Seattle Times* reported on 11 March that B-52s inflicted heavy damage to North Vietnamese forces in Laos. The B-52s were first used on 18 June 1965. They were so cool. Three U.S. helicopters were shot down in one hour during the operation in Laos. I sure did not want to fly one of those things. B-52s were safer. They said there was an average of 1,000 missions per month. The highest rate was in 1968, when they flew 1,800 missions a month. At the peak of the bombing, they were using 102 B-52s in Indochina. Another article mentioned that an army colonel said that VC were tortured to extract information. That was not very nice. Testimony in the Calley court-martial also came to a close.

The *Seattle Times* reported on 15 March that 12,000 Communist troops were moving on the Ho Chi Minh trail in Laos preparing to attack South Vietnam. The U.S. base of Khe Sanh was hit hard. Sixty-six American helicopters had been downed since February in the Laotian border-fighting. Those helicopters were dangerous. Also, Lieutenant Calley was convicted in the My Lai massacre. My dad said that the generals should have been convicted too. Lawyers even got involved in war. How did that happen?

My brother was in Quang Tri on 18 March. He said that Quang Tri was only nine miles south of the DMZ. The living conditions were bad and it was hard to get a shower or a good night's sleep. He sent an article from the *Stars and Stripes* about the operations at Quang Tri. He flew in an OV-10 to get there. The pilot did a few dives and rolls to impress him. He also flew to the DMZ and over North Vietnam at 2,000 feet. He saw a North Vietnamese flag as they flew over the river that separated North and South Vietnam. He sent us a picture of this river. He wrote that the red flag in the picture was worth a $10,000 bounty if captured. But judging by the size of the bomb craters and the moon-like landscape around it, the attempt would probably have proven deadly. The whole time he was flying, the pilot rolled from side to side to evade any enemy fire. He said that he was sitting on a seat that could be ejected, and he would be thrown into the air and hopefully a parachute would open. Mom would cry out "Aa herregud" whenever she read passages like that in my brother's letters home. It was Norwegian for "Oh Mr. God."

On 22 March Alf was in Khe Sanh, again supporting the ARVN in their Laotian operations. They were seven miles from Laos and the ARVN troops were six miles inside of the Laotian border. He was working a midnight shift directing gunships, flareships, and FACs into the area of Laos where the ARVN were being overrun. They tried to get choppers into Laos to pick up wounded, but some were shot down. Khe Sanh was dirty and there was nothing but C-rations to eat. Alf wrote that one day they took about ten rockets a few hundred yards away from his position. He said the sound was horrible as the rockets flew in and landed on the earth.

When my brother was in Khe Sanh taking a break outside of his radio bunker one day, a major came up and sat next to him on the sandbags to bum a cigarette. The major said that he was bored. He had been there during the Tet Offensive in 1968.

"I really saw some action then. I lost half of my unit during Tet. Yeah, this is nothing compared to that," he said.

My brother looked at him and said: "I think I would rather be bored sir."

On 3 April 1971, Alf wrote from Fire Support Base Sharon. It was about five miles from Quang Tri. What a dumb name for a fire support base, I thought. I did not tell Sharon at school about it because I thought she would just say something stupid about the war. My brother said it was better than Khe Sanh, where Charlie hit his base every day with rockets and artillery. The closest he was to an attack was fifty feet or so, when he was in a bunker. It blew up his jeep and killed two South Vietnamese. The Communist rockets were 122 millimeter. He went two weeks without a real shower or a decent meal. But the good news was that his mail finally caught up with him. Alf understood that Mom did not like him riding in helicopters, but he explained that it was the only way to get around sometimes. They were going to drive from one fire support base to Quang Tri (around forty miles) but there were too many VC ambushes. He said the roads were winding and the "gooks" liked to set up ambushes on them.

On 6 April my brother wrote to me personally and said that he worked up to thirteen hours a day and that Khe Sanh took rocket and mortar fire all the time. He hoped that the world would be at peace when I became eligible for the draft, so I would "have no need for the hassle of a senseless war." My brother closed his letter saying that the temperature was in the nineties and he needed to get inside. He signed the letter with a peace symbol. He had never done that before. I wondered what that meant.

FIGHTING FOR PEACE

On 7 April 1971, Alf wrote to tell us that he got the cookies Mom sent, but that they were crawling with bugs. This made Mom cry. I was not sure why. It was not her fault that the military postal system was so slow. He said that the C-rations were bad, but they were the only thing available sometimes.

My parents and I read in the paper on 19 April that the Vietnam Veterans Against the War protested on the Capital steps in Washington, D.C., and threw away their combat medals and ribbons. The paper also reported that there had been an increase in the number of fraggings in Vietnam—there were 69 in 1969 and 209 in 1970. I asked my parents what that meant. They told me that when lower-ranking soldiers killed their officers because they did not agree with their leadership, that was a fragging. When we played army in the woods here at home, sometimes I could not get the other guys to listen to me even when I was the captain. But they did not try to kill me. I did not understand why we would kill our own people when the VC were already doing a good job of it already. My dad said that if the veterans said the war was wrong, we had better listen to them.

On 21 April my brother wrote that Firebase 6, southwest of Pleiku, where he was stationed, was under heavy enemy attack. Also, the action was heating up in the A Shau Valley (site of the famous Hamburger Hill), where the 101st Airborne and the ARVN were fighting and lots of air strikes were being put in. Alf said that 21 April was one of the saddest days in his whole tour in Vietnam. Two hours before he wrote the letter, two majors crashed in their OV-10 Bronco at the end of the runway. One of them was leaving and that was his final flight before going home. My brother had just flown with him recently and had known him well. He said that everyone was walking around with sad expressions on their faces and were not talking. "These are things that happened," he said, "but it seemed wrong when it did anyway."

Alf was in Dong Ha on 26 April and said the weather was really hot. He was getting a chance to have his room organized. In Quang Tri on 30 April, my brother told my dad not to worry about how much the jungle fatigues he sent home cost. He got them free of cost. I sure liked to wear those uniforms when I played army. Mom sewed sergeant stripes on my uniform so I could be like my brother. I wrote and asked for jungle boots. I hoped that my brother could find them for me. He said he could not find a Mother's Day card in Quang Tri but that he thought of Mom on that day, and everyday for that matter. Mom also thought of him a lot. The other night she woke up in the early morning and was walking around the house totally upset. I heard my parents talking seriously. I got up and asked what was wrong. My mom told me that she had been restless and not sleeping, when suddenly she heard my brother's voice as if he was in the room with her. He was saying, "Help me Mom, help." She felt like he was in serious trouble. As it turned out, that was the night his firebase in Pleiku was being hit hard. My brother said that he was terribly afraid, and Mom had probably felt that.

Still in Quang Tri on 16 May, Alf wrote that he did not know what we were reading in the papers in Seattle, but he did not think there was a lull in the war as far as he could see. He said a lot of American soldiers died last week, more than there should be if there was a lull. The cease-fire in observance of Buddha's birthday ended almost as soon as it started, with more Americans dead. The NVA and VC were in the process of regrouping for a major offensive prior to the South Vietnamese election. Probably, more Americans would die. He had been putting in about ten to twenty sets (two fighters in a set) of aircraft daily on known enemy locations; troops in the open; antiaircraft sites; mortar, artillery, and rocket positions; food and arms caches; plus a lot of bunkers, bridges, trails, and enemy hootches. He said the FACs did a great job of locating these targets. On 15 May the FACs called in F-4s to an enemy location and got 12 KBAs (killed by air). "I don't know whether it was something to be proud of or not," he wrote, "I only wish that there was no need for war."

On 18 May Alf rode for three hours in an FAC and watched the pilot put in four sets of air strikes. He wrote that it was interesting and exciting and nice to know what happened up there. He bought a fan at the Da Nang PX and should be able to sleep again. The temperature was around 95 degrees in his hootch. It did not get that hot in Seattle very often.

In June 1971 the *New York Times* began publishing the Pentagon Papers. It was all over the news. I was not sure what it meant, but I knew that my dad was not happy with our national leaders. On 6 June my brother asked for cookies again. Mom had already sent some, but he had not yet received them. He said that barbecue corn chips and Snackpak puddings would be good too. I liked the chocolate Snackpaks and the caramel flavor Space Food Sticks. He was going to go on R and R (Rest and Recuperation) in Bangkok. He wanted to get away from the war for a while even though it would cost him $200 to $300. "The other night," he wrote, "three different companies of Vietnamese marines came under heavy attack by the enemy and I had to call in fighters for the FAC." By the time the fighters came in from Da Nang (about twenty minutes), the South Vietnamese were completely surrounded and had several dead and many wounded, who were left behind in retreat. The F-4s dropped napalm and daisy cutters. Daisy cutters, Alf explained, were bombs that exploded six feet above the ground and threw shrapnel straight out instead of up. Twenty or thirty NVA were killed and, of course, some of the South Vietnamese marines were as well, by our own bombs. He said it really made him wonder why we were doing all this. He reminded me to study hard and make good use of my time so I did not have to do what he had to do. He said that participating in war was not always the best thing to do. He signed his letter with a peace symbol again. I bought a peace symbol at Woolworths and wore it to school. A bully yanked it off, threw me into a mud puddle, threw the peace symbol into the woods at school, and said that I was a sissy hippie. War sure did make people mad, even those who were not fighting in one.

On 19 June Alf wrote that the cookies finally arrived and only lasted two days. Everyone who had one said they were great. The packaging kept the ants out that time. Father's Day cards could not be found in the PX so he wished Dad a happy Father's Day. My brother wrote to me and asked if I would have liked to fly in an O-2. Of course I would have liked to fly in one. But a B-52 would have been better. He flew for three and a half hours in an O-2 the other day. The pilot was diving, rolling, and it did not bother him. The pilot seemed surprised. My brother said that he had to move his radios to another bunker for security reasons.

Alf sent us some more cool articles from the *Stars and Stripes* newspaper. On 26 June, North Vietnamese troops drove South Vietnamese infantry off a key firebase just below the DMZ. American Chinook helicopters pulled artillery pieces out. For six days, firebase Fuller had been under heavy shelling. The two bases, Fuller and Sarge, were the westernmost outposts held by the South Vietnamese in the area just below the DMZ. The North Vietnamese increased their attacks as U.S. forces continued to leave. The Americans sent in Cobra gunships and fighter-bombers to bomb and strafe the North Vietnamese on the overrun bases. They struck every ten minutes throughout the day. One American was killed in the operation. They estimated that three NVA battalions took part in the attack. Fuller was fifteen miles northeast of Khe Sanh. A South Vietnamese officer said that NVA shelling from positions north was too much to take. My brother was not far from those places. He was only fifteen miles from Quang Tri. It did not seem to us that the war was being won or that peace was coming.

Another article from the 26 June *Stars and Stripes* displayed the headline "Red Gunners Jolt Allied Bases Near DMZ." The article indicated that seven bases were attacked in the Quang Tri Province. At Alf's base in Quang Tri, Communist rockets hit an ammo dump and the fires burned for days. There were also attacks by Communist sappers using satchel charges. Cobras killed seven NVA soldiers and destroyed an antiaircraft position. B-52s were also used. South Vietnamese political officials said that the Communists were applying pressure to influence the elections in October. Politicians in America were busy calling each other names in their campaigns. All those politicians just did not get it—they did not understand what was really important. Soldiers were dying while they argued.

The *Stars and Stripes* also reported that NVA attacks on U.S. Marines atop Ba Ho Mountain by Quang Tri proved unsuccessful and led to many Communist casualties. SAC sent B-52 missions in an area twenty to twenty-five miles west-northwest of Quang Tri.

On the DMZ, Alf got a report that an NVA tank came across the border. The ARVN said it was moving south, so bombers and fighters were sent in to destroy the tank. After the smoke cleared, the FAC reported that it was just an abandoned U.S. tank. My brother said the ARVN sometimes would call in U.S. ordinance just to watch the fireworks show. Who was the bigger dumb-dumb? I thought, the U.S. military or the ARVN?

Alf wrote on 4 July 1971 that he had just prepared everything for that day's air strikes. He said that he would order a movie camera for Dad through a catalog of stuff that came from Japan. He said that he was looking forward to applying to college in Norway. He was excited about getting out of Vietnam and the air force. He said that what he was doing in Quang Tri was the most important thing he had done in the service. He knew what it was like to be in the field and live in constant fear of losing your life. The grunts came back from the bush and told him thank you for sending in the air strikes. Alf felt that the group of guys he worked with were like a big family and they took care of each other. He wrote "not to worry and let us hope for peace and an end to the needless killing."

THE MACHINE

In July 1971, the 26th Amendment was passed, allowing eighteen-year-olds the right to vote. If they could be drafted, they should be able to vote, I thought. Alf wrote on 23 July that he had a great seven-day R and R in Bangkok. He was impressed with the Thai people and was able to forget about the war for a while. He said that many of his army friends were getting their Vietnam tours cut. So far the air force had not been doing likewise. At the end of the month, all of the air force FACs would be moved to Phu Bai, where Alf was on TDY three years ago. The radio operators would be in Quang Tri all the time instead of traveling back and forth between Dong Ha and Quang Tri. That would be better since Quang Tri was protected by U.S. soldiers instead of the ARVN. Nobody was being overrun at the moment, so it seemed as though things had quieted down. He hoped that both the South Vietnamese and North Vietnamese governments could reach some sort of compromise and coexist peacefully. "Hopefully," my brother wrote, "the White House will realize that it is wrong for us to be in Vietnam and that we have to put an end to the killing in Southeast Asia."

My mom and I went down to Fort Lawton the last week of July. She had heard that there were some Indians protesting down there. The Indians wanted the army to hand over the old fort to them. It was closing down and they felt that it should be handed back to the indigenous people. Hundreds of Indians were standing, sitting, and marching with signs around the front gate to the fort. We parked and walked up to them. My mom spoke to some of the Indians. It was then that I noticed that my mom was wearing a headband just like the Indians. She always wore something like that in her hair. She told me that the government should give the land back to the Indians so they can build a community center and do whatever they wanted with the land. She said it was not fair that the United States took the land in the first place. My friends and I would sometimes play Cowboys and Indians at home. I never played the Indian because I would have to be barefoot and the pebbles would hurt my feet.

Still in Dong Ha on 2 August, Alf wrote that the mail was getting slower because there were fewer and fewer Americans in Vietnam and because a DC-8 mail carrier crashed on the way over to Vietnam. He looked forward to coming home and skiing and camping with us. He said that other air force radio operators were getting tour cuts up to ninety days. He thought that the air force might reestablish his original discharge date of 26 October 1971. He said Mom should send another "out of sight" package of cookies and snack items. The food, he said, was getting worse every day.

We did not hear from my brother again until 18 August, when he wrote to tell us that Army Post Office (APO) 96477 just packed up and left without warning. And since the postal personnel were going back to "the world," they did not care about those people who remained behind, awaiting mail. The mail was just held in San Francisco. Alf was able to find another APO that would handle his mail, and gave us the new address. He was now in a deluxe hootch that even had an air-conditioner. He caught a cold from the cool air though.

On 29 August Alf wrote and said the mail had started coming through, but he had not seen the Lady Golden Glow cake my mom made for his birthday. It was the world's most delicious cake. It was chocolate and yellow cake, slightly dry, with icing that was opaque and had a slight orange peel taste. Semisweet chocolate shavings were on top. It was so good. He remembered that in five days it would be my birthday. One thing I remembered about my birthdays was that the Jerry Lewis Telethon was always on during the Labor Day weekend. The military activity, Alf wrote, was building up in the Quang Tri Province. The ground troops still needed air support, and the South Vietnamese Air Force (VNAF) was supposed to be taking over the U.S. role. But, my brother noted, the whole Vietnamization program was very slow and the South Vietnamese liked to sit back and watch the Americans do all the work. It was especially bad in Vietnam because of the national and local elections. They were fixed, according to my brother. President Thieu was assured of reelection before the elections actually took place, and it was all a big farce. Alf thought that the United States supported a nation with the most crooked politicians in the world. A Vietnamese captain told my brother that his vote would be changed by the time it got to Saigon. I wondered just whom we were supporting anyway. Were they really the good guys?

Mom wrote and asked Alf not to go up in the FACs. But he said that they were at 1,500 feet and fairly safe. Besides, he wanted to see what they were doing and he liked to fly. Mom was also worried about how thin he was. My brother told us that the food was so terrible and there were only a few places left to eat, since most of the Americans were leaving. He occasionally stocked up on can goods from the PX, but they rarely came anymore. He asked to send more care packages. When we played army in the woods by my house, we sometimes brought food and water or Kool-aid. But when we got hungry for real food, we went home to eat. If soldiers had moms with them, they probably would not get so skinny.

On 15 September my brother wrote about his working twelve-hour days in support of a new ARVN operation. The operation started on 6 September 1971 and was called Lam Son 810. They were bombing targets 500 yards from the Laotian border. If the ARVN pushed into Laos, the operation would be extended, but he did not think that the ARVN would succeed. The ARVN, Vietnamese marines, rangers, and Hac Bao (Black Panthers) had not had a great deal of contact with the NVA, but they believed that the North Vietnamese were massing on the southern part of the DMZ and near the Laotian border prior to the monsoon, which began in late September. According to Alf, there were approximately 20,000 South Vietnamese troops in the operation and the generals were asking for massive air strikes. He was hoping that they did not decide to invade Laos again. One of the FACs, Alf wrote, the other day reported 10 KBA. The ARVN on the ground later found that four of the NVA were chained to their antiaircraft guns. Wow, slave soldiers. I thought it would be hard to beat an enemy that stopped at nothing to win. It has been said that good guys always finish last. I did not want to think that was true. But maybe it was okay to finish last, so long as you could still be a good guy. His cake finally arrived but it was flat and stale. The APO struck again.

Alf wrote on 19 September to say that Operation Lam Son 810 was over and that he could not believe the number of choppers flying in with South Vietnamese and American troops. He knew that at least 150 to 200 American GIs were involved and that they probably were inside of Laos. He talked to one GI who was on a reconnaissance team that took heavy casualties. The GI had been wounded in the leg and most of the others were wounded as well. My brother wrote that "the war was wrong and that the authorities lied to the people." It gave him a sickening feeling; yet, he felt it was good that he was there to know the real truth of the war. "The VNAF was supposed to take over in November," Alf wrote, "but the way the colonels were calling air strikes you would never know that it was winding down." He had very serious doubts about a total Vietnamese takeover of the war. In a way, it was not the fault of the South Vietnamese because the Americans had been running the show for over five years. "Anybody would get lazy, or maybe smart, after that much observation," my brother wrote.

Alf got to see a touring U.S.O. show and spoke to a girl drummer named Judy from Los Angeles. She was the first "round-eyed" girl he had seen in a very long time. He said that it was quite a morale booster and one that more Americans who were not part of "the machine" should visit. He told Dad not to worry about the drug situation in Vietnam. He said that some of the guys at Quang Tri had heroin habits but he would not do something like that. The heroin was as easy to get as candy was in the States. The pushers were usually only ten to fifteen years old. My brother wrote that the drug problem would not exist in Vietnam if it were not for the war. Until the United States got out of the war, the problem would exist.

Mom was still worried about how thin my brother looked in the pictures he sent home. Alf wrote on 25 September that he was back up to 180 pounds, even though the army mess halls served only garbage. Operation Lam Son 810 was completed and the compound was getting back to normal. At the peak of the operation, there were seventeen pilots flying for them and ten aircraft to maintain. An average of ten missions a day required a lot of support. He guessed that the ARVN were satisfied. They killed 175 NVA soldiers and lost 75 themselves. They claimed to have blunted the threat of a major enemy monsoon offensive. However, just the other day, the Quang Tri Combat Base took nine incoming 122-millimeter rockets. Even though my brother was a heavy sleeper, he said that the sound of the rockets definitely woke him up in the morning.

In the end of September, I was coming home from school when I stopped at my friend's house, where some of the other neighborhood kids had gathered to play football. We were playing in a new kid's yard. He was the only black kid on the block. We were having a great time until I was accidentally elbowed on the head. I was hit hard enough to where a blood vessel beneath the surface had broken, and blood was pumping out of my wound. I fell to the ground while the other kids looked on in horror. The black kid yelled in to his dad, who came running out. He immediately put pressure on my wound to stop the blood from spurting out. He then tore apart his T-shirt and made some bandages. He kept applying pressure until the bleeding stopped and I was calm. He talked to me in a reassuring voice that led me to believe that he knew how to deal with that sort of thing. He told me he had been a combat medic in the army and that he had returned from Vietnam just a few months earlier. He had some of the other boys help me get home, and as I walked away I turned around and looked at him. He was kneeling on the ground where I fell. The blood was all over the grass in that spot. He looked at the blood and then to the sky. He looked as if he were not really there. I said thank you to him and he looked up and smiled.

IT AIN'T OVER TILL IT'S OVER

Alf wrote on 29 September 1971 that the air force announced it would be packing up the Quang Tri base on 27 October. Even the U.S. cavalry troops would be leaving. The only Americans up north after October would be the advisors to the ARVN. He was not sure what they would do with the five radio operators at Quang Tri. They could move to Thailand, they could be dropped from the service early, or they could end up at Da Nang, where Alf did not want to be. Da Nang was just too crowded, he wrote, and it got hit by rockets all the time. He thought they would send him home because almost every twentieth TASS field location was closing down and there really was not much of a job anymore. He said that in twenty-seven days he would have spent four years in the air force. He had learned a lot about Southeast Asia if nothing else. He had his discharge physical and got dental work done at Da Nang, since there were no dentists up north. I thought that was cool. I hated the dentist. If I were there, I would stay up north. "No more Freedom Birds would be leaving from Da Nang after November," Alf wrote, so he would more than likely be leaving from Cam Ranh Bay. That would mean he would land at McChord AFB. He said he did not care where he landed as long as he landed in the United States in one piece. He enjoyed reading the *Northshore Citizen* newspaper we sent him. I thought that it was probably very lonely being in a place where hardly anyone knew your name or cared about you.

My brother wrote on 6 October that the concert with the U.S.O. band that toured U.S. bases up north was an event that did not happen very often. They were leery of traveling that far north. Alf wondered if the entertainers could imagine living there for seven months like he had. He said that the military did not treat the band nice. The army shuttled them around on helicopters and made them sleep on cots. The performers were going to visit the hootch area where they lived at Quang Tri, but the army lifers stopped it.

The air force pilots were leaving Quang Tri on the 20th of October but the radio operators had to stay behind, Alf was told. They may get to move into the city at the MACV team compound, where there were clubs and good chow. Or they would stay on at the base with the ARVN. But since his major was a "stinking Air Force lifer," they would probably have to stay with the ARVN and guard their valuables all the time. Alf thought that he would be home for Christmas.

Alf wrote from Da Nang on 23 October that he was soon to leave the country. There were twenty or thirty radio operators at Da Nang with nothing to do. The air force said that they would give him an early tour cut. Of course, the air force, in their infinite wisdom, had brought in twenty-five new radio operators to add to the pool of "old salts" who were sitting around with nothing to do. Of course, the first sergeant had people pulling details—painting, cleaning, and picking up cigarette butts. My brother was mainly trying to stay dry because a typhoon had hit and dumped nine to ten inches of rain on them. He had to stop his letter because they had no power. His trip to Bangkok was not approved because he was leaving so soon and because the squadron took so long to complete the paperwork.

On 3 November Alf was still waiting for word from the 7th Air Force Headquarters in Saigon on when he would be sent home. It would probably be in December, he thought. He said that we did not have to be at the airport to meet him at McChord AFB because it would take eight hours to out-process. He was looking forward to the rest of his life and seeing all of us again.

While he was waiting for his orders at Da Nang, my brother killed some time by walking around the base. One day, a big staff car drove by him with a two-star general's flag on it. It went past him slowly and then screeched to a halt. As my brother walked by it, the window was rolled down and the general began yelling:

"Hey airman, don't you salute authority?"

My brother told him that he had just returned from the field and that they did not salute officers unless they wanted them to be shot. The general glared at him and then shouted, "Get a haircut," as the car sped off.

On 7 November my brother went back up to Quang Tri to say goodbye to his friends there, Americans and Vietnamese. He said it looked like a ghost town. The few Americans left were being protected by regional forces; even the ARVN had left and moved further south. He said the great news was that he could leave as soon as he could process out and find a seat on the Freedom Bird. On a sad note, his friend Jerry was nowhere to be found. He was also a radio operator. He had a bad heroin habit and could not break free. To go back to the States, the soldiers had to pass a urine test. Jerry was supposed to leave at the same time as my brother.

My brother said that he would take me to some Supersonic basketball games when he got back. We had gone to a game before, when he was home on leave, but we left early. Five seconds to play and the Baltimore Bullets had the ball. The Sonics were down by five.

My brother said, "No way are they going to come back," so we left early to beat the crowd. As we were leaving the Coliseum and were outside on the sidewalk, the crowd roared.

"See," I said, "the Sonics stole the inbound pass and scored." Then again the crowd screamed, but my brother said that we should just go home. Later we found out that the Sonics did come back and tied the game to send it into overtime. The famous New York Yankee catcher Yogi Berra once said, "It ain't over till it's over." I wondered if our leaders understood that. I knew my brother understood that when he got home from Vietnam. My brother arrived home on 30 November 1971. U.S. troop strength in Vietnam was at 140,000. His friend Jerry did not make the flight home.

MY BROTHER'S KEEPER

D. B. Cooper, the world's first skyjacker, struck on a cold rainy Thanksgiving eve in 1971. Our family had plenty to talk about around the holiday table, with my brother Alf coming home from the war and the dramatic skyjacking of the Northwest 727 jetliner. D. B. Cooper (his real false name being Dan Cooper, the press mistakenly used D. B.) fascinated people around the whole country with his demand for $200,000 and four parachutes. We all figured that if he had only asked for one parachute, it might have been rigged so that he would die if he used it. With four, he could make some other people jump as well and no one could be certain which of the four chutes he would use. D. B. Cooper jumped out of the tail-section exit door somewhere over southern Washington. Officially, he was never found, although $5,880 in bills showed up on a sandbar in the Columbia River. Some researchers believed that Richard McCoy, who was captured after skyjacking a United 727 flight under similar circumstances in Reno, may have been D. B. Cooper. McCoy was an army veteran who flew helicopters as a warrant officer in Vietnam.

When Alf came home from Vietnam just a few days after Thanksgiving 1971, I wanted to talk with him about the war, watch TV with him, and play catch with him. I just could not wait to do all of the things the way we used to before he left. When we picked him up at the airport, I noticed that Alf was different than the last time I had seen him. His eyes seemed dark and deep set, he was deathly thin, and he seemed anxious to dispense with the homecoming festivities. He was withdrawn. I was upset: Why was not Alf as excited as I was? What had that war done to him?

After we had our homecoming dinner of pork roast with Lady Golden Glow cake for dessert, Alf's friends arrived. They were mostly veterans as well. They all disappeared into his room. I stood outside of the door and listened to them swearing and telling raunchy war stories. The Woodstock tape was playing Jimi Hendrix and I could smell smoke coming from under the door. I guessed that my brother was not afraid to have Mom and Dad find out he was smoking. I supposed that he was not afraid of too many things anymore because he had been in a war.

Alf lived with us for a month or so and then he found an apartment in the University District. He never really wanted to talk very much. I wondered what happened to the brother who had left home several years ago—the brother I knew from his letters home. This brother was different. He seemed to be irritable most of the time.

I watched a show on TV that said some Vietnam veterans were having trouble adjusting after arriving home. Some of them had been treated unfairly by protesters. Maybe my brother was having trouble and he was just trying to hide from everyone. I never figured that war would affect people like that. Being a soldier was more complicated than I had originally thought.

Our lives at home went along as usual after my brother moved out. Alf had grown up and could not live with us anymore. I could not wait for baseball to start in the spring. I knew my brother would come to my games. He visited a few times a week to eat dinner with us, pick up cookies from Mom, and leave some laundry. When spring finally came, Alf met a young girl named Judy, who was just finishing high school. Judy seemed very nice even though "she was a hippie," as Dad said. They were married after a brief courtship. They moved into a small house in Seattle, where we all assumed everything was going to be okay. Alf's hair and beard started to grow very long—he looked like a college guy. He wore headbands and all kinds of necklaces and stuff. He sure looked different than when he was in the service.

I remember going with Alf to buy his car. He bought an old VW bug. We went to the seller's house somewhere in Seattle. The man who was selling the car looked at my brother strangely and would not accept a check. We had to go to the bank and get cash. Maybe he did not like Alf's long hair and beard. We then came back and gave the man $400 in cash. My brother handed him the brand new, crisp one hundred dollar bills. That stupid man did not know that my brother was a veteran. How could he treat him so disrespectfully? I wondered why Alf did not just tell the man that he had just recently come home from Vietnam. My brother just seemed to want to hide his identity.

One night Judy called and told my mom that we better go down to the county jail and pick up Alf. Judy did not say what had happened. My mom and dad wanted me to stay home, but I could not stand the thought of Alf in jail, so I insisted on going with them. When we got downtown and parked by the jail, my mom and dad were arguing in Norwegian. I could hear that they were wondering if it was a terrible thing that my brother had done. The desk sergeant told us that my brother had been booked for assault. Apparently, they had had a bit too much to drink and Alf had pushed Judy and caused her to fall. We paid the bail and Alf was sent down from the top floor of the county building where the jail was. When they released him to us he looked terrible. His hair was all messed up and his eyes were bloodshot. All that my brother said was, "Please take me home," and, pointing to me, "Why did you have to bring him?" At first, what my brother said hurt my feelings. But then I thought about how he must have felt with me there. Alf was my big brother, my hero, and he knew that. He did not want anything to take that away. I just could not understand what was happening to him. Maybe he was not my real brother, I thought to myself. Had someone replaced him? I felt sorry for Alf and wanted to help, but he did not want my help or pity. The world was not a safe and protected place like I once thought it was.

Time went by quickly as I graduated from high school and started at the University of Washington. I spent the summer of 1978 living back in my brother's garage and generally doing nothing productive at all. Little did I realize that all of that time I spent playing army when I was a kid would come in useful. My decision to join the military in the fall of 1978, almost seven years after my brother had returned from Vietnam, was not really a decision. It seemed more like an accident. Of course, my life in general at that time also seemed like an accident. I graduated from high school in 1976, our nation's bicentennial. Bad clothes, bad hair, bad music, bad ideas—what more could be said of the mid-1970s? The oil crisis had shaken America's sense of economic superiority just as the Vietnam War had shaken its sense of military invincibility. Even the presidency, the very symbol of U.S. power and prestige, hung in the balance. Richard Nixon had resigned amid an impeachment crisis and, for the first time in U.S. history, our president was appointed, not elected. The war in Vietnam came to an end in 1975 when the Communist North Vietnamese forces entered Saigon. No surprise there. Without the United States, the South Vietnamese did not stand a chance. This failure to achieve victory was not due to the soldiers' lack of courage, but rather the government's lack of foresight. A bitterness and a sense of loss prevailed. We felt a need to hide away.

Americans elected a democratic president in 1976, who seemed like he was "just plain folks." He had a down-home sensibility and a boyish smile. The world, unfortunately, was not as friendly as our president. Even his attempts to heal the nation from war, such as the presidential pardon for draft evaders, only polarized the country again. It was in this atmosphere that I joined the army—the aftermath of Vietnam, or the "national malaise," as some called it. Was I searching for our innocence and integrity that we had lost in that faraway place called Vietnam?

I felt as if everyone was passing me by and I was standing still, or worse yet, going backward. I could not succeed in school, work, or love. What was left? After I went through basic training in the fall of 1978, my girlfriend wrote to me and told me that she had slept with her boss's brother, a forty-four-year-old man. I was heartbroken. I left for Germany in March of 1979, having been rejected by the only girlfriend I had ever had.

BE ALL YOU CAN BE

It all comes back to me now like the opening sequence of a bad movie—a speeding truck, the door opening, a body rolling into an open ditch. I was arguing with my father as we drove to work when I decided that a change was needed. I worked with him as a carpenter and hated it. I was not a natural carpenter. My hands were always hurting and I daydreamed too much. Anyway, I decided to jump out of my dad's truck—it seemed to be my only escape. I did not want to explain anything to him; I just wanted to take action. I planned to sleep in that day, but my dad made me get up and go to work. To my father, there was something irritating about a twenty-year-old living at home and unwilling to work. After jumping into the ditch, I hid in the bushes until I was sure he would not return. But then it hit me—what was I going to do? I needed a place to stay, and I needed money—preferably a free place to stay and some spending money without work required. After entertaining thoughts of living in the woods and eating what I could catch, I came to my senses and started walking into town. It occurred to me that there was a navy recruiter in the strip mall. This was rather ironic because two years earlier I had turned down a Navy Reserve Officer Training Corps scholarship, deciding that military life was not for me. The navy recruiting station had moved, and in its place was the army recruiter. Why not? The military was the military, I figured. After spending a few minutes trying to select my career field, the recruiting sergeant said:

"How about working in a prison?"

"Cool," I said, remembering that my father once told me how he had worked at a brig when he was in the Norwegian navy. I was sworn in on Halloween 1978. A real nightmare was about to begin.

Just as my brother Alf had done eleven years earlier, I boarded a plane at Sea-Tac International Airport bound for a new life in the military. It was

November 1978. Before I left home, my brother came up and told me that I should not volunteer for anything. Too late for that, I thought, I had already made the big mistake. He told me to be careful and that he was proud of me serving the country. I flew to Atlanta and then took a bus to Anniston, Alabama. On the bus ride from Anniston to Fort McClellan, I met several GIs who had recently completed basic training. They knew that I was a cherry, or an FNG (fucking new guy), and proceeded to tell me horror stories about the drill sergeants. I took each story with a grain of salt, not like the other new guys who were a few years younger than me. When I got to the fort I was sent to a gym complex, where I was greeted by a masculine-looking female Specialist Four (SP4). She bossed me around for a while, made me fill out forms, took all of my records that I had with me, and then gave me a round white pill from a bottle in her desk.

"Take it," she said, "it'll help you breathe."

I looked at her in amazement, never having had someone other than a doctor or my mother order me to take a pill. "What is it, sir, err, mam?" I said.

"Shut up and take the pill or I'll report you to the drill sergeant," she said. I put the pill under my tongue and swallowed the dixie cup of water she offered. As she began to sort through my paperwork, I slipped the pill out of my mouth and put it in my pocket.

During the next few days, all of the guys who were to be in my company arrived and the rumors flew. They too had been offered the pill. Most of them thought it was to control our sex drives. Only a few of the guys believed that it would actually help us breathe.

"I could breathe well enough on my own," I told the guy we called Hamster. "I'm not going to take any pill that isn't prescribed by a doctor."

Hamster looked at me like I was the stupidest person in the world. "Shut up Solheim, what if it is an antidote for some kind of nerve gas that they're going to give us in training?"

A few others looked concerned as he said this. "Nah," I said, "they wouldn't use nerve gas on recruits." It was then that I remembered hearing something about atomic testing in the 1950s and how soldiers were told that radiation would not hurt them.

Next came the haircuts. I thought it was wrong that they made us pay for a haircut that I would not give a pig. Also, you notice the weirdest things about people's heads when they get their hair shaved. Moles, scars, and growths of all kinds emerged that had been hidden before. Finally we all got our uniforms. We felt like real soldiers, no more marching in formations that looked like rainbows.

Then came the big day that we would be sent to our basic training companies. The bus pulled up in front of the barracks, where two mean-looking drill sergeants stood with their smokey bear hats. One was of medium height with a mustache and glasses, the other one was tall, at least six feet five inches. They jumped on to the bus and started screaming:

"Get off the goddamned bus you fucking pukes."

We grabbed our duffel bags and all tried to get off at once. Our bags and our bodies could not occupy the same aisle so some of us went flying against the side of the bus. All the time, the drill instructors kept yelling. They were grabbing guys by the scruff of their necks and tossing them out. Half a dozen guys were sprawled out on the ground by the bus. They had us line up and march into the company break room. They played the "stand up sit down" game for about twenty minutes. And then they made us unload and load our gear. The tall drill sergeant, Sergeant Mock, yelled at me to grab my shit and go into the other room. I did it so quickly, and without looking, that I did not see the senior drill instructor in the doorway. I knocked him over and he had me doing push-ups for about fifteen minutes as Sergeant Mock and Sergeant Everest laughed. Several of the recruits were busy looking through their bags for their military bearing. "I wasn't issued any," said one bewildered recruit.

During some of the downtime in our training, Sergeant Everest told us stories about being an MP in Vietnam. He told us that it was a "fucked up war where you didn't know your friend from your enemy." We were taught to pay particular attention to keeping our M-16 rifles clean because they jammed so much in Vietnam. Later I found out that the United States military always plans and trains based on the last war that it had fought.

Basic training went by pretty quickly and I got an expert badge in grenade tossing—I thought that all of my years playing baseball helped. It was a skill that might come in handy at the prison, I thought. Sergeant Everest was my nemesis during basic. He thought I was too fat and would come up to me just as I would sit down with my tray of food in the mess hall. He would stick his fingers in my food and yell, "You're finished fat boy." On my last day in the company, he brought me into his office and told me that I had not shaved close enough. He took out his buck knife and dry-shaved my face. What an asshole.

There was something strange about Fort McClellan. I noticed that the soil was very red there, red ladderite, I believe it is called. The soil seemed to be the same color as the soil in Vietnam that I saw in all of my brother's slides he brought home from the war. It was eerie to be receiving combat training in soil that looked just like we were in Vietnam. I felt very close to that war, uncomfortably close. The drill sergeant always told us that war could break out at any time and we better be ready. It is funny how military people expect war all the time and civilians never do. Somewhere in between is probably when war breaks out.

I never did find out what was in that pill, whether it was a sex-drive suppressor or not, but with the selection of women available on the fort, I really did not need anything to keep me celibate anyway. Of course, to be fair, they probably would have said the same of us guys too.

My first assignment in the army was as a jail guard in Mannheim, West Germany. Having joined the army in 1978 on a whim, I found myself facing three years of "hard time" in the Mannheim Confinement Facility. I gave about as much thought to my chosen career field (MOS, or Military Occupational Specialty, in army jargon), as I did to joining the army itself. I ended up as a 95C or 95 Charlie—a jail guard. Everything went according to plan throughout basic training. But I began to think that something was wrong when my platoon was separated into two groups after we completed basic. I seemed to be in the group with all of the "geniuses." Among them was a guy we called the "space turtle." I do not remember why we called him that. However, I do remember that his hat size was 8 3/4—a cruel waste of space, I thought. He told everyone he had a job driving forklifts at the Campbell Soup Company waiting for him when he got out. I had no such promising opportunities awaiting me. Anyway, the drill sergeant came up to us in a rather unusual mood. He seemed to be exhibiting some kindness, sort of. "I know you poor shits wanted to be road duty MPs (military police), but you were too god damned stupid and did not score high enough on the entrance exams. Now don't feel bad, this man's army needs good screws."

Now, this was news to me. I chose the 95C MOS. I did not want to be a road duty MP. Thinking out loud, I said: "Hey, drill sergeant, I maximized the entrance exams and I am a 95C."

As soon as I opened my mouth, I began to look more closely at the group I was in. Everyone grew suddenly quiet. The drill sergeant's "pleasant" mood was transformed by my disruption. "Solheim, shuuut upp you shit."

The rest of the group giggled softly. Either they thought I was lying and was just as stupid as they were, or they thought I was telling the truth and was even more stupid than they were.

I completed my advanced individual training (AIT) at Fort McClellan, Alabama, and was then considered a "correctional specialist." The rigorous training involved learning how to count silverware, ripping apart bunks in order to look for contraband, riot control techniques (stay out of the way and do not be an asshole), and tower duty (my personal favorite). The tests were not written; we simply demonstrated a particular duty after it was shown to us two or three times. Any written tests would have weeded out over half of our group due to the high rate of illiteracy.

In March 1979 I was sent to Charleston, South Carolina, to await overseas movement to Germany. I thought about my brother's assignment at Charleston AFB during the war. Alf had hated South Carolina. But the air force seemed more low-key than the army. I met an air force firefighter at the airport and asked him what his MOS was. He told me that in the air force people have jobs, not MOSs. I had a twenty-four-hour layover, and it was during this time that I met two other young soldiers awaiting travel to Germany. They kind of looked like trouble, but I was game for an adventure. One was short and white, the other was tall, black, and had startlingly blue eyes—Sam and James, respectively. So we hired a cab and headed toward the old district in Charleston. James told me that he had met the son of a rich man and that he had been invited over. We thought he was probably bullshitting, but then the cab stopped in front of a huge mansion on the water overlooking Fort Sumter. "This is it!" he said, "let's go in." I was beginning to get suspicious.

We walked into the grand, old house, and on an old antique chair sat a white man in his sixties. He was barely conscious and a bottle of whiskey was lying near his feet. He grumbled something and waved to us. James hurried upstairs and came down with a young man who told us he was the son of the old guy. James introduced him as Rick. "He's always drunk," Rick said as he pointed toward his father.

There was talk of getting some marijuana and getting the young man's sister to come with us on some adventure. I grew more anxious. When Rick left to get some pot, James went upstairs again and it sounded like he was rifling through their drawers. I told Sam that I had to leave. After all, this was the deep south, we were in a rich white man's mansion, one of my companions was black, dealing with drugs and planning a liaison with the rich guy's daughter. All of this seemed to indicate that there might be trouble. I left the mansion and my companions to walk down the broad street overlooking the bay. A taxi drove by and I hailed it. I returned to the base and slept a little. The next morning I took my flight to Germany. I did not see my two companions on the flight.

I really did not think much about that day until one year later, when I was already working at the confinement facility in Mannheim. I was walking in the hallway of the prison when someone said, "Hey, don't I know you?"

I turned around and there was James in his prison garb. After he explained how he had eventually made it out of the sticky situation in Charleston (essentially he took some money and ran, before the guy, and likely the police, came), he told me how he became a drug dealer in his infantry unit in Germany and was finally caught. "I had a BMW though," he told me. "Yes indeed, I was livin' mighty high." He was heading for the military prison at Fort Leavenworth, Kansas, to make big rocks into little rocks for a few years.

THE FOOL

After a few weeks in Germany, working at the confinement facility, I began to resent being in the army. I thought back to how I came to join the army—the argument with my father and the recruiter's willingness to go along with my youthful impetuousness—and I felt that I had been taken advantage of. I felt that I was in an unstable emotional state at that time, which prompted me to make a rash, life-altering decision. I was bent on righting this injustice and securing my release from the military on those grounds. I began by reading the army regulations on discharges. I eventually came to know the discharge regulations better than anyone in the unit, including the commander. I stirred a shitstorm. I could not stand the fact that I had nearly three years yet to serve in the army. Most of the enlisted men had short-timer calendars on their wall lockers. Once you hit one year, you began the countdown. The last block on the calendar had a big jet airliner next to it—the Freedom Bird that took you back to the world. All of this was Vietnam era jargon, but we accepted it without thinking how it related to the war.

As part of my scheme to get out of the army, I decided to become a conscientious objector. I figured this would make me pretty useless to the army and prompt my release. To do this I had to document my nonviolent convictions. But it was nearly impossible for someone already in the military to be granted the status of a conscientious objector. They were suspicious of my having had such a sudden change of heart. My behavior began to irritate the sergeants and the company commander. One time I was ordered into the tower at the prison because they did not trust me to work inside. I told the guard commander that I was a conscientious objector and that I would not touch any weapons. Well, the tower guard is required by SOP (standard operating procedure) to have a shotgun and three rounds of ammunition while on duty. I proceeded to my tower as ordered, only without the weapon or any ammunition. An hour later, the guard commander and another sergeant came out to the tower on a perimeter check. I stepped out on to the catwalk in front of my tower.

"Halt, who goes there," I said in a booming voice. I thrust my arm up with my hand making a stop signal as I yelled.

"Where is your weapon, soldier?" the guard commander yelled up to me.

"I told you I was a conscientious objector, sarge, I don't believe in instruments of violence," I said in my most irritating voice.

"God damn you Solheim, get down out of that tower!" The guard commander was not pleased. I was put on permanent CQ (charge of quarters) duty at the barracks. Not a bad job. Fuck up and move up as they said.

As a permanent CQ runner I was off of work all day and began my shift around 4:00 p.m. when the company commander and first sergeant went home. I worked for the CQ sergeant. My job was to help the sergeant keep the barracks in order, sign people in and out of the unit, clean up, run messages to other units, and various other menial tasks. I liked it because all of the big brass were out of your hair. And, in my case, that was a good idea because my hair was getting rather long.

The administration did try to harass me during the day, however. They would have surprise room inspections and I would have to get up even if I had worked all night. On one such inspection, Lieutenant Grover, the company executive officer (XO), came into my room and found a brick with some charred incense on it. I used the brick to burn incense in my room to get rid of the rancid smells that seem to develop in army barracks.

"Ahh hah," Lieutenant Grover said, "we've got you now, Private Solheim." He held the brick up like a prized trophy. "Look Top (addressing the first sergeant who was accompanying him on the inspection), a controlled substance, probably hashish. Yes, we've got you Solheim." Lieutenant Grover was so happy with himself that I almost hated to spoil his good mood.

"Sir," I said, "that is incense on that brick, frankincense and myrrh to be exact . . . you know, the kind the three wise men gave to the baby Jesus."

Lieutenant Grover wheeled around: "Wise ass, we'll take this to the lab and have it analyzed." He then stormed out of the room with my incense brick.

A week later, I was inspected again and did not pass because my area was considered to be too messy. As punishment, the commander restricted me to the barracks and took away my civilian clothes. The sergeant who came to give me the orders and inventory my civilian clothes seemed apologetic. "I have never seen a soldier treated like this—maybe a prisoner, but not a soldier," he said. He told me about how draftees were treated in Vietnam and how I seemed to have an attitude like a draftee.

I ran down to the commander's office and asked him why they were taking my clothes away just for not passing an inspection. The prison commandant was there and told me that they had information that I was planning to go AWOL and defect. After about two weeks I was allowed to have my clothes back and I was determined more than ever to get out of the army.

The sergeants and officers who took their jobs too seriously, we called "lifers." The lifers would always give me a hassle because of my antics in trying to get out of the army. I told one old sergeant that I was going to write to my congressman about what went on in the prison and at the unit. He told me: "You are crazy Solheim, you think they're gonna read a letter from some lowly enlisted man."

It was only one month later that my letter writing paid off. My congressman brought a congressional investigation down on the unit. This was a very serious thing for a company commander to have done to him. It brought the attention of the commanding general and that was not the kind of attention the company commander wanted from the general. Eventually, I decided to stay in the army and finish my enlistment period. The day I told the company commander, he seemed ecstatic. He laughed, told me what he thought were funny stories, showed me his awful attempts at oil painting, and sent me on my way with a big slap on the back. It made his day.

Part of the reason I decided to stop the congressional investigation and stay in the army was that I had met my girlfriend (later my wife). Another reason was the advice, comments, and general influence from Vietnam veteran sergeants. One sergeant, after hearing about some of my antics, took me aside and told me: "Solheim, you are spoiled. You chose to join the army. I was drafted against my will and now I am fucked up and I have no other place to go. Stay in, do your time, live up to your obligations, then get the hell out." My brother said exactly the same thing when I talked to him on the phone. Was this some kind of Vietnam veteran conspiracy? I thought.

Another time, I was ordered to clean the latrines in the barracks—not my favorite assignment. One of the Vietnam veteran sergeants, Sergeant Isch, came in and started hassling me about the half-ass job I was doing. He was right, but I did not care. Annoyed with him, I snapped: "I'm surprised you were not shot by your own men in the war, sarge."

I regretted the statement almost as it rolled out of my vicious little tongue. The sergeant lunged at me and pounded me up against the wall of the latrine. His hands began to reach for my neck as if to choke me. Then he pushed me away and I sprawled out on to the floor. I was momentarily stunned by the suddenness of his reaction. He then began to sob gently, his face against the wall, his fist pounding slowly. I sat on the floor staring at the urinal. After a few minutes he collected himself. He turned to me and said, "Just clean the mother fucker, okay Solheim." "Yes sergeant," I said, unable to look up.

SANTAYANA'S WARNING

Driving through Heidelberg in the summer of 1981, I noticed that some German workers and their trucks were situated by the front entrance to the United States Army in Europe (USAREUR) headquarters. As I waited at a traffic light, I noticed that they were eating their lunch, smoking, joking, and drinking some beer. German workers were allowed to drink beer for lunch. The German version of the song "Sandman" was playing on the radio.

The workers had removed the USAREUR crests from the massive stone pillars at the front gate of the headquarters compound. These giant shield-shaped crests depicted the flaming sword insignia. As I drove by the front gate after the light had changed, I got a closer look at the pillars. I began to make out some faint shadows on the stone, shadows made from a previous orifice that had been attached to the pillars. As I came closer I could see it clearly—the shadows were the swastika and eagle symbol of the Nazis. These Nazi symbols had adorned the entrance pillars to this compound during World War II.

I must have slowed down too much to look because a few drivers behind me honked. I sped up past the front gate, but the shadowy symbols haunted me. That night at the prison I told my guard commander about what I saw.

"So what, Solheim," he told me, "almost all of our stuff here belonged to the Nazis. Nothing surprising about that." Even though it did not bother my guard commander, I kept thinking about how we could so easily step in and take over Nazi buildings without even bothering to sandblast those shadowy swastikas from the pillars. At the very least, I thought, not removing them would be bad luck, since the Nazis lost.

I continued to think about what I saw for the next few weeks, and then one day I went to the American Express bank near the PX facility in Mannheim. I had some special business that day and I needed to go upstairs instead of dealing with the tellers as I usually did downstairs. As I went into the hallway and headed toward the stairs, I noticed the ornamental wrought-iron railing that was fixed to the beautiful spiral stairs that led to the second floor. Fine work, I thought. Then, as my eyes followed the railing down to its terminus, where it curled around to the right of where I stood, I saw a black swastika. It was worked into the flowing design of the wrought iron. I put my hand on it to confirm that it was indeed real. I then followed the staircase up and found a similar swastika at the top of the railing.

We were supposed to be the good guys, I thought. How could we tolerate keeping those Nazi symbols around on the buildings we were using? A few weeks later, the Germans had an anti-American parade that we watched from our second-story apartment window. The protesters were hanging President Reagan in effigy and had paper mache nukes hoisted above their shoulders with signs that read, "Nuclear cowboys go home." Later that year, Red Army Faction terrorists attacked the USAREUR commanding general's car in Heidelberg with a rocket launcher. General Kroesen escaped unharmed and later said that he was lucky the terrorists attacked his car with Russian-made anti-tank weapons and not American ones.

AN OFFICER AND A GENTLEMAN

You cursed rotary-wing flying machine, your flight defied logic and common sense—bullshit and black magic kept you aloft. What drew me to you? I ended up flying the OH-58 helicopter in the 82nd Airborne Division Air Cavalry as an aeroscout. My mission was to fly, unarmed, into the advancing enemy line and identify hard targets such as tanks, armored personnel carriers, and air defense artillery (although they never told us, the assumption was that people are soft targets). We would then hand off the grid coordinates to the guns (army Cobra attack helicopters) or the air force or even the navy if we were close to the ocean. Most people have another word for this type of mission—suicide.

I did not want to be in the combat arms branch when I decided to join the army for a second time. I envisioned being a dustoff or medevac pilot. That was my dream based on what I knew from the Vietnam War. Of course, you rarely get what you want in the military unless you are well connected in Washington, so I was made an aeroscout and sent to the air cavalry at Fort Bragg.

I decided to join the army for the second time only one year after I completed my enlistment and tour of duty in Germany as a jail guard. I swore that I would never want to have anything to do with the military again. However, failing in engineering school, the Reagan recession, and facing a career working in the state prison system led me to reconsider the unthinkable—returning to the army (the big green weanie, as I used to call it). My thinking was that being an officer would make being in the army more tolerable—no more cleaning of latrines and no more orders from brainless sergeants. What I found out later was that it was the same "shit," only at a different level. There were plenty of brainless officers as well. And honor, apparently, had little to do with being an officer.

March 1983 and there I was at Fort Dix, New Jersey. I was in line getting new army uniforms. The army was now issuing BDUs (Battle Dress Uniforms), which were camouflaged. What in the hell happened? I had hated the military so much, how did I end up in the service for yet another tour of duty? Ah, but this time it would be different, I told myself. I would be an officer and nobody would push me around. And I was going to be flying helicopters, the ultimate icon of the Vietnam War. I could be a medevac pilot. I did not really think about it much at the time, but thinking back, most of my instructor pilots (IPs) were Vietnam veterans—their stories were from the war, we were surrounded by the war and did not know it. Twenty-four hours a day at Fort Rucker we heard the helicopters; the sound never went away. I still hear them.

The first thing I saw as we entered Fort Rucker in a taxi I took from the airport was the Huey monument by the Daleville entrance. From that point on I was living in a dream hatched during the war while my brother was in Vietnam. Although I had wanted to fly B-52s way back then, not having finished college precluded me from getting into the Air Force Officer Flight Program. My second choice was to fly medevac helicopters. The Warrant Officer Flight Program required candidates to have only a high school diploma.

Mack, one of my best friends in flight school, thought that all guys picked to be aviators by the army would be tall and good-looking like himself. He met Fred and myself at Fort Dix when we all were being in-processed into the army. We all had prior military service. Fred was tall and handsome, and I was, well, tall anyway. Mack went on endlessly about the movie *An Officer and a Gentleman* and how he saw himself as the Richard Gere character.

"These sergeants here at Dix treat us with respect because they know we are aviators," Mack would say. It was true that we did not have to pull any offensive details, but I told him it was probably because they were confused by our administrative status. Mack would hear none of that—we were hot shit. We had it all figured out until we got to Fort Rucker.

Warrant officer flight training involved four phases, taking approximately one year to complete. During training you are considered an administrative noncommissioned officer (NCO), and after completion you are awarded flight wings and the rank of warrant officer one (WO-1). The first phase was called WOC-D or warrant officer candidate development. This was like boot camp, only more intense. We did not fly or learn anything about flying during that six-week phase. It was mainly set up to weed out people before the army spent any money on teaching us to fly. The next phase was primary. In primary we learned about basic aerodynamics and flying the TH-55 training helicopter. These old two-seaters replaced the H-23 Hiller as the army's training aircraft. The third phase was the Huey transition, where we learned to fly the basic UH-1 helicopter—the icon of the Vietnam War. The last phase was tactics, where we transitioned into the helicopter that would be our permanent assignment. It was at this phase that I got the bad news that I would be an aeroscout and fly OH-58s.

As WOCs, we were locked up for sixteen weeks. Those WOCs who were married (like myself) would see their wives and children only during visiting hours on the weekends—it was like we were prisoners in a prison of our own making. Oddly enough, even though I longed for passes where I could visit with my family, I soon grew tired of the visits. I wanted real freedom with my family, not an hour here and an hour there. Of course, this irritated my wife Lucy to no end. She wondered why I did not want to see her, and why I acted so strangely when she came to visit. I had probably become institutionalized.

In the primary phase we had a senior TAC officer who got into trouble. He was a high-living, gregarious man. He drove a Ferrari and looked a little bit like the actor William Devane. It was no secret that he was a playboy. He was the only officer I knew who had his own personal photographer following him around. At the end of my primary training he disappeared, and we later found out that he was caught sleeping with the wife of one of the WOCs. We all knew that we were locked up and did not see our loved ones very much. That seemed to make it even more heinous. Apparently, the woman was led to believe that she could make things easier for her husband if she slept with the senior TAC officer. Although this was my first indication, it would be later when I would come to find out exactly what the aviator lifestyle was like.

Learning to fly was not easy. Although we were not required to know how a car works in order to obtain an automobile driver's license, we had to attain a certain level of proficiency in aerodynamics and aviation mechanics in order to earn our wings and obtain a pilot's license. Pilots never think of flying without doing a thorough preflight inspection of their aircraft. A frightening thought comes to mind: Who bothers to inspect their car before they head out on to the highway at sixty miles per hour, surrounded by others who could care less about the condition of their car or the quality of their driving? Yet the chances of being killed in an automobile accident are many times greater than those of dying in an aerial mishap. I suppose the difference is that aircraft disasters are more spectacular, usually take more lives in one fell swoop, and make the evening news. Meanwhile, we are slowly and methodically exterminating ourselves out on the freeways every day. It is inherently scarier being up in the air. That fact makes us fear flying more than driving. If something goes wrong in flight, your options are limited. On the ground, you tend to have more options in a crisis. The old aviation saying was, Take-offs are optional and landings are mandatory.

I had never flown in a helicopter prior to coming to the army flight school at Fort Rucker, Alabama. After completing our first phase of training, WOC-D, we were taken out to the flight line, introduced to our flight instructors, and given our first flight—the nickel ride. The tradition was that we would give our instructor pilots (IPs) a nickel after the flight. Mr. Swensen, my IP, wasted no time in putting the old TH-55 training helicopter to the test. When we took off and the old bird shuttered and jumped sharply aloft, I was facing toward the ground. I mean I was looking at the damn pavement on the runway. No one had told me that helicopters gain lift by tilting nose down. I was scared shitless. Then I thought to myself, if I was afraid of just getting a ride in one of these things, how was I going to learn how to fly?

I was not the only total rookie, however. The army also trained foreign pilots, and my IP told me a story about an Arab student pilot who was absolutely unfamiliar with modern technology. He took the student to the flight line and showed him a helicopter that was running up. The main rotor blades were turning and the tail rotor as well. Of course, when the tail rotor is spinning, you do not see it because of the speed at which it spins. Well, the Arab student headed toward the tail rotor in wonder. "Look," he said, "it has vanished." Mr. Swensen had to grab the student by the collar and pull him back so that he did not step into the spinning tail rotor.

During our training time together, Mr. Swensen taught me all the ins and outs of the old helicopters we were flying. One day, as we were studying the main rotor very carefully, he pointed to a large nut above the rotors:

"If this comes off, your goose is cooked," he said. I looked at the piece of metal in amazement.

"This is it," he said.

"What?" I asked.

"You dummy, this is your Jesus nut, pay attention Solheim." I thought about it for a moment. Then he continued:

"If this comes off boy, Jesus is the only one who can help you. Always make sure it is properly fastened."

Later in flight school, when we were transitioning into the UH-1 Huey helicopter, there was a crash, and two students and an IP were killed. The hydraulics had failed and they flipped over on landing. There was nothing they could do. They had followed all of the procedures and still ended up dead. It did not matter that the Jesus nut was intact.

After the initial six weeks of warrant officer development, we entered the flight portion of our training in June of 1983. It was then that we met our primary flight instructors. Most of these guys were pretty old. To give you some idea, my instructor was too old to serve in Vietnam—he was a Korean War veteran. Mr. Swensen was an experienced pilot to say the least. He had logged more than 17,000 flight hours. That is equivalent to flying twenty-four hours a day for two years. Mr. Swensen and the other IPs were very crusty and temperamental. When he was frustrated with my flying, he used to tell me: "Solheim, you need to concentrate, your head is in the fucking clouds."

My friend Flynt had an instructor we nicknamed "Jabba the Hut," from the huge slug-like character in the movie Star Wars. Flynt was very small and his IP was huge and fat. When they hovered in the small two-seat training helicopters we used, Flynt's aircraft would list to the side that Jabba was on. Flynt said that Jabba would always ask him why he could not keep the aircraft level and would then hit him in the helmet. Flynt was too afraid to tell Jabba that the aircraft was not straight because he was so fat. In spite of his weight, Jabba was a good pilot. One time, when Flynt was struggling to learn how to hover, Jabba grabbed the controls and using his little finger he hovered. He then proceeded to spin the aircraft in tight and precise pirouettes, all perfectly under control.

"What is so goddamned hard about that?" he asked Flynt.

It takes about ten hours to become proficient enough to hover and learn the basic things you need to do to take off and land. Learning to hover was called finding the "hover button." It is at that time that the IPs let you solo. You never know exactly when they will let you solo. "I remember my first solo flight," Mr. Swensen began to tell me. To myself I thought that his first solo flight was probably around the time Da Vinci was designing helicopters.

"I was so tight you'd need a sledgehammer to drive a mustard seed up my ass," he continued. It was a disturbing image to say the least.

Mr. Swensen was flying with me one day when he suddenly told me to hover over to the end of the taxiway. I did and he promptly unbuckled his harness and got out. Before he disconnected his microphone cord, he told me:

"Have a good solo flight Solheim," he said. And then he left. I was shocked. Was I ready? I told myself: yes. I began to get ready for take off and took off without any problems. As I was climbing out to altitude, I looked over to the empty left seat and the cyclic control moving all by itself as I moved mine. I suddenly felt terribly alone. I had really depended on this man, and now it was up to me. I had my life in my own hands, literally. Fear gave way to routine and I followed the procedures I had learned to the letter. Mr. Swensen was waiting for me back at the briefing room, where he shook my hand and gave me my solo wings.

E PLURIBUS UNUM

I have only met one Medal of Honor winner in my lifetime. This is not unusual since so few of these medals are awarded to the living. I met Chief Warrant Officer Novosel during my Huey transition in flight school. He was an older man, sixty-two or so, with tanned leathery skin and bright blue eyes. His white hair was cut close in a flattop. One day I was doing some details outside and he happened to walk by. It was my birthday, the 3rd of September, and I later found out that we shared the same birthday. A group of us then began talking to him. The first thing I noticed about him was the fact that he was very short and did not strut around like I imagined a living Medal of Honor winner would. He was very unassuming. He spoke in low tones—sincere, honest, and without hubris. Someone had told me before the story of how he won the medal, so I knew more than what he told us at that time.

He had been a medevac/dustoff pilot in the Vietnam War. In October 1969, ARVN (South Vietnamese army) and U.S. infantry companies took heavy casualties in a fierce firefight with the North Vietnamese Army in the Kien Tuong Province near Cambodia's Parrot's Beak. One medevac helicopter had gone in to pick up the wounded but was shot down in the unrelenting rain of enemy bullets and mortar fire emanating from around the landing zone (LZ). Heavy enemy fire from the surrounding area had brought down two Cobra gunships and two air force F-100 jets. No one would volunteer to go in and pick up the wounded men—it was, after all, a suicide mission. Mr. Novosel decided that he would go. But he did not make just one flight; he flew in to the area fifteen times until all twenty-nine wounded men were evacuated. He himself was wounded in the process. A NVA bullet pierced through the Plexiglas chin bubble and fragments embedded themselves in his right calf and thigh. It was a miracle that he made it and that all of the wounded men were saved. During his two tours of duty in Vietnam, Mr. Novosel extracted more than 5,500 casualties. Few could match that record.

To hear Mr. Novosel tell the story, it was not so heroic. "It was not right to let wounded men suffer," he said. He did not think that he really deserved the medal. "I was just doing my job. Many other pilots have had missions just as tough." His demeanor was difficult for some of my fellow WOCs to understand. "Some hero he is," one said. But I thought carefully about his interpretation of the story. His modest appraisal made sense. Heroic deeds seem to be accomplished by ordinary people in extraordinary circumstances. A sense of humanity and integrity—wanting to do one's job to the best of one's ability to help others—that is what seemed to be really important. In that sense, anyone can be a hero who lives their life in such a manner. However, not everyone is recognized for their humanity and integrity. A man like Mr. Novosel knew this and paid homage to those unrecognized heroic people through his quiet and humble nature.

Our UH-1 transition IP decided to take my flight partner Flynt and me on a cross-country flight one day in November 1984. Mr. Johnson was a great guy—he had been a 727 pilot for Continental before the deregulation of the airline industry and (like many other IPs) had flown Slicks (troop-carrying Hueys) in Vietnam. It was a glorious day for flying, sunny and crisp with a light wind. Sweet home Alabama beckoned us. "Kick the tires and light the fires," and we flew south toward the Florida border. After flying for about fifteen minutes, Mr. Johnson said that our destination was a small civilian airport near the border. Why he wanted to stop there, we did not know.

As we approached the airport, our IP took the stick from Flynt. "I'll take her in," he said. No sooner had he taken the stick than we sped up to 140 knots. We were screaming into the airport faster than either Flynt or I had ever experienced in a Huey. I thought to myself that maybe all of these long hours with dumb student pilots had driven him mad. Perhaps he was having some sort of Nam flashback or something. We dropped down to the tree line on our approach at maximum speed. I felt as if the bottoms of my feet were scraping against the treetops. Then, as we cleared the tree line, we dropped suddenly to the runway. My stomach remained at altitude for a while longer, though. My God, he was maintaining his speed but now only inches from the ground. He is going to kill us, I thought. We came to the end of the runway and he hit his right pedal simultaneously pulling up the nose of the Huey and executing the forbidden "pedal turn"—dangerous, yet most impressive. The blades popped loudly as we decelerated and came to a hover near the tie-down area. By this time everyone in the hangar and terminal buildings had come out to see what was going on. We shut down and stepped out onto the tarmac and headed for the terminal. In our flight suits, helmets, and survival vests, we looked like conquering warriors.

"Nice flying, son, you must have learned that in the war," said an old fuel farm worker. Our IP nodded and smiled as we continued to the terminal still not knowing why we were there. As we entered the terminal building, it became clear. There she was—a beautiful blonde in a tight blue jumpsuit. She giggled and called his name. Flynt looked at me and we both laughed. Now we know why we had risked our lives on the approach, the display was for her benefit. They went off into a corner somewhere while Flynt and I grabbed sodas and made a general spectacle of ourselves for the locals. We were aviator gods that day.

By the end of flight school, we figured that there seemed to be no way to win as a pilot. If you were perfect, you would have nothing to worry about. If you were human, like the majority of us, you were going to make mistakes. If the machine broke down, you would be blamed anyway. We developed a sort of fatalism; no matter what, the pilot would get screwed. Later I developed the idea that it was better for the army to lose a few pilots than ruin a cozy deal with a defense contractor. I suppose it was all part of what Eisenhower called the Military Industrial Complex. I always thought that the tail-rotor problems with the OH-58 observation helicopter were a case in point. While I was flying the OH-58, several accidents occurred throughout the army. Always it was blamed on the pilot. If only the pilot would follow the correct emergency procedure, then the aircraft would not crash. The problem was that the emergency procedure changed every time some poor SOB drilled a helicopter into the earth.

I flunked my last phase of flight school and almost did not make it for my wings or warrant officer bars. I did not tell my TAC officer before they gave me my warrant officer bars, so they could not kick me out. The captain who flunked me on my night-vision goggle check ride did so mainly because I did not call him sir once during our preflight briefing. I was retested the next day and passed. It was time to move on to Fort Bragg, North Carolina.

SUCK, SQUEEZE, BANG, BLOW

"God damned jet jocks and their fast movers, they think their shit don't stink," an old army warrant officer whispered to me as we watched the air force pilots enter our flight line briefing room. I was one of the warrant officer helicopter pilots at the air cavalry in the 82nd Airborne Division at Fort Bragg in April 1984. There we all sat in our OD (olive drab) green flight suits with subdued rank and flight wing insignia as the air force pilots strutted in with their gaudy uniforms adorned with colorful patches displaying lightning bolts, tigers, and other virile things. Their rank and flight wing insignias were the shiny dress uniform type encased in plastic on their chests and shoulders. Around their necks they wore bright blue scarves. Of course they arrived late and made a dramatic entrance. Army helicopter pilots were the working class of the aviation world. The jet pilots were the upper crust.

After the briefing, we headed out to the firing range for a joint service exercise. We were handing off targets to the air force pilots. I did my handoff and waited for the F-15 fighter jet to make its run. Without warning, it came screaming in from behind us at about one hundred feet, but it seemed like it was only a few feet from the top of our helicopter. The noise was deafening even though I was wearing a helmet and earplugs. The jet made its pass and was gone in a flash. It was then that I realized exactly why they called them fast movers. As army aviators we knew that our maximum speed was only 140 knots or so. It was this difference in speed that made the helicopter pilots feel inferior to the jet pilots. From the bigger perspective, of course, the air force and the army were both in the killing business; it's just that the army did it at a slower pace.

The Wild West outlaw Gret Dalton's great-grandson was a cobra pilot in my air cavalry squadron. Somehow, it fit. The air cavalry had quite a reputation. Popularized in the Francis Ford Coppola film *Apocalypse Now*, the air cavalry continued to perplex, amaze, and baffle its admirers and detractors alike. I knew that things were getting weird when I went to our first squadron hail and farewell party in June 1984. Dress blues, swords, stetsons, and spurs. All the married guys were given yellow garters to place on their lady's thighs. I was given a heavy coin with the 82nd Airborne insignia and the Air Cavalry inscribed on it. This coin was to be carried at all times or else you would have to buy all the drinks.

My aeroscout platoon consisted of myself (a misplaced history professor in the making who really wanted to be a medevac pilot), Rodriquez (a Latin version of Fred Flintstone), Lieutenant Genius (finished last in his class at West Point but had a silver spoon up his ass), Lieutenant Booboo (also West Point, but cool), Mr. Druk (test pilot, his crustiness had crustiness), Captain Monday (master of hackneyed expressions), Pender (the human pretzel), Hemmer (unfortunate hemorrhoids), and Fred (my pugilist buddy from flight school). The cobra platoon used to walk by our briefing room and make noises like sheep.

"Baaah, baaaaah. Hey you fuckers, did you know that you are the sacrificial lambs? You guys draw the fire, and then we know where to attack. Hey, what kind of armament you guys got? Oh yeah, you are not armed, I forgot. You can pull the .38 out of your survival best and shoot out of the side vent, ha ha ha ha." Funny stuff, I thought. They never got tired of their material either.

"Suck, squeeze, bang, blow. That is how the turbine engine works, gentlemen." I could still hear those words when I thought back about flight school. Our instructors liked to use sexual allusions to help us remember. Aviators need that, I suppose. The turbine draws air in the intake, it squeezes it through a venturi chamber, mixes air with fuel and ignites it, then blows it through the turbine blades creating power to turn the drive shaft and, thereby, the rotors. My mind wandered back to those days in flight school when I still had hope of being a medevac pilot. As I sat in that hootch, listening to the other pilots and the hard-core porno they consumed, I thought how cruel my fate was—instead of flying with the medevac pilots carrying wounded men from the battlefield, I was going to be with a bunch of assholes killing people on the battlefield. Things went from bad to worse when I transferred to the 82nd Combat Aviation Battalion.

Our motto at the Combat Aviation Battalion was "Kill Tanks." Every time our unit would gather, the commander would have us scream the unit motto. After a few months at my unit, my misplacement in a combat role was jeopardizing my flying career. As a result, I began to have doubts about my being in the army and being a pilot. I was taking college courses at night and my interests seemed to be far from the flight line. The war training and the mindless mottos began to wear on me. I started asking forbidden questions of those around me: "Shouldn't we say kill people in tanks, isn't that what we are really doing?" They would tell me to shut up and not think so much about it. But I could not help but think about it. I ended up sharing my doubts with our chaplain. How could I deal with the fact that my mission would eventually lead me to kill someone? The chaplain, in a reassuring voice, said: "My son, remember, you would be killing godless Communists." That incident pretty much solidified my view. I had to get out.

I started having more reoccurring nightmares during this time. One of the nightmares would begin with me on the ground somewhere in what appeared to be Southeast Asia. I was surrounded by small children in torn and ragged clothing. Then, suddenly, there came terrible noises and explosions all around us. The cobra attack helicopters were coming. The cobras were attacking the children and me. I grabbed two babies and had the others follow me as we ran toward some thatched huts that stood on stilts. The cobra gunships swooped in again and began firing rockets with fléchette rounds (tiny razor-like projectiles). We reached the huts and entered just as the fléchettes ripped through the walls. The children and I were shredded—death was everywhere and I began screaming. That is the point at which I would wake up. In another reoccurring nightmare I would be flying in a helicopter by myself when, all of a sudden, an explosion destroyed the aircraft around me. I continued flying through the air without the helicopter for a while until I began hurtling toward the ground. I always woke up before I hit the ground. I decided to leave the military and was discharged in 1986.

UNACCEPTABLE LOSS

I left the military only to take a job at Boeing, working on military contracts. As a corporate wage slave at Boeing, I was depressed and miserable. I really wanted to be a teacher. When I was stationed at Fort Bragg, I took night classes and met Dr. Evans, a professor who served as my first mentor. I imagined myself teaching a class. I thought it would be the ideal job. My wife Lucy was very upset about my plan to sell our house and move to the Midwest so I could get my doctoral degree and be a professor. I did not really confer with her, I just had to do it. Little did I know that the move would set off a chain of events that would bring me crashing down hard.

A month before we were to leave for Ohio, my mom called me at home. She sounded afraid—something did not sound normal in her voice.

"Come home, your brother said that he is on drugs," she said. I immediately told Lucy that I needed to go and see what was wrong. I had suspected that something was going very badly for Alf. Debbie, his second wife, and Alf were always fighting and they were about to lose their house to the bank. Debbie said that Alf was using cocaine, but I did not believe her.

When I got to my mom and dad's house, everyone was sitting in the living room and had very serious looks on their faces. Mom said that she was glad I came over. Alf asked why I had to come. I told him that I just wanted to help. He had asked Dad for a loan to pay some bills and could not tell a lie when Mom asked what the problem was. I offered to help him find an appropriate treatment program that would allow him to continue working during the day, and get counseling at night. He was making too much money to get into a VA program, so we found a program at a Catholic hospital. I sponsored my brother and told him that he had always been my hero and would still be when he completed the program. We sat in the counseling center cafeteria, drank coffee, and talked about the old days.

After a few weeks I noticed a change in Alf. He was friendlier, more talk-ative, and seemed to be like the old brother I knew before he went to Vietnam. I was so happy that I finally got my big brother back. The counselor said that the drug acted like a shell that enclosed the old personality of the addicts and changed them. When they quit, their true self once again bloomed. I left for Ohio knowing that my brother would be okay.

All went fairly well the first semester, and I was working on designing my first final exam in April when disaster struck. I came home one day to find my wife crying. I looked at her tears and saw the message before she spoke. I had played it over in my head many times. I never wanted to be caught off guard, so I imagined what it would be like if one of my loved ones were to die suddenly. It was a morbid game, but it assured me that I would never be surprised.

"It's your mom, she called, she says she has cancer," Lucy said sobbing. I did not say anything, but I went immediately to the phone and called my mom and dad.

"Looks like the Big C," my mom said. She had been on jury duty for a few weeks and had come down with what she thought was a cold. The doctors thought it was a severe cold or maybe even pneumonia. She was put on anti-biotics. But she kept getting worse. They finally did an ultrasound and found a problem with her liver. I talked to my sister, my brother, and my dad, but no one knew that much. I even went to the science library at the university to study up on cancer. Then I called my mom's doctor and asked him to be honest with me.

"How bad was it doc, should I come home now?" I asked.

"Your mother's liver is cancerous, it is inoperable, she may have a few weeks, or a few months," he said. He advised me to come home as soon as possible. The next day my family and I all flew back to Seattle. On the flight I was very quiet. My wife did not ask me anything, she knew better than to push me. I was a time bomb. I was afraid to see my mom. I was afraid to face death. I was afraid to face my own mortality. When we arrived and we all went to see her, she was lying down in bed. She was cheerful and was glad to see us, but I could see death in her eyes. We spent ten days with my mom, listening to her, praying with her, and just enjoying our last days with her. She was hospitalized when we left to complete finals week. I was going to come back after finals and be with her. On Friday, the 4th of May, I had just finished grading my last final when the phone rang. My sister had been trying to get through to me all day. Mom had died that morning.

The evening before my mom died, I had called her at home because the doctor had allowed her to go home with a hospice nurse. I told her that I loved her and that she was the best mom in the whole world. She laughed a little and then told me she was tired. That was the last time I heard her voice when she was alive.

Before we left I had met with her doctor and he had explained how it was better to send her home with a hospice nurse than leave her in the hospital.

"A natural death is preferable to a chemical one," the doctor said. "In the hospital we could keep her medicated, but she would not die comfortably." Natural death would come when her kidneys and liver shut down. The kidneys would send a toxic substance into the blood that would give her a natural euphoria as she died.

I knew what was happening, but I did not want to know. Intellectually I understood the doctor's words, but emotionally I just sat there like a bewildered child. I felt the pain, but I did not want to feel it. I wanted to be numb. I saw my mom fading, but I did not want to see her slip away. Time seemed to lose its meaning and I became stuck. One thing was certain: as she lay dying, I could do nothing. Her heartbeats were numbered. But I did not know how many remained. What would happen to her mind and soul? I remembered my visions of heaven in Sunday school—a light and cheerful place in the clouds where the sun never set and people were happy forever. Is that where she was headed? She was a good woman. She slipped ahead in time as I sat helpless and thought. Back in school during finals week, I went through the motions while she saw the light and reached with both hands. This left me in the darkness—knowing, feeling, and seeing. After the memorial service I fell apart emotionally, and my brother was there to hold me up and keep me walking straight ahead.

TEACHING

My dream of teaching came true when I started as a part-time teacher in the fall of 1992, but I continued to apply for full-time work. One full-time job that I interviewed for was in Barrow, Alaska. Exactly fifteen years after the brief month that I worked in South Naknek, Alaska, I arrived for summer in the North Slope—the ice frontier. When my plane landed in Barrow I was shocked at the condition of the place. My first impression was that Barrow was the most rundown, messy town that I had ever seen. The houses were little more than glorified shacks with no paint—just worn and weathered boards. And there was junk strewn everywhere—old cars, washers, and other trash. The roads were dirty and dust blew over everything leaving a fine light brown coating on the entire town. Later I figured out that the severe weather would strip paint off of the walls of the buildings, so it was useless to spruce up your house.

Barrow is the northernmost town in North America. The Arctic ice hugged up against the beach year-round. Barrow had grown remarkably since the 1970s with the opening of the North Slope oil drilling at Prudhoe Bay. The townspeople were mostly Inupiat (Eskimo). One of the teachers at the college met me at the airport. He told me a little about the town and then put me up in the Arctic Hotel. It looked like a hotel from an old Western movie. My window overlooked the beach and the ice. The Inupiat people, whom I had seen since my arrival, impressed me with their calmness and gentle, smiling nature.

It was about 11:30 p.m. when I decided to take a walk. It would be light all night so I did not have to worry about it getting dark. I walked down by the shoreline and noticed how dark and coarse the sand was. I wandered down the beach for a while, leaning in to the gusty, freezing wind. My thoughts drifted back to my walks around the abandoned canneries at South Naknek. Then I heard a voice from the sandy ledge above. An Inupiat man with a black baseball cap smiled down at me as he sat cross-legged on the ledge.

"Where you are standing was the old village," he said.

"Really," I said, "What happened to it?"

"The sea takes away what it gives sometimes," he said with a grin that revealed several missing teeth.

"Come up here and sit for a while," he said.

I climbed up the ledge and stood next to the Inupiat man. He was about forty-five years old, very small, and had black horn-rimmed glasses. He told me his name was Billy.

"Are there polar bears around here?" I asked. Billy looked at me with another big grin.

"There is probably a big one about one hundred yards away sniffing you now. You were polar bear bait for sure on the beach," Billy said. We shared a laugh, although mine was a bit nervous.

"Here, I'll share this spot, the turf keeps you warm," he said pointing to the grass patch he was sitting on. I sat down next to him in a cross-legged fashion and felt warmer. I had the strange feeling that he knew that I was coming, even though I did not know where I was going. After I told him my name he began to tell me stories about living in Barrow. I knew that these stories had a purpose. They seemed to have no real endings or beginnings. He told me about the ice flows and the whale hunting. "The Inupiat believe that you had to be a good people to get a whale. The whale gives himself to good people," he said. I had been against whaling, but I found his explanation of the sacred hunt satisfying. "The whale respects good people and rewards them with his body to sustain life," he continued.

I was surprised to learn that Inupiats did not swim. They would hunt whales in tiny seal-skin boats and if they fell down, they would drown. "The Great Spirit would take you when he wanted to, it did not matter whether you could swim or not," said Billy.

Billy seemed to be about my brother's age, so I asked if he was a Vietnam War veteran like my brother. Billy told me that he did not like to talk about the war. "The army took me from my grandfather and the ice flows and put me in a hot, steamy jungle," he said.

"It was alien to me. I could only hear my grandfather's heart, and when I returned, he was gone," he added. A tear ran down his weathered brown cheek as he looked out over the ice flows.

He then began to ask me questions about what he had told me. I remembered almost everything.

"Which way is north?" Billy asked. I pointed in the wrong direction. "You are lost," he said as he moved my hand so that it was pointed north. "Remember, north is where your heart leads you," he added.

I told Billy that I had to get back to the hotel room. As I stood up to go, he made a circular motion with his hand. "All the living creatures, the water, and the land are as one," he said. I did not get the job in Barrow, but the experience left me feeling closer to my destination in life.

It was another gray, rainy, fall day in Seattle. I was on my way to a poetry reading, when I walked past a hideously scarred homeless man who was sitting on a street corner by the Public Market. After passing him, I heard a whispery voice: "We are all scarred, either emotionally or physically." I stopped, turned, and looked at the homeless man. Did he say that, or did I imagine the voice? He sat next to a cardboard sign that read, "Pete—Vietnam Veteran." Pete's legs were crossed and he was looking down, his dirty jeans were tattered, and he wore jungle boots that may very well have begun their journey in Vietnam. He wore a faded blue baseball cap and his graying long hair fell to his shoulders. Pete's field jacket was covered with dark greasy blotches. Just as I was about to look away again, he tipped his head up and smiled at me. I felt a burning sensation inside of my body, like I usually do when something bizarre or unexplainable happened. I smiled back at him and continued on to my poetry reading.

The poetry readings provided healing for me, especially after my divorce and losing custody of my children. Poetry had become a way for me to better understand myself and the world. Poetry was a language and forum by which I could reach toward the infinite. I read somewhere that to find the Creator, you had to reach both outwardly and inwardly because the universe was both infinitely large and infinitely small at the same time. In a way, this made sense to me. This was probably because as a small boy, I had believed that we were all in the belly of a giant, and we had people in our bellies, and the giant was within the belly of an even larger giant. My confidence in understanding infinity in either sense, large or small, eroded as I grew older, and I quickly resigned myself to the fact that life would present me with more questions than answers.

After the poetry reading, I walked back home with Gene, a Native American friend of mine. I mentioned something about luck and he stopped in his tracks.

"Define good luck," he said. I looked at him rather oddly, thinking it was a tricky question. I bought into it anyway.

"When you get something unexpectedly," I said.

Gene looked away for a moment, then he raised his hand to scratch his forehead. In his usual, carefully chosen and deliberate speech he continued.

"In a Western sense, yes, but my people think of good luck as being able to help someone." I thought for a long moment as I looked down at my wet sneakers, then I understood. As we continued our walk, I told Gene about my dreams, and what I thought they meant.

"There is a message, a connection to another world in those," he said. He encouraged me to find a symbolic understanding.

"You are a seeker and a person who is gifted with the ability to see visions...you have a purpose and a big responsibility," he added. When we arrived at his apartment and were prepared to part company, I asked if we could talk more about spiritual things. Gene kept walking toward the entrance to his building as if he did not hear me. Then he turned around.

"Find yourself, find the Creator, the time to talk is over, now it's time to act," he said rather abruptly. And then he opened the door and went into his building.

Teaching became my life, especially the Vietnam War course. The most important part of the course came on the last day. I invited students to bring in friends and family members and we would have a special speaker that day. One time, during a Family Day, a girl and her father could not make it to the event. They sat out in the parking lot and talked for three hours. Her father talked for the first time about the war. Another student's father broke down once during the Family Day. He had been a marine in Hue during the Tet Offensive in 1968. Haunted by his memories, his life had been spent since that time covering and concealing his emotions. They all came out in a remarkable forty-five-minute metamorphosis. It was the first time his son had heard him talk about the war. The other students and guests sat in astonishment.

Many of my students, veterans and nonveterans, have become friends of mine. Peck, one of my veteran students, once came back to the class to speak and told about his nightmarish experiences as a marine. In the battle of Hue in 1968, he came upon a pile of rotting corpses. The stench was incredible. There, at the bottom of the pile, stood a large pig feasting on the human remains. Someone in his platoon shot the pig. Peck said that he felt sorry for the pig. He said that the killing in war did not seem real to him until he went on leave back home. During an acid party in the University District, where he was the only GI, a few long-haired guys came up to him and asked him if he knew what he was doing over there. Up to that point, Peck had not really paid much attention. It was as if he was on a hunting trip, he said. Although Peck was supposed to return to Vietnam, he never made it back.

My brother came into the class often to show slides and talk. This has helped him and me. I now understand how I came to join the military and what I was looking for. Watching him present his story and show his slides brought me back to those times when I felt proud of him serving his country and afraid that he would not return home. When Alf spoke to my class, I saw the fears were still there. The presence of my mom was overwhelming in those memories as they unfolded in the form of slides and his matter-of-fact narration.

My Vietnam course offered students many different perspectives. Usually, I had combat veterans, REMFs, officers, reporters, nurses, and others coming to speak to the class. Some of their stories were so powerful that I often had to get up and walk outside to gather myself together.

Nurses in Vietnam suffered a great deal. Combat soldiers saw more than their share of blood and guts when they fought, but nurses and doctors saw much more. They saw the flower of youth reduced to legless, armless, and faceless patients without futures or dreams. Lara, my nurse friend, told the class about her friend who suffered from PTSD. Lara's friend would, as a matter of routine in Vietnam, wash surgical sponges in a series of water and soap solutions contained in drums. She began to experience nightmares after her return to the States, nightmares where faces appeared in each of the drums of water. The surgical sponges contained bits of skin, other tissues, and blood clots. These things would rise to the surface of the water in the drums and Lara's friend would see them form slowly into the faces of dead soldiers she had treated in the hospital.

Another friend of mine, Max, was in three wars—World War II, Korea, and Vietnam. "The Eternal Warrior," as I call Max, had a happy-go-lucky attitude that was infectious for the younger students. He was like their grandpa. The only war experiences that bothered him and gave him nightmares were from Vietnam. Max would tell the class about the twelve-year-old girl that he shot near a village in the Central Highlands. He had nightmares every night over the shooting. Max was not, however, bothered by others whom he had to kill in other wars.

BRUCE'S RETURN

As the wheels of the airplane touched down on the rain-soaked runway at Sea-Tac airport in Seattle, I was jarred back into reality. Thoughts and memories about my dad filled my mind during the short flight from southern California—my new home. I had finished graduate school and found a job in California. I was a busy college teacher and had achieved something my dad was proud of. So why did I feel so guilty? It was true that I did not live near my father, and I did not visit him as often as I should. I knew that he spent his days staring out the window of his retirement-home room. His once-powerful hands shook uncontrollably and his once-muscular body was now withered and weakened with age and disease. I feared seeing him. I picked up my rental car at the airport and went to visit my father. He recognized me with a smile. We sat down at the kitchen table, where the retirement-home manager had set out some coffee and sandwiches. We sat in silence for a few moments; then, as he struggled with his shaking hand to bring the coffee cup to his mouth, I saw that his eyes reflected unfamiliarity. I could see him fade out and slip into a combination of vague memories, cloudy recollections of past experiences, and emotions as he began to stare into the trembling coffee cup.

"I once had a son who was a teacher," he said.

"I am not sure where he is . . . he doesn't visit anymore," he said wistfully, tears forming in his eyes. "Do you know him?"

Dad was kicked out of his residential retirement home a few days later because he kept escaping and because he got very hysterical one day. He was convinced that people were going to kill him and all of the others in the home. He began throwing dishes and yelling. The police were called and Dad was sent in for psychiatric evaluation at the Swedish hospital in Seattle. The nurse told me that he had been talking about Nazis when they brought him in. He thought that the Nazis were coming to get him in his home. That was why he got so upset. He was just trying to protect what he thought was his home and family. The war was still haunting him, and now manifesting itself in his dementia.

Dad passed away on 20 August 1999. I was holding his hand and rubbing his forehead, just like he did for me when I was a young boy. It has come full circle. He was my greatest hero. I miss him more than these words can even come close to expressing. Whatever good I do in this life is because of what my parents taught me, the rest is my own damn fault.

THE WAR COMES HOME

What was my direction and where was my destination? From being a child growing up in the 1960s and 1970s during the Vietnam War, to my own service in the military from 1978 to 1986 searching for something that I was not sure of, to teaching about the war in the 1990s, my journey has led me faraway only to return to the beginning. What have I learned?

Storytelling is an ancient method of healing. Indigenous cultures around the world rely on their traditional storytelling to instruct the young and to comfort the older generations. Modern societies, unfortunately, have mostly forgotten the purpose and power of the story. What I came to believe was that the Vietnam War had affected more than just the generation that experienced it firsthand—the effects of that war were intergenerational. And this was true not only for the Vietnam War, but for every war the United States has ever fought. We were a nation born of war that has never really stopped warring.

On the first day of the Vietnam War class that I taught, I would ask the students to write down the reason(s) they took the course. The overwhelming majority of students wrote that they had relatives involved in one aspect or another of the war and that they needed to understand more. No other class that I have taught has had such personal meaning for my students.

People never fully recovered from the effects of war. The "video game generation" should see that war was not all fun and games like *Desert Storm* portrayed. The horrors of war could be dulled by reliance on technology. A reliance on technology in warfare could make war more palatable. This would consequently diminish the need for peacemakers and peace.

The children, nephews, nieces, and other relatives and friends of the Vietnam veterans should be added to the list of those affected by the war. In some ways, the children of the Vietnam era folks (veterans and nonveterans) are the ones who have suffered the most. They have no war stories to tell; they only feel the war indirectly through their parents and other relatives. Because few people suspect that the effects of war are intergenerational, these indirect victims must suffer in silence, the war insidiously contaminating their lives. By their sheer numbers, this indirect group is significant.

The young inner-city street gangs of the 1980s and 1990s said they were going to "bust a cap" in someone when they meant to shoot somebody and kill them. This terminology was from the Vietnam War. American soldiers in Vietnam (especially black soldiers) used to refer to setting the selector switch on the M-16 rifle to fully automatic as "busting caps." Also, a refrain from a popular, early 1990s rap song, "Woop, there it is," was borrowed from the Vietnam veteran's vocabulary meant to express hopelessness and to minimalize emotional responses.

Because we never seemed to have enough time and are not allowed to heal from each war we fight, our society becomes ever more violent with each generation. We were all victims of war and have been since this country was founded. The decline of the middle class since the end of the Vietnam War has increased the separation of the rich and poor. The most economically vulnerable have been the inner-city minorities. These inner-city kids fought for each other, for themselves; they had no nation behind them, no family; they merely survived day to day. Recruiters today target the poverty-stricken neighborhoods to find fresh recruits for the armed services. This situation was not unlike the plight of U.S. soldiers in the Vietnam War, especially after 1968. Those soldiers no longer fought for their country; they felt abandoned, there were no convictions left, and they fought to keep themselves and their buddies alive. It was well known that murder rates in the United States soared after wars were over. Violence spiked again as the children of the Vietnam generation came of age. Racism in the form of dehumanization—calling the Vietnamese gooks, dinks, slopes—carried over to race relations in America and has helped spur the rise of neo-Nazi and militia organizations. All of this was also fueled by a growing lack of trust in government.

The United States was like one large extended dysfunctional family. War has made us that way. We never seem to recover from the last war we fought before we get engaged in another one. The effects overlapped, and the cycle continued. I think that the generation that comes of age during the end of the decade after the last war was over had the opportunity to stop the cycle of war, to end this dysfunctionality. History has given us the Discontented Intellectuals of the late 1920s, the Beat Generation of the late 1950s, and Generation X of the late 1980s. All of these generations have had it within their power to change this horrible cycle. But now we are embroiled in a global war on terror, and our country is once again debating whether to stay the course in order to honor those who have fallen or to get out to save the lives of those still alive. There is no peace anywhere in sight. I can only dream.

Conclusion: That Faraway Place in All of Us

Reality is not a function of the event as event but of the relationship of that event to past and future events. We seem to have here a paradox: That the reality of an event, which is not real in itself, arises from other events, which likewise, in themselves are not real. But this only affirms what we must affirm: That direction is all. But only as we realize this do we live, for our own identity is dependent upon this principle.
— Robert Penn Warren, *All the King's Men*

War is the bankruptcy of policy.
—John Keegan, military historian

PROFILE OF U.S. FORCES

Because this is a people's history, we need to look at who fought in Vietnam. To put the Vietnam War into perspective, demographically, of the 27,000,000 draft-age men during Vietnam War era, 8,700,000 enlisted, 2,200,000 were drafted, 500,000 illegally evaded the draft, and 2,700,000 physically served in Vietnam. The poor were twice as likely to be drafted as the middle and upper-middle class, and twice as likely to be in a combat role as well. Enlisting meant you were less likely to go to Vietnam.

In 1965, 16 percent of military in Vietnam were draftees, and by 1967, 65 percent were draftees. Many who went to Vietnam believed in what they were doing. One could avoid the draft through an educational deferment, and by 1967, nearly one in five were in college to avoid the draft. In effect, millions bought their way out of military service.

According to the Department of Defense, 7,465 women served as active duty military personnel in Vietnam. The Veterans Administration says that the number is 11,000. The discrepancy could come from the fact that DOD did not count women on hospital ships off the coast of Vietnam. There were also 50,000 nonmilitary women serving as volunteers and in other positions. There are eight military women listed on the Vietnam War memorial wall.[1]

There was a sense of futility while in Vietnam. The soldiers were different in Vietnam than in World War II. They were younger and the forces were undergoing constant turnover. A soldier would serve twelve months while a marine would serve thirteen-month tours. They would return to the United States alone, just as they had left alone. They did not travel together on huge troop ships or transports like in World War II. Only one in three saw any combat; most were in support roles, but in danger nonetheless. The main emphasis for GIs was survival in Vietnam. Body counts made killing the focus, instead of gaining territory from the enemy. And they really did not know who the enemy was, so no one could be trusted. Often the conclusion was, "Waste all the gooks." Morale was low at the end of the war and fraggings began. Over 300,000 Americans were physically wounded and over 500,000 got in trouble and received Bad Conduct Discharges or Dishonorable Discharges. Oftentimes, the psychological trauma of sudden return to the World made adjustment after the war even worse. They faced many at home who were critical of the war and blamed those who served.

Because of the Vietnam War, we now know a lot more about what has come to be known as PTSD—Post Traumatic Stress Disorder. In previous wars, this condition for returning veterans was called Shell Shock, Battle Fatigue, and other names. The condition is well documented back to ancient times. What we now know is that any type of extremely traumatic event (war, rape, child molestation, natural disasters) can create symptoms that generally fall under the diagnostic category, PTSD. Apparently, the traumatic event, being out of the normal experience, leaves a lasting imprint psychologically on a person, which continues to affect them for the rest of their lives. A frozen frame of time from the event is embedded and comes out and is exposed at certain unannounced and often unanticipated times. Often, smells, sounds, and objects can trigger flashbacks. Once in a flashback, the PTSD sufferers feel as if they are actually back in the time under the same conditions as when the traumatic incident took place.

PTSD sufferers often have trouble sleeping, have nervous ticks, heightened startle responses, hyper-vigilance, inability to maintain close personal relationships, and drug and/or alcohol abuse. Many veterans have returned to civilian life and have done well in spite of their traumatization. However, a significant number have not adjusted and continue to suffer (estimates are 20–30 percent). No one who goes to war is unaffected, and many who claim they have no effects suffer in silence and often in a state of denial.

President Clinton opened up trade and diplomatic relations with Vietnam more than twenty years after the war ended. This impacted veterans especially. Many felt it was time, others felt that Vietnam should never be recognized. The Gulf War was fought very much with Vietnam in mind, and lessons learned from Vietnam guided policy (e.g., the use of the Powell Doctrine). The Vietnam War will continue to affect us for many years to come.

U.S.-SOUTH VIETNAMESE RELATIONS

At the heart of any discussion of what went wrong in the American War in Vietnam is the relationship between the United States and South Vietnam. President Ngo Dinh Diem, who led South Vietnam from 1955 to 1963, in one sense, met the American criteria for leadership in Vietnam—he was intensely nationalistic and vehemently anti-Communist. But he was also very wary of U.S. influence in Vietnam and the dangers of large-scale U.S. military intervention. "South Vietnam would not be a protectorate," he insisted. Americans, on the other hand, did not like to be pushed around, least of all by those whom they hoped to exercise control over. The Vietnamese did not like to take advice from Americans who did not respect or understand their ancient culture. To make matters worse, Americans never really understood Buddhists or what they wanted. In the midst of these cultural and political misunderstandings and disagreements, the pressures of the Cold War made everything more desperate and deadly and created a tendency for policymakers to see everything in apocalyptic terms.

With unfortunate shortsightedness, JFK approved the coup that ultimately killed Diem and Nhu. This left a power vacuum in South Vietnam that was never adequately filled. The Americans stepped in and created a dependent puppet state. Nguyen Cao Ky and Nguyen Van Thieu were no comfort to U.S. policymakers, even though they were glad to be rid of Diem. The flamboyant Ky seemed more like a comic book character than a leader. One thing was certain: The South Vietnamese did not have someone like Ho Chi Minh to lead them.

A National Security Council (NSC) study in 1964 noted problems with U.S. nation-building efforts in South Vietnam:

1. Negative colonial heritage in Vietnam
2. Inadequate preparation for self-government
3. Nationalist movement taken over by Communists
4. Communist opposition having a better army and leadership.

By the spring of 1965, South Vietnam was on the verge of collapse. Undersecretary of State George Ball argued that South Vietnam incompetence required total U.S. withdrawal. Ball wanted us to cut our losses and go. He noted that the South Vietnamese leaders were "clowns" and we could not build anything on such a faulty base. Ball was, unfortunately, a minority of one among Johnson's advisors. Other officials felt South Vietnam was weak, but thought that U.S. strength could more than make up for it. The key point was that they were concerned with humiliation if they withdrew from Vietnam. The international context of the Cold War figured prominently in any policy decisions.

This unwillingness to withdraw presented a curious reversal of previous strategy, which was that intervention would be ill advised if South Vietnam was too weak. The United States disregarded the wishes of its allies in the decision to intervene. To throw money, men, and resources at a problem is a typically American way of doing things. In the process, the United States molded South Vietnam into a submissive and dependent nation.

In terms of military cooperation, South Vietnam did not agree to a joint command structure with the United States. They had badly coordinated missions and numerous friendly fire incidents. The U.S. forces took the big jobs and left mop-up and security operations to the ARVN. General Maxwell Taylor observed that by the United States becoming the primary combatant, it would absorb the highest number of casualties, thus threatening domestic support for the war, and it would demoralize the South Vietnamese people—why should they fight when the Americans do it for them?. The ARVN became a carbon copy of the U.S. Army, including a large logistics infrastructure—one combat soldier for every five support troops. The ARVN wore U.S. uniforms, had U.S. equipment, were financed by the Americans, and their leaders were selected by the Americans all the way down to the village level. Not surprisingly, many people viewed the Americans as colonialists. Interestingly enough, all of these points are being revisited today in our current war in Iraq.

The sudden infusion of money in to the South Vietnamese economy had disastrous effects on a weak and divided country. There were ships in line way out to sea, waiting to be unloaded in Saigon and Cam Ranh Bay. Signs of U.S. presence were everywhere—brothels, GI bars, and discarded American beer cans. There was corruption on a massive scale. The dilemma for the U.S. government was that if they took total charge they would completely undermine South Vietnamese confidence; if they did not, nothing would get done. Relations between South Vietnam and the United States worsened with increasing U.S. presence. There was a definite lack of trust. Since it was believed that the ARVN had been infiltrated by the VC, U.S. officers did not share intelligence information with the ARVN. The Americans looked down on the South Vietnamese as the Vietnamese resented increasing U.S. dependency. The Tet Offensive was a turning point in U.S.-South Vietnamese relations just as it was a turning point in U.S. public opinion.

General Giap's strategy for the Tet Offensive did not quite work the way he had planned it to. He wanted to increase discord between U.S. and ARVN forces and cause a collapse of the ARVN. This would then intensify the pressure for the United States to get out of the war. But a mass uprising did not occur in South Vietnam, and the U.S. and ARVN forces fought back hard turning the NVA and VC advances around. The Americans could not distinguish friend from foe during and after Tet, and this led to many friendly fire incidents through an indiscriminate use of firepower. The ARVN were given larger combat roles, but the political damage had been done with Tet. The massacre at My Lai was proof for critics of the war that the United States had lost its focus and now felt hostility for all Vietnamese. The South Vietnamese saw

Nixon's plan for Vietnamization as a fig leaf for abandonment. U.S. morale deteriorated rapidly under surreal conditions of Vietnamization. Accordingly, the Americans and the South Vietnamese blamed each other.

Henry Kissinger talked of the 1973 peace agreements as providing a decent interval between U.S. withdrawal and North Vietnamese victory. The U.S. government was heavy handed in dealing with President Thieu—Nixon even went as far as to remind Thieu of what happened to Diem. The ARVN, based on U.S. support, had no strategy of their own and no force doctrine other than what the Americans had taught them. Tragically, even as the North Vietnamese tanks closed in on Saigon, South Vietnamese remained certain that U.S. B-52s would intervene and U.S. forces would come back to save them like the cavalry of old. The bottom line was that neither country, America or South Vietnam, understood the other. The Americans did not have a viable solution to the problems in South Vietnam. However noble the goals of the outside power, the act of intervention may bring more grief than benefit to the people who are to be saved. This lesson may be lost on the U.S. leaders dealing with the current war in Iraq.

What did Americans learn from the Vietnam War experience? Even though the Americans dropped more bombs on Vietnam than were dropped in all theaters of battle in World War II, the bombing only disrupted transport of supplies by the North to the South, but did not stop it. Enough got through. We learned that bombing a Third World country is not as effective as bombing an industrialized country. In terms of the ground war, the enemy was everywhere and nowhere. It was difficult to distinguish friend from foe. A U.S. general argued with an NVA officer after the war and told him that the United States was never defeated in open battle during the entire war. The North Vietnamese officer remarked that that may be true, but it is also irrelevant since the United States lost the war.

What were the U.S. war goals and how did Vietnam become so important to the United States?

1. Containment and the domino effect
2. The Munich analogy
3. Investment trap
4. U.S. sense of moral mission forced Americans to look at international problems in absolute terms.

American policy leaders were drawn into Vietnam partially through a sort of misguided application of the overarching containment policy and a weak and silly corollary, the domino effect. As strange as it sounds today, many Americans believed that if Vietnam were to become Communist, we would eventually fall under Communism as well.

To further galvanize the decision for war in Vietnam, U.S. policymakers looked back to World War II and remembered that the British attempted to appease Hitler and his aggression. This, of course, backfired on the British and the rest of the world. But the application of the Munich analogy in Vietnam was quite a stretch.

An investment trap is created when a country invests heavily in another country and government. The more invested you are, the harder it is to disengage politically. One can also think of this in terms of lives lost. The argument that we must continue fighting in order to honor those who have died echoed throughout America during the Vietnam War and does again today with our war in Iraq.

The last reason given above, the sense of moral mission, is deeply rooted in U.S. foreign policy, and perhaps one can look all the way back to the influence of the Puritans. By looking at foreign policy in such visionary, religious terms, one runs the risk of departing from realism and seeing everything as black and white, good and evil.

COMPARISON OF THE IRAQ WAR TO THE VIETNAM WAR

There are many comparisons being made between the Iraq War and the Vietnam War. Yet both are very different. In some ways, Iraq is a more difficult situation for the Untied States. At the same time that the U.S. presence in Iraq may be necessary to preserve what little security there is for the Iraqis, this same U.S. presence is fostering the insurgency. Public opinion in Iraq is 80 percent in favor of U.S. troops leaving. More than half of those Iraqis polled believe that it is okay to kill Americans. I have to ask this question: Is it really democracy that we are fighting for in Iraq?

By focusing on war as an extension of policy, Americans have lost much of what they have fought and died for. Eisenhower warned us of the Military Industrial Complex. I have concluded that Eisenhower's fear of misplaced power and undue influence by the Military Industrial Complex has come to pass. Its ascendancy has started what I call the Devolution of Democracy in America.

In a totalitarian political system, journalists are essentially propaganda tools used by the regime. All news is approved and censored to fulfill the needs of the regime. Any journalist who dares to defy the regime faces death or imprisonment. In a modern corporate capitalist society, a journalist does not have total freedom of speech. He or she must work within a narrow range of acceptable reporting, or face banishment, blacklisting, and firing. Although the punishments are different, censorship is present in both systems. This is but one element of the devolution of democracy.

Consider the erosion of privacy. In today's world, even in democratic societies, your privacy is waning. The interest of the ruling corporate elite in your privacy stems from their will to control. Insurance companies, for instance, can access your medical records and, accordingly, make corporate decisions as to your insurability. We are but one step from discriminating against people based on genetics now that the human genome has been mapped. Surveillance is easy and data are simple enough to store and search. Now, with the fear that gripped our nation after 9/11 and the passage of the Patriot Act, we cannot run, we cannot hide, and we cannot make it stop.

There is also the imposition of state-sponsored (tacit though it appears to be) religion. Senator Elizabeth Dole of North Carolina said at the 2004 Republican convention that we do not have the right to freedom *from* religion. The reinterpretation of the Constitution to impose religion on Americans is considered acceptable to those who subscribe to the religion in question. But liberty is based on what is not comfortable for the majority. That is the key to freedom. The movement in America to teach Intelligent Design alongside Evolution in public schools is but a ruse to infuse religion in the classroom. Even the Vatican has said that Intelligent Design is not science and is really not religion, and should not be taught. Public policy decisions based on religion take us further from democracy and liberty and closer to the theocratic states of the Middle East—ironically, the very states we are trying to democratize.

From an economic perspective, the family is under attack. Union wages allowed blue-collar workers to support a family of four in the 1950s and 1960s. It takes two incomes to do this today for most families, leaving children with no primary caregiver (I do not mean to imply that women have to play this role; it does not matter if this primary caregiver is a man or a woman). The middle class has been artificially maintained at the expense of children. We leave it to our government and corporate leaders to care for our children. This is a perfect opportunity to raise the next generation to accept the erosion of civil liberties and democracy as if they never really existed in the first place.

Voting is supposed to be the guarantee of liberty and freedom and democracy. Yet, voting is restricted to two political parties that maintain an artificially narrow choice. The system itself is undemocratic. Consider the Electoral College. When a candidate can lose the popular election and still become president, something is definitely wrong (e.g., 2000 election). Fraud in elections is rampant, and now that electronic voting is becoming the norm, it is even easier to hack systems and rig elections.

As for who must serve in our military, we do not ask all of our able-bodied citizens to fight our wars through conscription. We ask the working class, the poor, the disadvantaged, and the disenfranchised to do the fighting for all of us. Our all-volunteer fighting force is maintained by keeping the underclass down through the perpetuation of an economic system that is inherently unfair. The poor simply have fewer alternatives and so they often choose the military.

Only five major corporations control all news and media consumed by Americans. Paul Kennedy, in his book *Preparing for the Twenty First*

Century, said that corporations are controlled by stock holders who are most interested in profits, not in benefiting humankind. It is government's responsibility to take care of its people. Corporations should be left to do what they do best—making money, not setting or unduly influencing public policy.

The current war in Iraq and the dramatic shift in U.S. foreign policy from containment and coalition building to unilateralism and preemption practiced by President George W. Bush and his cadre of neo-conservatives have put the United States in a very precarious situation. The moment after 9/11 could have been the point at which America could recapture what it had lost in Vietnam. The idealism, the support of our like-minded allies, and the source of inspiration to new democracies around the world were lost in our pursuit of the Iraq War. I cannot help but think about the Gulf War, where Bush the elder did not topple Saddam and charge into Baghdad in 1991 because

1. The coalition allies (including Arab countries) would have dropped out
2. It would have led to a prolonged occupation
3. The occupation would result in guerrilla warfare by regime holdouts and others
4. There was no clear exit strategy
5. Most importantly, the breakup of Iraq with all of its ethnic and religious factionalism would destabilize the Middle East and the world balance of power. Specifically mentioned was that the lack of a strong Iraq would embolden an openly hostile (to the West) Iran.

None of these considerations seemed to have been passed down from father to son.[2] The current Bush administration has the desire to impose order in the world and transplant its political and economic system abroad, but it lacks the long-term capacity to do so.

In early October 2005, the U.S. government announced that they had found a letter in Iraq from Ayman al-Zawahri (Osama bin Laden's second in command) to Abu Musab al-Zarqawi (the al Qa'ida leader in Iraq). The discovery of this letter coincided nicely with President Bush's dropping approval ratings, a majority of Americans believing that the war in Iraq was not worth it, and increasing comparisons between the Iraq War and the Vietnam War. The letter serves to reinforce the Bush policies in Iraq. Here are the highlights from the intercepted letter:

1. The centrality of the war in Iraq for the global jihad
2. From al Qa'ida's point of view, the war does not end with America's departure
3. An acknowledgment of the appeal of democracy to the Iraqis
4. The strategic vision of inevitable conflict, with a tacit recognition of current political dynamics in Iraq, with a call by al-Zawahiri for political action equal to military action

5. The need to maintain popular support at least until jihadist rule has been established

6. Admission that more than half the struggle is taking place in the battlefield of the media.

The first point fits in nicely with the emphasis that the administration has put Iraq in the War on Terror. This point basically proves that the administration's pursuit of war in Iraq was the right decision. The second point reinforces the administration's determination to stay for an undetermined time in Iraq. Points three through five prove that building a democracy in Iraq is a threat to al Qa'ida and that they plan to stay the course. The sixth and last point refers to the importance of the media and public opinion, both in the United States and in the world. The fact that this supposed letter covers all of the administration's current talking points on the Iraq War is more than coincidence in my opinion. The al Qa'ida letter also refers directly to U.S. policy in the Vietnam War:

> My answer is, firstly: Things may develop faster than we imagine. The aftermath of the collapse of American power in Vietnam—and how they ran and left their agents—is noteworthy. Because of that, we must be ready starting now, before events overtake us, and before we are surprised by the conspiracies of the Americans and the United Nations and their plans to fill the void behind them. We must take the initiative and impose a fait accompli upon our enemies, instead of the enemy imposing one on us, wherein our lot would be to merely resist their schemes.[3]

This is nothing but blatant propaganda on the part of the U.S. government. I expect this from nondemocratic governments and from organizations like al Qa'ida, but not from the U.S. government. President Bush and Vice President Cheney are criticizing politicians and others in America who advocate bringing the troops home. They call this a cowardly "cut and run" strategy that plays into the hands of the enemy. It is interesting that the letter from al Qa'ida uses the words "ran and left" to describe what America did in Vietnam. I suppose operative theory here is that it is easier for people to believe a big lie than a little one.

We must keep in mind that the War on Terror was forced on us by the 9/11 attacks; the Iraq War was a choice on our part. Looking at previous wars, we can see that successful outcomes are obtained when the president (1) defines the necessity of war, (2) builds popular support, (3) obtains congressional approval for use of force, and (4) gets backing of allies and the UN. Vietnam was ill defined, had lost popular support, and did not have the backing of key allies. Subsequently, this led to a negative outcome. In Iraq, President Bush defined the necessity of war based on intelligence we now know was faulty. He was able to harness popular support based on the perceived threat and the emotional connection to 9/11 and used this to obtain a nearly unanimous

196
Conclusion

congressional approval for the use of force. Bush was able to get a "coalition of the willing," which included Great Britain, but was lacking the support of the Middle East or other key allies or the UN. The outcome may not be what we hope for.[4]

I cannot help but think about Hitler's regime and his focus on controlling all aspects of society while harnessing the corporate machine. Industrialists went along with the program because they were still allowed to do what they did best: create capital. Hitler saw children and the arts as the two most important elements in cementing his thousand-year Reich. The Nazi party determined art and music and books that were considered heretical. They forced their ideology on schoolchildren, who had no alternatives. This is what a one-party system will do. We should consider a secular and pluralist government, the greatest gift from our founding fathers. Yet the party in power does everything it can to utterly destroy the other party. We have not learned.

This book started out with the following questions: (1) What is the meaning and significance of the Vietnam War for Americans today? (2) What lessons have Americans learned from our defeat, and how should we apply that knowledge in implementing current foreign policy? (3) Who or what is to be blamed for the loss in Vietnam? (4) How can we heal our nation from the Vietnam War syndrome? and (5) How do we fit the Vietnam War era into our greater historical narrative?

Vietnam is often used as an analogy for almost any military operation the United States has undertaken since 1975. Oftentimes the analogy is stretched too thin. Most historical analogies are used inappropriately as convenient tools to promote a given political position or agenda. The interesting thing about the use of the Vietnam analogy is that it can be used for opposite reasons. This is a testament to how divided our nation was during the Vietnam War. The failure in Vietnam can be used by peace activists to point out the folly of all wars, whereas those who support war warn us that we need to go to war with overwhelming force, unified in public opinion, and we must give a free hand to the military to fight to win without political interference. So, the meaning of the Vietnam War for most Americans is really one of two competing visions:

1. Defeat came because of arrogance, immorality, and the ascendancy of the Military Industrial Complex and its influence on policy.
2. Defeat came because of lack of military control over war policy and strategy, lack of clear objectives, and unhindered use of force to achieve victory.

As for lessons we can apply, it depends on the analogy one chooses from the Vietnam War experience. The current war in Iraq is defended as a war for freedom against tyranny and an attempt to plant the seeds of democracy in the Middle East. President Bush has said that it is better to fight the terrorists over there, than here at home. This was the essence of the Domino Theory that led us into Vietnam. The debate over returning our troops is similar to the debates during the Vietnam War as well. Do we send the troops home and dishonor those who have died? Or do we save the ones that are left to be used more appropriately? It all depends on your political perspective. So the lessons are many, and often at odds with one another. I believe that we are becoming as divided today as we were during the Vietnam War.

In terms of blame in the Vietnam War, it also depends on your perspective and which analogy and lessons you seek to apply. The media has been blamed, the government has been blamed, the military has been blamed, and the South Vietnamese have been blamed. There is no shortage of blame in other words. As JFK said, "Victory has many fathers, but defeat is an orphan." But perhaps the very *nature* of war is to be blamed. As the quote by John Keegan states at the beginning of this chapter, "War is the bankruptcy of policy." In my understanding, war is failure, failure to maintain and preserve peace. One war always leads to another—even the so-called good wars.

Healing is really at the crux of this whole problem of war. Politics should be put aside to heal from war. True healing would help to prevent future wars. Ancient people understood this. Native American warriors returning from battle were put through purification rituals by the tribe. Oftentimes, these ceremonies and rituals were sweat lodges, wherein the warrior sits in absolute darkness and high humidity until he reemerges into the world, born again. We have to realize that all of us suffer when we go to war.

The Vietnam War can either be seen as the turning point for us in understanding the failure of war as a mechanism of positive social change, or it can be a launching pad for the militarization of foreign policy. It depends on how we look at it and which analogy and lesson is internalized by our society. It seems to me that the hawkish Vietnam War analogy is more pervasive in America today.

Having looked at different historical analogies drawn from the Vietnam War, it is time to see the different ways that historians have interpreted the war. The Vietnam War story is a lengthy one. It has been told in fragments more so than in its entirety. Most literature is from the American perspective. The following interpretations capture the major schools of thought on the war from the American side (they are arranged chronologically as they developed). These interpretations have emerged in the years since the end of the Vietnam War.

1. Orthodox: This interpretation was the first to emerge; it came together during the war. The main theme is that the United States engaged in a mindless anti-Communist crusade that it could not win.
2. Revisionist: This interpretation holds that the United States did not blunder in to the war; the government was aware of each obstacle, did only the minimum required to avoid defeat, and was largely successful in doing so until it lost the

most essential domino—U.S. public opinion. Many military writers have used this interpretation to criticize a civilian-run war.

3. Advanced Revisionist: There are three subgroups of advanced revisionists.

   A. Clausewitzians: The civilians misunderstood the war and sent the military off to wage the wrong kind of war. Had the government attacked and invaded North Vietnam directly, the United States would have won the war.

   B. Hearts and Minds: There was too much emphasis on conventional warfare and too little emphasis on pacification. These writers blame the military leaders for wasteful and ill-conceived strategy (i.e., Search and Destroy).

   C. Legitimacists: This interpretation emphasizes the geopolitical, moral, and ethical legitimacy of waging war in Vietnam. U.S. national interests were at stake and the South Vietnamese government was viable until Diem was assassinated in 1963. That was the turning point.

4. Neo-Orthodox: The United States misread its own interests and Vietnamese realities in a doomed effort to build an independent Vietnam (a flawed form of containment).[5]

To me, neo-orthodoxy makes the most sense. Robert McNamara seems to express views that are close to this thought. This school of thought may also apply to the current war in Iraq.

At no time since the Civil War had American society been so divided as during the Vietnam era. Tremendous changes took place in America, changes that affect us to this day. Americans do not look at their government the same way as they did before. We were humbled by the outcome in Vietnam. Unfortunately, the public backlash went against those who were not in a position to set policy—the soldiers. Homecoming was not a pleasant event. Soldiers came home to a society that had for all intents and purposes abandoned them. The trauma of war can be lessened when there is support for the returning veterans. This did not happen in the case of the Vietnam War.

In the escalation phase of the war, we did not acknowledge the advice of our western European allies, who did not see the threat we felt in Vietnam. We had the entire French experience at our fingertips, yet did not consult them or bother to study their history of failure in Indochina. We were blinded by the fact that our war was not a colonial war, it was a war to stop Communism and create democracy in South Vietnam. Our imperialism, as was the case in the Spanish-American War and subsequent Philippine Insurrection, was anti-imperial imperialism.[6]

What is often forgotten in the Vietnam War literature is that the war was fought based mainly on international considerations. The projection of American credibility and difficult relations with alliance partners played a major role in setting American Vietnam policy in Vietnam. Unfortunately, the war that was supposed to enhance the United States' position in the Cold War and advance democracy and freedom in the world ended up as a lost crusade that nearly destroyed U.S. international prestige, alliances, and economic viability. The American Cold War alliance was a lot more fragile than U.S.

policy planners imagined. Johnson was not equipped to deal effectively with American allies and balance their advice, concerns, and policies with our own to develop a concerted effort in Southeast Asia.[7]

For ten thousand years of human history . . . young and old alike have felt that the way of the world offers no one any alternative to the death of its young men under arms. May the world, in the next ten thousand years, find a way of working that spares the old the need to ask the young that sacrifice.
—John Keegan, *Soldiers: A History of Men in Battle*

Notes

INTRODUCTION

1. Robert J. McMahon, "Contested Memory: The Vietnam War and American Society, 1975–2001," *Diplomatic History*, vol. 26, no. 2 (Spring 2002), p. 163.

2. McMahon, p. 159.

3. Ernest W. Lefever, "Vietnam's Ghosts," *Wall Street Journal*, 21 May 1997.

4. Robert A. Divine, "The Persian Gulf War Revisited: Tactical Victory, Strategic Failure," *Diplomatic History*, vol. 24, no. 1 (Winter 2000), pp. 129–130; Colin Powell, *My American Journey*, New York: Random House, 1995, p. 303.

5. McMahon, pp. 160–161.

CHAPTER 1

1. Sun Tzu, *The Art of War*, New York: Oxford University Press, 1984. *The Art of War* is the oldest military treatise in the world. Available online at: http://all.net/books/tzu/tzu.html.

2. Common Era or CE was formerly known as AD. Before the Common Era or BCE was formerly known as BC.

3. *Vietnam: A Television History*. Episode 1. Prod. Judith Vecchione. 1983. VHS. WGBH Educational Foundation, 1997.

4. Ibid.

5. Nguyen Khac Vien, *Vietnam: A Long History*, rev. ed., Hanoi: The Gioi Publishers, 1993, pp. 14–19.

6. Gary R. Hess, *Vietnam and the United States: Origins and Legacy of War*, Boston: Twayne Publishers, 1990, pp. 1–2; Vien, pp. 20–29.

7. Trung Trac and Trung Nhi, born of a family of military chiefs northwest of Hanoi, led a revolt against the Han dynasty. Although they were crushed, they left an indelible imprint on the history of Vietnam. See Vien, pp. 25–26.

8. Hess, *Vietnam and the United States*, pp. 1–2; Vien, pp. 3–5, 28–29, 41–49; D.G.E. Hall, *A History of South-East Asia*, 3d. ed., London: Macmillan, 1968, p. 419;

William J. Duiker, *The Rise of Nationalism in Vietnam, 1900–1941*, Ithaca, NY: Cornell University Press, 1996; Huynh Kim Khanh, *Vietnamese Communism, 1925–1945*, Ithaca, NY: Cornell University Press, 1982, p. 32; Stanley Karnow, *Vietnam: A History*, New York: Viking, 1983, pp. 99–106.

9. Vien, pp. 139–140.

10. Karnow, pp. 76–88; *Vietnam: A Television History*.

11. *Vietnam: A Television History*.

12. Ibid.

13. Vien, pp. 170–171; Karnow, pp. 110–113.

14. Vien, p. 194; Karnow, p. 124.

15. Vien, pp. 198–199.

16. William J. Duiker, *Sacred War: Nationalism and Revolution in a Divided Vietnam*, New York: McGraw Hill, 1995, pp. 22–27; *Vietnam: A Television History*; See also David Halberstam, *Ho*, New York: Knopf, 1987.

17. Fourteen Points Speech by President Woodrow Wilson, 8 January 1918. http://history.acusd.edu/gen/text/ww1/fourteenpoints.html.

18. Vien, p. 191.

19. *Vietnam: A Television History*.

CHAPTER 2

1. Vien, pp. 228–232.

2. *Vietnam: A Television History*.

3. Karnow, pp. 139–140.

4. Ibid., p. 169.

5. Vien, pp. 282–291; Karnow, pp. 199–205; Hess, *Vietnam and the United States*, pp. 43–47.

6. Hess, *Vietnam and the United States*, pp. 47–50.

CHAPTER 3

1. Farewell Address to the Nation by President Dwight D. Eisenhower, 17 January 1961. http://www.luminet.net/~tgort/ike.htm.

2. Foreign Relations of the United States (FRUS), vol. 13, Washington, DC: Government Printing Office (GPO), p. 929.

3. *Vietnam: A Television History*.

4. Karnow, p. 219; Hess, *Vietnam and the United States*, pp. 59–60; George C. Herring, *America's Longest War: The United States and Vietnam, 1950–1975*, 3d ed., New York: McGraw Hill, 1996, pp. 60–61.

5. An example would be the summary execution of a suspected VC by the Saigon chief of police. The famous picture can be found at: http://www.news-journalonline.com/photo/2000/.

6. The full correct name for the organization is National Front for the Liberation of South Vietnam (*Mat Tran Dan Toc Giai Phong Mien Nam Viet Nam*). The NLF served as an umbrella organization for many political, religious, professional, and ethnic groups that had major grievances with Ngo Dinh Diem's regime in South Vietnam.

7. Robert K. Brigham, *Guerrilla Diplomacy: The NLF's Foreign Relations and the Viet Minh War*, Ithaca, NY: Cornell University Press, 1999.

8. Americans have a tendency toward what is called "anti-imperial imperialism." The United States often moved into areas of the world ostensibly to clear out colonialist or imperialist nations only to themselves become imperialists in the process. The Spanish-American War period is an excellent example.

9. Gary R. Hess, "Commitment in the Age of Counter-insurgency: Kennedy's Vietnam Options and Decisions, 1961–1963," in David L. Anderson, ed., *Shadow on the White House: Presidents and the Vietnam War, 1945–1975*, Lawrence: University Press of Kansas, 1993, pp. 68–69.

10. FRUS, vol. 13, p. 553; Anthony Short, *The Origins of the Vietnam War*, New York: Longman, 1989, pp. 118–119.

11. John F. Kennedy, "America's Stake in Vietnam," *Vital Speeches* 22 (August 1956), pp. 617–619. See also Lawrence J. Bassett and Stephen E. Pelz, "The Failed Search for Victory: Vietnam and the Politics of War," in Thomas G. Patterson, ed., *Kennedy's Quest for Victory*, New York, Oxford University Press, 1989, pp. 112–129; Herring, pp. 36–37; and Arthur M. Schlesinger, Jr., *A Thousand Days: John F. Kennedy in the White House*, Boston: Houghton Mifflin, 1965, pp. 320–323.

12. Johnson to Kennedy, May 23, 1961, United States Department of Defense, *The Pentagon Papers: The Defense Department History of the United States Decision Making on Vietnam*, Senator Gravel edition. Boston: Beacon Press, 1971, 2:58–59; Chester L. Cooper, *The Lost Crusade: America in Vietnam*, Greenwich, CT: Fawcett, 1970, p. 208; John L. Gaddis, *Strategies of Containment: A Critical Appraisal of Postwar American National Security Policy*, New York: Oxford University Press, 1982, p. 212; Short, pp. 234–235; Speech to American Newspapers Publishers Association, April 27, 1961, *Public Papers of the Presidents of the United States: John F. Kennedy, 1961*, Washington, DC: GPO, 1962, p. 336.

13. Schlesinger, pp. 537–538.

14. McNamara-Taylor Report, October 2, 1963, *Pentagon Papers*, 2:751–766.

15. Short, pp. 248–249; Excerpts from Taylor to Kennedy, November 3, 1961, *Pentagon Papers*, 2:92–93; Chester Bowles, *Promises to Keep: My Years in Public Life*, New York: Harper, 1971, p. 409;FRUS, 1961–1963, vol. 1, pp. 322–325.

16. Karnow, p. 291. This photograph can be found at: http://www.uwec.edu/aca demic/curric/greidebe/BMRB/culture/student.work/hicksr/.

17. Transcript of broadcast, September 2, 1963, *Public Papers: Kennedy, 1963*, p. 652; *Vietnam: A Television History*.

18. CIA to Lodge, October 9, 1963, FRUS, 1961–1963, vol. 4, p. 393.

19. The Library of Congress collection of JFK assassination files can be found at: http://www.nara.gov/research/jfk/index.html. Some other JFK assassination sites can be found at:

http://mcadams.posc.mu.edu/home.htm

http://www.jfk-online.com//garrison.html

http://mcadams.posc.mu.edu/bestof.htm

20. Transcript of broadcast, September 2, 1963, *Public Papers: Kennedy, 1963*, p. 652.

21. See James K. Galbraith, "Exit Strategy: In 1963, JFK ordered a complete withdrawal from Vietnam," *Boston Review*, October/November 2003; Robert McNamara, *In*

Retrospect: The Tragedy and Lessons of Vietnam, New York: Random House, 1995; John M. Newman, *JFK and Vietnam*, New York: Time Warner, 1992; and Howard Jones, *Death of a Generation: How the Assassinations of Diem and JFK Prolonged the Vietnam War*, New York: Oxford University Press, 2004.

22. Hess, "Kennedy's Vietnam Options and Decisions," pp. 82–83.

CHAPTER 4

1. Available online at: http://mcadams.posc.mu.edu/viet16.htm.

2. The peasants, often helped by the VC, destroyed the Strategic Hamlets built by Diem's regime.

3. Kennedy's inaugural address, 20 January 1961. http://www.historyplace.com/speeches/jfk-inaug.htm.

4. "The Phantom Battle that Led to War," *U.S. News and World Report*, 23 July 1984, pp. 56–67; McNamara, pp. 128, 133–136.

5. McNamara, p. 135.

6. Scott Shane, "Critique of Intelligence on Vietnam Kept Secret," *New York Times*, 1 November 2005.

7. Joint Resolution of Congress, H.J. RES 1145 August 7, 1964. Text available at7 http://www.luminet.net/~tgort/tonkin.htm; Herring, p. 142; Maxwell Taylor, *Swords and Ploughshares: A Memoir*, New York: Diane Publishing Co., 1972, p. 330.

8. *Vietnam: A Television History*. Episode 2.

9. Larry Berman, *Planning a Tragedy: The Americanization of the War in Vietnam*, New York: W.W. Norton, 1983, pp. 51–56.

CHAPTER 5

1. Hess, *Vietnam and the United States*, pp. 95–96; Phillip B. Davidson, *Vietnam at War: The History, 1946–1975*, New York: Oxford University Press, 1991, pp. 422–423.

2. Karnow, pp. 438–439; Hess, *Vietnam and the United States*, p. 98; Bernard William Rogers, *Cedar Falls/Junction City: A Turning Point*, Washington, DC: U.S. Army Center of Military History, 1974, p. 78.

3. Hess, p. 98.

4. A popular motto on the defoliant spraying planes in Vietnam was, "Only You Can Prevent Forests."

5. Hess, p. 96.

6. Bill Moyers in *Vietnam: A Television History*.

7. *Vietnam: A Television History*. Episode 2.

CHAPTER 6

1. Duiker, *Sacred War*, New York: McGraw Hill, 1995, pp. 1–4, 188–204.

2. David G. Marr, "Bringing the National Liberation Front Back into the History of the Vietnam War," *Diplomatic History*, vol. 25, no. 3 (Summer 2001), p. 525.

3. Ibid., pp. 526–528.

CHAPTER 7

1. Department of State Bulletin, 11 December 1967, pp. 786–788; Karnow, p. 535; Hess, *Vietnam and the United States*, pp. 103–111; Herring, p. 192; Dave R. Palmer, *Summons of Trumpet: U.S.-Vietnam in Perspective,* New York: Presidio Press, 1995, pp. 217, 247, 256.

2. Herring, p. 235.

3. You can listen to Cronkite's report from 1968 at the following site: http://www.npr.org/templates/story/story.php?storyId=1147965.

4. Herring, p. 231; McNamara, pp. 295–302.

5. Karnow, pp. 447, 450, 529; *Vietnam: A Television History.* Episode 6.

6. Herring, p. 208.

7. Karnow, p. 548; *Vietnam: A Television History.* Episode 1.

8. Karnow, p. 558; *Vietnam: A Television History.* Episode 1.

9. Hess, p. 110.

10. Truong Nhu Tang, *A Viet Cong Memoir*, New York: Vintage Books, 1985, pp. 201–202.

CHAPTER 8

1. Kissinger served as national security advisor until 1973, when he became secretary of state.

2. Karnow, pp. 584–586.

3. Herring, pp. 244–247; Marilyn B. Young, *The Vietnam Wars: 1945–1990,* New York: HarperCollins, 1991, p. 241.

4. Karnow, p. 489.

5. Myra MacPherson, *Long Time Passing: Vietnam and the Haunted Generation,* New York: Doubleday, 1993, p. 43.

6. MacPherson, p. 340.

7. MacPherson, p. 88. To illustrate the futility and senselessness of the Kent State shootings, one can consider the case of one of the shooting victims—nineteen-year-old Allison Krause. She was just walking to class with her boyfriend, not protesting, when she was shot dead by an Ohio National Guardsman. Just the day before, she had placed a flower in the gun barrel of one of the guardsmen.

8. Cal Woodward, AP Wire, 16 November 2005.

9. Karnow, pp. 249, 398, 633.

10. Gabriel Kolko, *Anatomy of a War: Vietnam, the United States, and the Modern Historical Experience,* New York: Pantheon, 1985, p. 343.

CHAPTER 9

1. Herring, p. 275.

CHAPTER 10

1. Reese Williams, ed., *Unwinding the War*, Seattle, WA: Real Comet Press, 1987, pp. 427–440.

2. Christian G. Appy, *Working-Class War: American Combat Soldiers and Vietnam*, Chapel Hill: University of North Carolina Press, 1993, pp. 26–28; Young, pp. 197–198.

3. MacPherson, p. 92.

4. Tom Wells, *The War Within: America's Battle over Vietnam*, New York: Henry Holt, 1996, pp. 116–117, 272.

5. *Vietnam: A Television History*. Episode 10.

6. Jane Franklin, H. Bruce Franklin, Marvin E. Gettleman, eds., *Vietnam and America: A Documented History*, New York: Grove Press, 1995, pp. 310–318, 322, 342.

7. Wells, pp. 276–280.

8. See James S. Olson, Randy Roberts, *My Lai: A Brief History with Documents*, New York: Bedford Books, 1998; MacPherson, p. 340.

9. James M. Washington, ed., *I Have a Dream: Writings and Speeches That Changed the World*, New York: HarperCollins, 1986, pp. 136–138.

10. Ibid., pp. 176–177.

11. Wells, pp. 13–14.

12. Wells, pp. 424–425.

13. Hess, *Vietnam and the United States*, p. 109; Young, pp. 193–197.

14. I had a friend who worked for the AP during the war and he told me that a story he wrote about Joan Baez was "spiked" or killed because the editor said, "I don't want to give that commie bitch any press."

CHAPTER 11

1. Karnow, p. 638.

2. Kolko, p. 343.

3. Phillip B. Davidson, *Vietnam at War: The History, 1946–1975*, New York: Oxford University Press, 1988, pp. 728–731.

4. Kolko, pp. 499–501; Herring, p. 289; See also Stanley Kutler, ed., *Watergate: The Fall of Richard M. Nixon*, New York: Brandywine Press, 1996.

5. Herring, p. 289.

6. McMahon, p. 165.

7. *New York Times*, 19 August 1980.

8. *New York Times*, 2 March 1991.

9. McMahon, p. 170.

10. Ibid.

11. McMahon, p. 172.

12. Chicago Council on Foreign Relations, American Public Opinion and U.S. Foreign Policy 1983, Chicago, 1983, 29; Thomas G. Paterson, "Historical Memory and Illusive Victories: Vietnam and Central America," *Diplomatic History*, no. 1, vol. 12 (Winter 1988), pp. 1–18; Richard Sobel, *The Impact of Public Opinion on U.S. Foreign Policy Since Vietnam: Constraining the Colossus*, New York: Oxford University Press, 2001. Also see: http://www.usatoday.com/news/polls/2005-11-15-iraq-poll.htm.

CHAPTER 12

1. Oral history based on numerous stories told on various occasions by the author's father. Asbjorn Solheim died in August 1999, but his stories live on.

CONCLUSION

1. Joe P. Dunn, "Women and the Vietnam War: A Bibliographic Review," *Journal of American Culture*, vol. 12, no. 1 (Spring 1989), p. 79.

2. Divine, p. 134.

3. Al Qa'ida letter, 11 October 2005. www.fas.org/irp/news/2005/10/dni101105 .html.

4. Gary R. Hess, "Has Bush Learned the Lessons of Other War Presidents?" April 5, 2004, History News Network Web site: http://hnn.us/articles/4378.html.

5. Gary R. Hess, "The Unending Debate: Historians and the Vietnam War," *Diplomatic History* 18 (Spring 1994), pp. 239–264.

6. Serge Ricard, "Europe and the Vietnam War: A Thirty-Year Perspective," *Diplomatic History*, vol. 29, no. 5 (November 2005), p. 880.

7. Kevin Boyle, "The Price of Peace: Vietnam, the Pound, and the Crisis of the American Empire," *Diplomatic History*, vol. 27, no. 1 (January 2003), p. 39.

Selected Bibliography

Anderson, David L., ed. *Shadow on the White House: Presidents and the Vietnam War, 1945–1975*. Lawrence: University Press of Kansas, 1993.

Appy, Christian G. "The Muffling of Public Memory in Post-Vietnam America." *Chronicle of Higher Education*, vol. 45, no. 23 (12 February 1999): B4–B6.

Appy, Christian G. *Working-Class War: American Combat Soldiers and Vietnam*. Chapel Hill: University of North Carolina Press, 1993.

Arnett, Peter. *Live from the Battlefield: From Vietnam to Baghdad; 35 Years in the World's War Zones*. New York: Simon & Schuster, 1994.

Berman, Larry. *Planning a Tragedy: The Americanization of the War in Vietnam*. New York: Norton, 1982.

Browne, Malcolm W. *The New Face of War*. Indianapolis: Bobbs-Merrill, 1965.

Bundy, William. *A Tangled Web: The Making of Foreign Policy in the Nixon Presidency*. New York: Hill & Wang, 1998.

Caputo, Philip. *A Rumor of War*. New York: Holt, Rinehart & Winston, 1977.

Casey, Michael. *Obscenities*. New Haven, CT: Yale University Press, 1972.

Chomsky, Noam. *Rethinking Camelot: JFK, the Vietnam War, and U.S. Political Culture*. Boston: South End Press, 1993.

Clifford, Clark. *Counsel to the President: A Memoir*. With Richard C. Holbrooke. New York: Random House, 1991.

Colby, William E. *Honorable Men: My Life in the CIA*. New York: Simon & Schuster, 1978.

Colby, William E. *Lost Victory: A Firsthand Account of America's Sixteen Year Involvement in Vietnam*. With James McCargar. Chicago: Contemporary Books, 1989.

Duiker, William J. *Ho Chi Minh*. New York: Hyperion, 2000.

Duiker, William J. *Sacred War: Nationalism and Revolution in a Divided Vietnam*. New York: McGraw-Hill, 1995.

Dunn, Joe P. "Women and the Vietnam War: A Bibliographic Review." *Journal of American Culture* 12 (Spring 1989): 79–86.

Edelman, Bernard, ed. *Dear America: Letters Home from Vietnam*. New York: Norton, 1985.

Ellsberg, Daniel. *Papers on the War*. New York: Simon & Schuster, 1972.

Elwood-Akers, Virginia. *Women War Correspondents in the Vietnam War, 1961–1975*. Metuchen, NJ: Scarecrow, 1988.

Emerson, Gloria. *Winners and Losers: Battles, Retreats, Gains, Losses, and Ruins from the Vietnam War*. New York: Random House, 1976.

Fall, Bernard. *Street without Joy*. Harrisburg, PA: Stackpole, 1961.

Fitzgerald, Frances. *Fire in the Lake: The Vietnamese and the Americans in Vietnam*. Boston: Little, Brown, 1972.

Fonda, Jane. *My Life So Far*. New York: Random House, 2005.

French, Albert. *Patches of Fire: A Story of War and Redemption*. New York: Anchor, 1998.

Hackworth, David H., and Julie Sherman. *About Face: The Odyssey of an American Warrior*. New York: Simon & Schuster, 1989.

Halberstam, David. *The Best and the Brightest*. New York: Random House, 1972.

Halberstam, David. *The Making of a Quagmire: America and Vietnam during the Kennedy Era*. Rev. ed. New York: Knopf, 1988.

Hammer, Ellen J. *A Death in November: America in Vietnam, 1963*. New York: Dutton, 1987.

Hasford, Gustav. *The Short-Timers*. New York: Bantam, 1980.

Hayslip, Le Ly, and Jay Wurts. *When Heaven and Earth Changed Places: A Vietnamese Woman's Journey from War to Peace*. New York: Doubleday, 1989.

Herr, Michael. *Dispatches*. New York: Knopf, 1977.

Herring, George C. *America's Longest War: The United States and Vietnam, 1950–1975*. 3rd ed. New York: McGraw Hill, 1996.

Herring, George C. *LBJ and Vietnam: A Different Kind of War*. Austin: University of Texas Press, 1994.

Hersh, Seymour. *Cover-Up: The Army's Secret Investigation of the Massacre at My Lai 4*. New York: Random House, 1972.

Hess, Gary R. *Presidential Decisions for War: Korea, Vietnam, and the Persian Gulf*. Baltimore: Johns Hopkins University Press, 2001.

Hess, Gary R. *Vietnam and the United States: Origins and Legacy of War*. Rev. ed. New York: Twayne, 1998.

Hixson, Walter L. *The Lessons and Legacies of the Vietnam War*. New York: Garland, 2000.

Hunt, Michael H. *Lyndon Johnson's War: America's Cold War Crusade in Vietnam, 1945–1968*. New York: Hill & Wang, 1996.

Johnson, Lyndon. *The Vantage Point: Perspectives of the Presidency, 1963–1969*. New York: Holt, Rinehart & Winston, 1971.

Jorgenson, Kregg P. J. *Acceptable Loss*. New York: Presidio Press, 1991.

Jorgenson, Kregg P. J. *Very Crazy G.I.: Strange but True Stories of the Vietnam War*. New York: Ballantine, 2001.

Kahin, George M. *Intervention: How America Became Involved in Vietnam*. New York: Knopf, 1986.

Kane, Rod. *Veteran's Day: A Combat Odyssey*. New York: Pocket Books, 1991.

Karnow, Stanley. *Vietnam: A History*. New York: Viking, 1983.

Kissinger, Henry. *White House Years*. Boston: Little, Brown, 1979.

Kolko, Gabriel. *Anatomy of a Peace*. New York: Routledge, 1997.

Kovic, Ron. *Born on the Fourth of July*. New York: McGraw-Hill, 1976.

Lliteras, D. S. *613 West Jefferson*. Charlottesville, VA: Hampton Roads, 2001.

MacPherson, Myra. *Long Time Passing: Vietnam and the Haunted Generation*. Garden City, NY: Doubleday, 1984.

Mansker, Dennis. *A Bad Attitude*. Olympia, WA: Writer's Showcase Press, 2002.

Mason, Patience. *Recovering from the War: A Woman's Guide to Helping Your Vietnam Vet, Your Family, and Yourself*. New York: Viking, 1990.

Mason, Robert. *Chickenhawk*. New York: Viking, 1983.

Mason, Robert. *Chickenhawk: Back in the World*. New York: Viking, 1993.

McMahon, Robert. "Contested Memory: The Vietnam War and American Society, 1975–2001." *Diplomatic History*, vol. 26, no. 2 (Spring 2002): 159–184.

McNamara, Robert S. *In Retrospect: The Tragedy and Lessons of Vietnam*. With Brian VanDeMark. New York: Times Books, 1995.

Merritt, William E. *Where the Rivers Ran Backward*. Athens: University of Georgia Press, 1989.

Moore, Harold G., and Joseph L. Galloway. *We Were Soldiers Once . . . And Young*. New York: Random House, 1992.

Newman, John M. *JFK and Vietnam: Deception, Intrigue, and the Struggle for Power*. New York: Warner Books, 1992.

Nguyen, Khac Vien. *Vietnam: A Long History*. Rev. ed. Hanoi: The Gioi Publishers, 1993.

Nixon, Richard M. *No More Vietnams*. New York: Arbor House, 1985.

O'Brien, Tim. *If I Die in a Combat Zone*. New York: Delacorte, 1973.

O'Neill, Susan. *Don't Mean Nothing: Short Stories of Vietnam*. Amherst: University of Massachusetts Press, 2004.

Parks, David. *GI Diary*. Washington, DC: Howard University Press, 1982.

Patti, Archimedes. *Why Viet Nam?* Berkeley: University of California Press, 1980.

Powell, Mary Reynolds. *A World of Hurt: Between Innocence and Arrogance in Vietnam*. Cleveland: Greenleaf Enterprises, 2000.

Puller, Lewis B., Jr. *Fortunate Son: The Autobiography of Lewis B. Puller, Jr*. New York: Grove, Weidenfeld, 1991.

Quintana, Leroy V. *Interrogations*. Chevy Chase, MD: Burning Cities Press, 1990.

Salisbury, Harrison E., ed. *Vietnam Reconsidered: Lessons from a War*. New York: Harper & Row, 1984.

Schell, Jonathan. *The Village of Ben Suc*. New York: Knopf, 1967.

Sheehan, Neil. *A Bright Shining Lie: John Paul Vann and America in Vietnam*. New York: Random House, 1988.

Spencer, Ernest. *Welcome to Vietnam, Macho Man: Reflections of a Khe Sanh Vet*. New York: Random House, 1991.

Steinbeck, John IV. *In Touch*. New York: Knopf, 1969.

Stockdale, James B. *A Vietnam Experience: Ten Years of Reflection*. Stanford: Hoover Institution, Stanford University, 1984.

Summers, Harry. *On Strategy*. Novato, CA: Presidio Press, 1982.

Taylor, Maxwell D. *Swords and Plowshares*. New York: Norton, 1972.

Taylor, Sandra C. *Vietnamese Women at War: Fighting for Ho Chi Minh and the Revolution*. Lawrence: University Press of Kansas, 1999.

Terry, Wallace. *Bloods: An Oral History of the Vietnam War by Black Veterans*. New York: Random House, 1984.

Troung Nhu Tang. *A Vietcong Memoir*. With David Chanoff and Doan Van Toai. New York: Harcourt, Brace, Jovanovich, 1985.

Van Devanter, Lynda. *Home Before Morning: The Story of an Army Nurse in Vietnam*. New York: Beaufort Books, 1983.

Vo Nguyen Giap. *Unforgettable Months and Years*. Ithaca, NY: Cornell University, Southeast Asia Program, 1975.

Wells, Tom. *The War Within: America's Battle over Vietnam*. Berkeley: University of California Press, 1994.

Westmoreland, William C. *A Soldier Reports*. Garden City, NY: Doubleday, 1976.

Willson, David A. *In the Army Now*. Woodbridge, CT: Burning Cities Press, 1995.

Willson, David A. *A Short History of the Vietnam War: And Other Tales of Sex, Death, and Military Might*. Glendora, CA: Viet Nam War Generation Press, forthcoming.

Willson, David A. *REMF Diary*. Seattle, WA: Black Heron Press, 1988.

Willson, David A. *The REMF Returns*. Seattle, WA: Black Heron Press, 1992.

Wolff, Tobias. *In Pharaoh's Army: Memories of the Lost War*. New York: Knopf, 1994.

Young, Marilyn B. *The Vietnam Wars, 1945–1990*. New York: HarperCollins, 1991.

Index

Names in **bold** have featured biographies starting on the page number in **bold**.

ABOUT THE AUTHOR

BRUCE O. SOLHEIM is Professor of History at Citrus College in Glendora, California. He is a veteran of the U.S. Army. Solheim is the author of *The Nordic Nexus: A Lesson in Peaceful Security* (Praeger, 1994), and *On Top of the World: Women's Political Leadership in Scandinavia and Beyond* (Greenwood Press, 2000).